THE ROAD WET, THE WIND CLOSE
Celtic Ireland

High Cross, Moone Abbey, Co. Kildare

The Road Wet, The Wind Close

CELTIC IRELAND

JAMES CHARLES ROY
'JE'

'Peregrinus expectavi pedes meos in cymbalis'

DUFOUR EDITIONS

First published 1986 by
Dufour Editions Inc.
Chester Springs, Pennsylvania 19425

First paperback edition 1987
Reprinted 1989, 1990

Library of Congress Cataloguing-in-Publication Data:

Roy, James Charles, 1945-
   The road wet, the wind close.

   Bibliography: p.
   1. Ireland—History—To 1172. 2. Celts—Ireland—
History. I.Title.
DA930.R68   1986   936.4   85-31100

ISBN 0 8023 1283 7

Print origination in Ireland by
Keywrite Ltd., Dublin

Cover design by Q Design

Printed and bound in the United States of America

This book is dedicated to the memory of
Grace Mary O'Brien Roy
(more Irish than she ever realised)
and to
James Charles Roy

Contents

One of the difficulties with which the Irish historian will always have to deal is to discriminate where the imaginary ends and the actual begins. It, in fact, ends and begins nowhere.

Eleanor Hull
1908

Introduction: Skellig Michael

A Monday in the spring

It took most of the afternoon to arrange for a boat. I tried first in Caherciveen. Most of the fishing fleet was in because of the weather, but even had the day been fine no one would have taken me out. Their trawlers were too big, the captains said, to attempt a landing on Skellig Michael, especially if the swells were running to the west as they were today. They all said to try a charter fisherman, a collective friend of theirs. No matter the weather, he'd go.

And he would have, for £55. I said that was too much and he smiled at me in a way I can only describe as benevolent. 'And have you been to Ireland before?' he asked. Yes, several years ago. 'And things were cheaper then, for you Americans, bargains and all?' I admitted this to be true. 'Well those days are done,' he said with a friendly smile, 'gone and buried. It will be £55.'

He called after me as I left his house, suggesting a neighbour of his wife's family as an alternative, a lobsterman who had a small boat moored in Knightstown on Valentia Island across the channel. I telephoned him at dinnertime, negotiated a more reasonable fare, he said if the seas were right we'd leave first thing in the morning.

I drove to Portmagee, a squalid little fishing village that before power boats came along had always been the point of departure for Skellig Michael. Eighteenth- and nineteenth-century travellers and pilgrims would engage curraghs here for the nine-mile voyage. Depending on the size of the party, from four to six men were usually hired to row them out and back. Nowadays there isn't a single job in the town. Most of the villagers are older fishermen who work out of Caherciveen on the trawlers.

A small unclassified road runs southwest from the town up to Bolus Head. The first half mile or so is fairly level, after which it seems to accelerate, straight into the sky. Pulling over I park in a drainage gully, leave the car in gear, then collect some flat stones to wedge behind the wheels. The sea cliffs are about a ten-minute hike, the last fifty yards of which are nearly vertical. Reaching the top, I take my first look at the Skelligs.

The day has calmed down considerably. As dusk approaches, a dark, almost purple sky veils the horizon. Puffs of clouds provide a contrast as they skim across with the westward Atlantic winds. Shafts of sunlight occasionally break through to blazon small patches of the sea below. The ocean seems steady. Like two soot-black fingers the Skelligs arise from the water. They seem in total command.

I sit down and take a sandwich from my haversack, surveying the boundless expanse of water all around me, interrupted first by an ocean crag called Lemon Rock, about three miles offshore, that at high tide is barely above water. Then come the Skelligs: Little Skellig, the famous bird refuge, seven miles out, and beyond it the Great Skellig, over nine miles away — supporter of no life save rabbits and a few species of birds, totally deserted but for a lighthouse crew. A dead piece of rock, a memorial of sorts to a history that is itself dead and forgotten.

We leave from Knights Town at 8.30. I stow my sleeping bag and some other gear up front, along with a small

Little Skellig and Skellig Michael
(from Bolus Head), Co. Kerry

parcel of food purchased at the local grocery. It looks to be a fine day, the sun blazing, hardly a cloud in the sky, a rarity for Ireland. As we enter the open ocean the swells run against us from the south-west, about four feet. We are in for a rocking voyage.

The captain is a small-time fisherman. I gather from talking with him that fish are plentiful around the Skelligs and that he goes there frequently, especially in the summer when tourists want to visit the island. He usually trolls with a few lines while his passengers explore the ruins. He has most of his lobster traps off the north coast of Valentia Island.

I tell him my plans to stay over and ask if he can pick me up in a couple of days. He looks at me as if I was crazy. What are you going to do, he asks, where are you going to stay? For some reason I won't answer him specifically, though I have planned all along to camp in the monastery ruins. He warns me that the weather is not to be trusted, I could be marooned there for days if my luck was bad. I try to explain that I wouldn't half mind, but the captain just shakes his head, off and on, for several minutes. After an hour and a half or so we approach Little Skellig.

At some point in our voyage one or two of the great gannets probably picked us out, a tiny speck in the sea. As we chugged closer certainly more and more eyes turned our way. But why, at one specific moment, several hundreds decided as if with one mind to plummet down upon us I cannot say. Nor can I really describe my feelings of astonishment as these huge birds, many with wing spans of over six feet, wheeled and dived about us close enough to touch. One, in fact, brushed my shoulder.

Gannets are ocean birds. For most of the year they stay at sea, often spending hours in the air gliding with the winds. At dawn and dusk they fish and only when exhausted will they rest on the water. They never touch land except in the spring when some amazing, primeval instinct guides them back to where they were born. And as befits a bird of the sea their breeding grounds are remote and exposed: Bass Rock in the Firth of Forth, St Kildas of the Hebrides and Little Skellig are typical of gannet colonies, and the most famous in the British Isles.

Twenty thousand pairs of gannets gather here each year between March and April to breed and then rear their young. The fisherman tells me that all of the colony have not yet arrived from their wanderings in the far Atlantic. Another third at least are due. Even so the hundreds of ledges and narrow walks seem full of birds, many of them busy constructing nests from seaweed and odd bits of flotsam plucked from the ocean. Soon each female will lay her single egg, and by a remarkable evolutionary technique few if any will roll away into the sea either by a gust of wind or an inadvertent kick from a neighbour. Gannets, with their long webbed feet, incubate their eggs by standing on them: they place one foot over the egg, then wrap the other over the first. Parents alternate their shifts regularly, one guarding the egg while its mate either fishes or sleeps.

As we round Little Skellig the din diminishes. We have no food or refuse to throw over and the gannets, after a while, realise this. First in droves, then in threes and fours and finally by ones and twos, they leave us to return home. The rock is stained white with their numbers.

Skellig Michael now stands before us, about a mile to go. Even from afar it looks menacing, unfriendly, barren, seemingly a perfect cone rising from the sea, jet-black in colour and everywhere jagged, sharp. There doesn't seem to be a smooth place anywhere.

As we come broadside I can distinguish not one peak but two: the first, fairly level, is separated by a gap from another, much higher and pointed. Little Skellig seems dwarfed in comparison.

After circling the island we approach from the north-east. In ancient times there were three landing spots, but only one has been modernised to the point of having a jetty. It is appropriately called Blind Man's Cove: there is barely room for a small boat to enter and none to manoeuvre. The captain eases in very carefully, even though we are protected from today's winds and swells by the bulk of the island. Getting ashore takes a good-sized leap. My things are tossed from the swaying boat, he promises to return, I am left alone, nine miles out in the open Atlantic on a wet concrete dock, my only company three dead fish, apparently fresh, lying in thin sunlight at my feet.

The power of the printed word, that's what I'm thinking as I watch the lobsterboat retrace its path to the mainland. The Pope would undoubtedly have fallen to his knees and kissed this holy ground, but the excitement I feel is more ironical in nature. I have been led here by books, by impressions recorded long ago in pages yellowing and falling apart with age — books no longer read, disintegrating on library shelves, looking now for the last chance (or so I imagine) to rekindle someone's interest. That is where the lure of Skellig Michael caught me, hundreds of miles away in a different, modern age, one unconcerned with the remote and desolate reaches of the past. One or two journals, a few sentences here and there, some scattered references in historical surveys — this is not exactly the mass persuasion that will move millions, though enough to join me with the handful of visitors who still pester this island. We have come to Skellig Michael because of what we've read. We find ourselves drawn to obscurities, or perhaps it's just the urge to go places where no one else sees value. For whatever reason, on this island, I think, is the very essence of Celtic Ireland. It is the best place to begin, and I move towards the path.

Originally a series of steps began here at the jetty, which led directly up the slope to the monastery. These have mostly fallen away though traces of that route can still be seen. I walk along the new track constructed by the Commissioners of Lights to reach the lighthouse. Rock slides must be frequent as the way is littered with debris.

I am so intent on trudging forward, and especially taken with vistas of the sea, that I barely notice the great cross until I'm upon it. It seems to be a monolith, hewn from a single rocky outcrop of the mountain. The cross is crudely cut and very primitive. It stands at an angle about seven feet tall and signals a second set of ancient stairs. I leave the modern pathway and start climbing.

There are over four hundred steps to the gap. Each is a single large slab of stone, hacked and shaped from the mountainside itself. Smaller rocks have been wedged beneath them to support their weight. They resemble tongues, each and every one, pitted with the sores and chancres of endless rockfalls, countless feet. They are the treadmills of sin, their burden the cross of fear, sorrow,

repentance. They lead me to Christ's Saddle where a brutal, searing wind blows my cap far below.

Christ's Saddle is what the monks called this spot, the breach between two peaks. Its form is that of a crescent. To the left is the Way of the Cross, the taller and more theatrical summit. To the right is the lower, less exposed plateau where the ancient monastery still remains. Christ's Saddle is open to the prevailing winds, which are in fact intensified by the funnel these two overhanging peaks create. It is, for me, the most extraordinary place on the island, more so than the Spit of the Pilgrim's Way. Christ's Saddle is a metaphor that works.

Crossing the floor of the Saddle to the western edge, I look for traces of a third major stairway that, according to maps of the island that I had studied, originally came up this side from another landing spot below. I can see no signs of steps or even where a landing would be possible. The drop to the sea is practically sheer, the water below noticeably more turbulent and the din thunderous. Puffins streak past my head, caught up in the wind, projected like missiles.

I take a long view of the Way of the Cross above me which culminates in the point known as the Spit. For centuries local people rowed out to the island as a penance, popularly known as the Pilgrim's Way. They would first visit the monastic ruins, then cross Christ's Saddle and scale the Way of the Cross. It was, in its basic format, a variation of the more traditional stations of the cross, although certain devotional customs gave this pilgrimage a unique flavour. For some reason, and many are given, the circuit here was discouraged, beginning in the 1720s. Some say it was the British, trying as they did less successfully at Lough Derg in Donegal to stamp out superstitious rites, while others attribute the decline to none other than the Church itself. I have not been able to determine the exact cause for sure. Whatever it was, the shroud of disapproval proved effective. Only tourists come here today, and not even many of them.

The stairway to the monastery above leads north. It too has a cross at the start, an ancient beacon warning all who approach that they enter sacred ground. About a hundred and fifty steps more bring me to a level ledge which approaches the gateway to the compound thirty yards ahead. To pass through is to step back fourteen centuries.

The monastery of Skellig Michael is a Celtic diorama — the Angkor Wat of early Christian Ireland. It is, perhaps, the most intriguing historical remain in the country, a miniaturised example of what the bigger and more famous monastic cities of Glendalough, Kells, Bangor, Iona, Armagh and Clonmacnoise must have been like. Over six hundred monastic settlements were founded in Ireland between the coming of the faith c.AD400 and the reform of the Cistercians in 1142. Most of these either lie in ruins or else have disappeared. Skellig Michael stands complete and in perfect condition. There is nothing about it that cannot be understood or recreated. It breathes a presence in much the same way as a concert hall, half an hour before the musicians appear. Where are the monks, you ask yourself, why have they left? One disbelieves the passage of countless generations.

Skellig Michael reveals to the traveller what Ireland was like before strangers swept aside almost everything native. The Normans left little imprint here, neither did the English. Only the Vikings truly made their menace felt, but stone cannot burn and Skellig Michael somehow survived. No one can say just how this monastery came to be. The first Christians to live here were solitary hermits whose shelters were little more than rough piles of stone. During some later age these ascetics were joined by others of like persuasion and inevitably a more defined settlement became the need. The *clocháns* and oratories we see today are the result. They betray no foreign influence in plan or construction. Everything about them not only reflects tradition but is tradition. The beehive design, the cashel wall, the incised crosses are all more or less a common thread that string together both ends of the native Christian era, 400-1142. Skellig Michael could fit anywhere in that span. An educated guess would be c. 650.

There are nine actual buildings in the complex, the whole of which is layered rather like a vineyard. The accompanying sketch, if examined right to left, explains the gradation. The monastery was first literally carved into the side of the mountain. The slopes falling off to the right are severe and abrupt: the sea is a long drop of over six hundred feet. The enclosures were created by building an ingenious series of support walls (called cashels) from loose stones, an engineering feat of some skill considering the angle of incline. While it is impossible to say exactly what they were for, the largest of the three has always been called the Monk's Garden. Soil analysis has proven the area arable, an interesting fact of itself since the only ground-cover on the island is a moss known as sea-pink, which is nowhere more than a single foot thick. The monks, it is thought, must have transported the soil from the mainland to create this artificial field, a type of labour characteristically Irish. The Fir Bolg of legendary times, for example, were apparently renowned for it: 'They made clovery plains of the rough-headed hills with the clay from elsewhere,' carrying the soil about in leather pouches from whence their name, 'men of the bags'. It is curious to note that in the legends the Fir Bolg were eventually overthrown by another race of people, the Tuatha Dé Danann, and forced to flee the mainland of Ireland for the safety of the Aran Islands, where even fairly recently you could see the men of Inishmore coping as their forebears had centuries ago with pastures of little more than barren rock.

The original entrance to the settlement was apparently through the garden, but the present gateway leads one in by the most impressive of the *clocháns*. This remarkable structure is the largest and finest beehive building in all of Ireland. It is circular in shape and while one must stoop to enter, the inside is over sixteen feet in height from floor to apex. The walls are nearly six feet thick at their base and the roof is corbelled, which means that as the stones were laid, one over the other, each new addition was positioned further inward than its predecessor. In this fashion the walls eventually met and a single capstone finished the structure. Furthermore every stone was inclined, forcing rain water to run off the roof instead of in. What makes the finished construction so striking is that not a single speck of mortar holds any of it together. It is, as the architects say, a dry dress.

This particular *clochán* is so big that its dome contains over two dozen additional corbels. These are simply large rectangular slabs of stone that project into the roof for extra support, rather like studs. The other beehives (five in

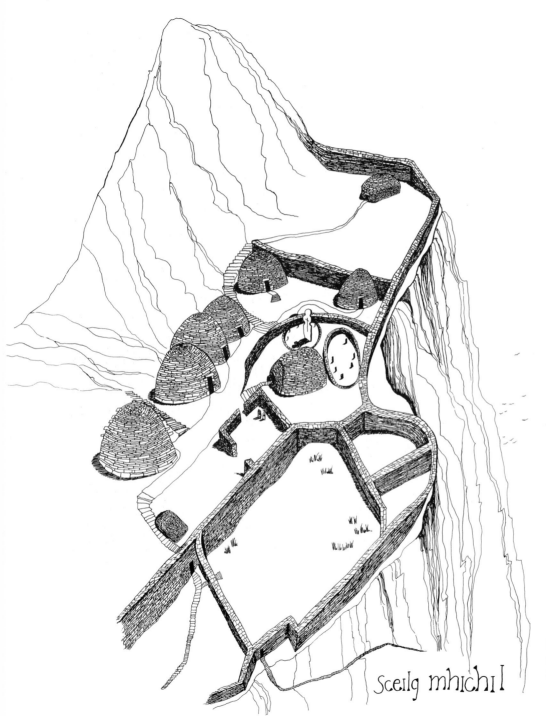

Sceilg mhichil

*Sketch showing reconstruction
of Monastery ruins,
Skellig Michael*

Monastic Clocháns, *Skellig Michael, Co. Kerry*

number) are smaller and their roofs are mostly smooth. All were used as living quarters. Some have wall cupboards.

The oblong buildings are oratories or chapels. Here the monks said mass and performed many of their devotions. Aside from a rectangular base they are similar in appearance to the *clocháns*. Clustered around the central chapel are two small plots of built-up ground. Both are graveyards, and grouped along their edges are several low crosses and one dominating monolith, about six feet tall. Across from it is a well. Antiquarians have previously noted the presence of two fresh water wells here on the northern plateau. There are apparently no others on the entire island (the lighthouse crew drinks rain water); this leads me to the question — and I can hardly believe it — whether the wells were dug. I decide to take a sip. The taste is sour and brackish.

A stairway climbs to a rocky slope above the buildings. As I approach the western height of this incline I can hear the deafening wind from the other side, and when I reach the lip its force pushes me back. I turn and take a seat, surveying the settlement below. The conceptual entity of it all is very clear from this vantage point. None of the *clochán* entrances, for instance, face my direction, the avenue of prevailing winds; all open out to the east or northeast. The site itself is also sheltered, being in the lee of the wind. The cashel wall, a characteristic of all Celtic monasteries, surrounds and defines any area not enclosed by the north-south cliff ledge where I am. The monastery's confines are thus precisely delineated. Its sense of order — fastidious in a way, but eccentric — is the most revealing thing about this place.

Celtic Ireland in both pagan and early Christian times was a land of many kings. Every petty *tuath* or kingdom had a king who owed allegiance above him to an over-king, who was himself subordinate to a *rí ruirech* or king of over-kings. The complexity of relationships is at times impossible to sort out but at the core of everything is the *tuath* and the local king. There were, it is said, well over two hundred of these kingdoms, all of which were controlled or fought over by numberless local dynasties. The prize was land, valued not at all for its own sake but rather for the gold it foddered, cattle. There has, as a result, never been a race on earth more boundary conscious than the Irish. No matter how small the holding or how poor the land, ancient and modern Irishmen have bickered and contested its limits. The men of the church were just the same as the rest.

In the ruins of any purely Celtic monastery the outline of the cashel wall can usually be traced. Aerial photography in particular will generally pick out this feature. It represents the hereditary Irish obsession with order, classification, legal exactitude and class rights. At the same time there is something fragile and almost whimsical about it. The cashel wall was a legal entity. It spelled sanctuary and was meant to be taken seriously as a legitimate barrier to intrusion. Very few, I think, were ever naïve enough to put their trust in this wall *as* a wall, but many were the clergy who had faith in it as an idea, and in fact the concept proved a viable protection for centuries. Few Celtic warriors dared pillage or burn a monastic settlement until someone else showed them how.

In 823 a party of Vikings raided Skellig Michael. Eitgall, the abbot, was taken and dragged to the longboats below. There he was chained and there he died, on the high seas, starved to death for the amusement of his captors. Many of the monks were killed outright and the monastery was plundered. Those who had luck scattered about the island and evaded capture, waiting for the Norse to leave. When they saw them pull away they returned, one by one, to their cells. The shock they must have felt we can only imagine. No Irish king would have violated their *termonn* or sanctuary. But then again, what law, however strong, could bind the foreign Viking? Tradition has it that all the curraghs on the island were taken by the Norse to sea and sunk. The survivors probably didn't realise their plight until later, but without any means of reaching the mainland food supplies were soon exhausted, and every monk eventually died.

Towards evening, after tramping about this place for hours, I pick one of the *clocháns* for a berth. All have flagstone floors, very uneven, but this one seems the least punishing of the lot. At first I had thought of sleeping out on the sea-pink, which is luxurious and soft, but the

Monastic Cashel, Abbey of Mona Incha, Roscrea, Co. Tipperary

weather is turning and I figure there's rain in store for tonight.

It is cold and drizzly in the morning. The *clochán* is grim with moisture as I struggle to get up, stiff from the rocky floor and tacky from the mildew of my wet and now dirty clothing. After some breakfast and a quick tidying up of my things I go out into the mist and head down for Christ's Saddle.

Well before Christian times — indeed, well before Celtic times — the Great Skellig was inhabited. Its first visitors were priests and learned men of the various neolithic tribes which began coming to Ireland *c.* 3500 BC, a Stone Age people having no knowledge of metals, the wheel or writing. Their superiority to the inhabitants they found here lay in the ability to grow crops and breed stock. They were skilled workers with stone and understood the rudiments of navigation and maritime travel. The most sophisticated of their number settled around the Boyne, north of Dublin, where the vast city of the dead they built still remains.

These are shadowy limits in the arc of our knowledge. It will be, to some, an exaggeration to assume any of these people ever came to the Skelligs. But the finger of logic says otherwise. The tombs of the Boyne, and Newgrange in particular, reveal an attitude towards the sky that blends primitive awe with scholarship. Wise men were drawn to this remote and dramatic wilderness of rock for a single purpose, to study and track the movement of God through the heavens. No doubt they stayed here for months at a time, the high priest and his disciples, perhaps even years. Wrapped in the shroud of solitary observation they questioned the world directly, watching the stars and movements of sun and moon; studying clouds and patterns in the wind; noting migrations of birds and fish, seeing everywhere a cycle in life, the ways of God.

The Skellig became in itself a symbol of mystery. Any traveller today seeing it from the mainland far out to sea, motionless amid the foam and turmoil of endless waves, can easily share in that prehistoric aura. Its myth would certainly have been a priestly creation. Standing on the edge of the world, beyond which there was no being or foothold — what better place for God's servants, a pagan Sinai leading into his world, a sacred place. In his own mind the high priest might add — not only refuge but observatory.

The priest was looked to for a variety of reasons. In a life and death sense he intervened with God for his people. By interpreting the signs of earth and sky he learned the times of year for planting and harvest. He could say when the omens were good for hunting, when game and flocks of birds could be expected, when the fish was running. As God's messenger he also warned the flock of divine anger by predicting storms or the most sensational of celestial phenomena, the eclipse of sun or moon. In all these tasks knowledge preceded bravura, and Newgrange far away to the north is the most visible expression of neolithic ability. Here on the Great Skellig we feel more than see its strength. They left behind no footprints to follow or ruins, just the arena of their discipline.

In later centuries, when the race of these men had largely disappeared, druids came to the Great Skellig. Druids are, of course, a cult phenomenon. They have been so for centuries, ever since ancient writers such as Posidonius, Strabo and Caesar detailed the more gruesome aspects of their ritual. Diodorus Siculus, for example, described a typically 'strange and incredible custom: they devote to death a human being and stab him with a dagger in the region above the diaphragm, and when he has fallen they foretell the future from his fall and from the convulsions of his limbs and from the spurting of blood.' The fascination men have with human sacrifice, especially when neatly documented as in the case here, is largely responsible for the traditional association of druids with eerie stone circles in general, and with Stonehenge in particular. Almost by itself Stonehenge has kept the public infatuation with druids alive and prospering, even though the relationship between the two is a seventeenth-century invention. Such apocalyptic designations as the 'Slaughter' stone and the 'Altar' stone for two of its monoliths typify the fables.

Druids, quite simply, were an order of priesthood. They were specifically Celtic, coming to Ireland *c.* 300 BC when their tribes migrated from Continental Europe and flooded the island with new settlers. Newgrange by then was overgrown and deserted. The druids, it is said, had no idea what to make of it.

They worked from a more complicated base than their distant neolithic predecessors. There were more gods to be worshipped for one thing, as the universal sun god gave way to a host of smaller deities. More importantly the druids broadened their functions to include jurisdiction in political and secular matters. But one characteristic they did have in common: druids looked to nature for guidance and rulings. They too were seers and prophets.

The impetuosity and bravery of the Celtic race has often been noted. 'We should call a man mad,' wrote Aristotle, 'if he feared nothing — "earthquake nor billows" as they say of the Celts.' But a revealing conversation between Alexander the Great and a group of Celtic chieftains does indicate a certain primal terror they did feel. Alexander, ready to depart on his voyage of conquest into Persia and beyond, sought assurance that these Celtic mercenaries would protect Macedonia until his return. He asked them if there was anything they feared. Nothing was the reply, save the sky and heavens, should they crack and fall to earth.

To the priests fell the responsibility of forestalling such a disaster, and many were the ancient writers who observed how firmly the Celts believed in the power of the druids to do so, 'as though they were people who can speak [the gods'] language.' Their power was enormous, though high esteem was not easily won, training for the priesthood often lasting twenty years according to Caesar. 'Besides this,' he noted, 'they have discussions as touching the stars and their movements, the size of the universe and the earth.'

Legend has always indicated the Great Skellig as a place

of pagan meditations, a sanctuary where the teachings of druidic elders could be verified to master and novice alike. Once again the course of many lives depended on their skill. Druids could make war or peace, could sentence a man to death, all according to the flap of a wing or the flight of a star.

Looking beyond Christ's Saddle to the Way of the Cross on the other side, these musings on pagan priests and druids vanish altogether. Their candles are soaked by rain, their stars and moonlight lie hidden away in banks of mist. That is no druid on the Spit, nor a pupil of the skies. There is no inquiry, no interest in anything so vain. The Way of the Cross is a hermitage, closed, crabbed, sour and miserable. The man up there is Simeon of the Desert, arms outstretched crying to heaven 'Fall upon us,' and to the hills, 'Cover us.'

White martyrdom was a goal sought by many in Ireland for well over four centuries. It was called by some the Philosophy of Pain, by others the Pathway to Paradise or the Way of the Cross. Its thesis claimed that self-mortification and punishment of the body led directly to divine revelation and sometimes communication with God himself. 'When I am weak,' St Antony of Egypt believed, 'then am I powerful. The soul's energy thrives when the body's desires are feeblest.'

This principle is not, of course, unique to Christian thought. Hindu and Buddhist holy men have long believed that sensory deprivation results in mastery of the body, which in turn enables the ascetic to attain varying levels of spiritual ecstacy. Domination of the body became an art all to itself to a point never achieved in Christian realms. Holy men of India could remain in a fixed position for days without moving, eating or drinking. Their control of muscular function was such that rate of breathing could be regulated at will, and water taken in through the anus. The bed of nails is famous but lesser Hindu mortifications may not be. There is no Christian equivalent to the practice of clenching the fist perpetually, allowing the finger nails to grow into the flesh of the hand and out the other side. All this to show the mastery of spirit over body.

St Antony of Egypt was the most famous of the early Christian fathers, mostly because his friend and fellow saint, St Athanasius of Alexandria, wrote an enormously popular biography of his life c. 360 AD. The arid wastes of Egypt and the Holy Land were already crowded with hermits by that time, living in mountain caves and deserted tombs. St Antony found his refuge in a lonely Roman fort, barring the door and remaining there for over twenty years. 'It is well to think over what the Apostle says,' he told Athanasius, 'namely, "I die daily."'

Word of these aberrations from established religious conduct spread very slowly to the westward reaches of the Empire. Athanasius himself carried the news to Rome in 340, after being thrown out of Alexandria by adherents of the Arian heresy. He illustrated his talks with examples of the real thing — two genuine hermits. These bearded, filthy ascetics astounded the Romans by their piety and disdain of comfort. Like Antony their food was bread with salt sprinkled in to give it bitterness of taste, and their only drink, water. 'Meat and wine we need not even mention.'

Athanasius' book on Antony was the first significant exposure of asceticism to the west. Its popularity was such that many younger men travelled to Egypt to see the phenomenon for themselves. The best known of these was Palladius, who first arrived in the desert c. 388 and was to remain there for ten years. His *Lausiac History* portrays over eighty ascetics, many of whom found themselves trailed about by droves of dusty, determined followers. For some it was a burden, for others vainglory. For some the path did lead to paradise, for others it was caricature.

Palladius described Macarius of Alexandria who squashed a mosquito stinging his foot: 'accusing himself of having taken revenge, he condemned himself to sit naked for six months in the marsh of Scete, which is in the great desert. The mosquitoes there are like wasps, and even pierce the skins of wild boars. So then he was bitten all over and developed so many swellings that some

thought he had leprosy.' When he returned to his cell after six months only by his voice was he known to all as their elder, Macarius.

The most spectacular of the later ascetics was Simeon the Stylite, the 'Aerial Martyr' as the Emperor Theodosius called him. He had, early in life, shown a predilection for severity. His expulsions from settlements by jealous brothers (his zeal for mortification being an embarrassment) deterred him not at all. He fled to the hills and had himself chained in fetters, with a huge ball attached for good measure. Soon great crowds were following him as he dragged his body through the barren desert. In 423 he built himself a pillar, one of four, and took up residence on it. His last home was over seventy feet high, and the space on which he lived no more than three feet across. In such fashion he spent thirty-six years fasting, mortifying himself and preaching to the faithful who gathered to marvel at this 'great wonder of the world', this 'candle on a candlestick, which sheds its rays on every side.'

By Simeon's time the idea of ascetic retreat had taken hold in Europe. Hermits could be found in just about any cave in Italy and Sicily, but more important was the enthusiasm generated in Gaul. By 400 this Celtic province had been completely Christianised and was, moreover, taking up the intellectual slack that resulted from all the barbarian invasions of Rome. St Martin of Tours, regarded as the Father of monasticism, fused a tradition that has never really died — the merger of ascetic practice with a sense of community. In Egypt there was ample precedent for such a movement, but Martin was the first fanatic, in the Egyptian sense of the word, to put together a desert organisation in the west. Gaul even boasted the first and only pillar saint recorded in Europe. Gregory of Tours, a successor to Martin's bishopric, describes the heroics of Vulfilaic, a ferocious Lombard who found a tribe still worshipping the graven image of Diana. Beside the pagan sanctuary he 'built a column on which I stood in my bare feet in great pain. And when the winter had come as usual I was so nipped by the icy cold that the power of the cold often caused my toe-nails to fall off and frozen moisture hung from my beard like candles. And when a multitude began to flock to me from the neighbouring villages, I preached always that Diana was nothing, that her images and the worship they thought it well to observe were nothing.' But AD 550 was a century past Simeon's time and the bishops came 'who should have urged me the more to continue wisely the work I had begun,' but instead ordered him to come down since 'this way which you follow is not the right one, and a baseless man like you cannot be compared with Simeon.' When he obeyed they destroyed the column forever.

The significance of Gaul to the development of Irish monasticism cannot be overestimated. Contacts between the southern portion of Ireland and the Gaulish mainland were ongoing as early as AD 250. Certainly by the first decades of the 500s, when Irish communities were being established in great numbers, the interplay was steady and important. The biography of Antony, the writings of Palladius, the rule of the first Egyptian 'abbot', Pachomius (translated into Latin by Jerome), Cassian's commentaries on ascetic ideals — all these, it is certain passed back and forth. And in Ireland, as nowhere else in length or persistence, the foam of Egyptian faith found a nest. God was hounded from one corner of this island to the other, pursued by men as determined to possess him as Antony and even Simeon. The Spit is the finest pillar in Western Europe.

The Way of the Cross rises over seven hundred feet from the sea, and its peak is the most exposed portion of the island. As I start to climb the rain begins falling heavily and the wind, even more than usual, is incessant. I wonder if the early hermits went barefoot and suppose that they did. 'He is being punished,' wrote Palladius of an ascetic, yet 'God is curing his soul.'

Soon I come to the Needle's Eye, one of the more notorious devotional obstacles on the climb. This is a long shaft about twenty feet in height which most nearly resembles a chimney. It is four-sided and hollow, the idea being for the pilgrim to squeeze into and up. It is not recommended for those overweight or claustrophobic. Foot and hand holds have been cut into the 'flue' so in effect the passage is disappointingly easy. Once through I gain a small plateau which leads to the Stone of Pain, a smooth rock about fourteen feet high, up which the pilgrim must scramble. All the rocks by now are very slippery and a false step would, in the words of an early visitor, throw one 'headlong, many fathoms into the sea'.

Each of these obstacles, like a station of the cross, was attended with devotions. From what I can learn the form of prayer was basically the repetition of Our Fathers and Hail Marys, over and over again. As to the prayer of the anchorites, we know nothing.

Once the Stone of Pain is surmounted, the trail, though narrow, eventually reaches the summit. The 'tremendousness and awfulness of the prospect' is limited today because of the mist, but at times I can see through its swirling tendrils to the ocean far below, and the commotion is simply overpowering. Some atheist has planted a weather vane on the top, pointing the way north, south, east and west. Somehow I had expected something more fitting.

One final deed is required. In the words of Dr Smith, a physician from Cork City who came to the island in 1756, it 'is attended with the utmost horror and peril'. It is called the Spindle by some, 'and others the Spit; which is a long narrow fragment of rock, projecting from the summit of this frightful place, over a raging sea; and this is walked to by a narrow path only two feet in breadth, and several steps in length. Here the devotees, women as well as men, get astride of this rock, and so edge forward, until they arrive at a stone cross, which some bold adventurer cut formerly, on its extreme end: and here having repeated a pater noster, returning from thence concludes the penance.'

Smith fails to mention the usual kiss, traditionally planted on the cross and the most difficult part of the ordeal. I have a genuine fear of heights but straddle the rock anyway and inch forward towards the end. The drop is no exaggeration and the wind is so fierce that I find myself gripping on with fearful strength. My progress is very slow and far from steady. The wet of the rock is seeping through the pants of my rain gear.

Protestant historians of the eighteenth and nineteenth centuries had a field day with such excessive Catholic pieties, condemning them as idolatries and papist superstitions. A few went further back in time than that and

The Way of the Cross.
Skellig Michael, Co. Kerry

attacked the very principles of asceticism, even the holy saints themselves. 'Some were no more than low sluggards or gloomy misanthropes,' said one, 'who would rather company with wild beasts, with lions, wolves and hyenas than with immortal man.' He went on to comment that 'ascetic holiness...delights in filth,' reversing 'the maxim of sound evangelical morality and modern Christian civilisation that cleanliness is next to godliness'. This may have been germane for a Victorian Protestant ethic, but it misses the point where I am. A Catholic myself, I can recognise the absurdity of what I'm doing. This uncomfortable exercise, to say nothing of dangerous, given weather like this, is now but a ritual (albeit centuries old) yet corrupted, I would think, from a notion more daring and certainly more ancient. What is the basis of a ritual such as this? Taking measure of my own bodily signs — dry mouth, beating pulse, a flying imagination — it seems to me the answer must be fear.

The primary fear of historical men has always been of the unknown after death. Its many cousins are ranged below like a geneological table: the dread of demons and the terror of sudden, intimate murder by sword or fire. The ancients were never far from the reach of fear. Ritual has traditionally been man's way of dealing with fear, the fear of what lay beyond, which God, in the opinion of some, was created to remedy. God was the anchor in a sea of mystery, the only thing to be trusted or relied upon. But God too was an unknown, often more puzzling than even the original void. What shape, what size, what humour, what motives, what demands? No one knew for certain, though the histories of religion are full of seers and prophets who gave this awesome task a try. Ritual merely shook its wizened head. It didn't know. But its job never was to understand, only to guard the faithful through mime. Whoever dreamed up the idea of kissing the end of this rock, which juts out from the mountain top over a

thunderous, threatening sea? No one can say. Was there ever any connection between kissing the end of the stone and a religious truth or dogma? No, never a one. Ritual has always been a mystery of its own making, ritual never makes any sense — we must not expect it to.

Mystery's task is to inform our fear. It tells us what to be afraid of, not directly, but inferentially. The vastness of mystery is terrifying in itself, but through faith the thousands of pilgrims who have crawled like mice to the end of the Spit have experienced the reassurance of knowledge. Faith for them was knowledge, and while this may not be so for today's traveller there is no contesting the ancient hold or power of faith as an historical fact. Like fear, it enjoys a healthy pedigree. To use Sean O'Casey's term, however, no pilgrim ever came here to 'illumine' his fear through legendary ritual. There was no real desire to confront, in truly personal terms, what we call now the abyss. For that we should address ourselves to those whom centuries of pilgrims have imitated, in their own limited, almost timid fashion. Quite simply, the hermits themselves.

The hermits who came to Skellig Michael were admittedly a fairly strange group of men, and we must accept from the start, I think, that the majority of them suffered from obsession — their spirits were diseased with Christ. He was their cancer, the sickness was terminal, it destroyed their lives. But if you scrape away this tumour you arrive at two truths. The first is they feared nothing. No demon was so threatening, no task so hard, no discomfort of body so awful that it kept them out of combat. Theirs was a holy war. What saves them for us is a glimmer of humanity, very small indeed but there. They scorned the devil but, strangely, had what almost could be called respect for one of his snares. Not the lust for women or riches, which they feared but little, nor the hardships of meagre food or drink. Rather it was 'accidie' which John Cassian identified as the 'midday demon' spoken of in the 90th Psalm, 'the destruction that wasteth at noonday'. It was dejection, despair, the feeling that the fight was not going well, the idea that maybe it should be given up. Accidie resulted in irresolution and slackening of effort. It was a subtle trap, less glaring than ordinary vice, perhaps even forgivable. The only remedy was persistence and determination, the boldness of spirit that would not be pushed aside. Palladius once wrote of the advice an older hermit gave him when he was striken with accidie: 'I went to him and said, 'Father, what shall I do? Since my thoughts afflict me saying, "You are making no progress, go away from here." And he said to me, "Tell them, for Christ's sake I am guarding the walls!"'

The second truth is heretical. Conventional Christianity teaches that we are utterly dependent upon God: with him we have a chance, without him we are lost. In medieval terms this was best expressed by Augustine who emphasised over and over again that if we reject the gifts of God — namely, grace — we have no weapon with which to beat off the devil at play. We become a demon's pawn if we turn our back on the outstretched hand of God.

Augustine formulated these famous teachings in response to those of Pelagius, a Celtic monk born in Britain c. 350. Pelagius is remembered today (remotely) as the forefather of deism. In his own lifetime the theories he espoused caused endless strife and earned for him the hatred of many early saints. Jerome characterised him as a 'most stupid fellow, heavy with Irish porridge,' and the tides of condemnation arose to sweep the man away. He died an exile's death somewhere in the east, c. 429.

The crux of his teaching centred on the premise of free will and involved the rejection of original sin. Pelagius believed that man is uncontaminated by the fall of Adam and unaffected by the crucifixion of Christ. The movement of a soul towards goodness and God is determined completely by the will of the individual. Sin is therefore 'not born with man, it is not a product of nature, but of the will. Man is born both without virtue and without vice, but with the capacity for either.' Accordingly God is seen as the detached Creator, not the personalised extrovert whose aid we need for eternal salvation.

Augustine stumbled, however, when he was confronted with the sight of godly heathens. He sought to differentiate between their virtue ('corrupt') and that of a Christian by saying that the love of God alone inspires true goodness, but only grace permits us to love him. Heathen virtue, achieved without grace, is a lower species unlikely to be accepted by God, for it stems not from Christ.

Julian of Eclanum,[1] a disciple of Pelagius, took exception to this logic and commented that 'if the chastity of a heathen were no chastity, then it might be said with the same propriety that the bodies of unbelievers are no bodies; that the eyes of the heathen could not see; that the grain which grew in their fields was no grain'. Pelagius believed in the ability of man to be good, just and decent on his own merits. He could seek and find God himself, could lead a life of justice if he so desired. Jew, Christian or pagan alike became capable of moral goodness. All of these theories were suppressed c. 430. When I was in school Augustine was required reading. Pelagius had none of the 'rich, deep life of faith' to recommend him.

Now the hermits were clearly wilful men, guilty of pride, far from humble. Most cared not a bit for the outcome of theological argument, their beliefs were very much their own. The implications of Augustine's writings were serious, though, inasmuch as they struck at the very heart of what many ascetics held to be the truth. As the church emerged from the glow of evangelism and developed into a bureaucratic entity, the split between bishops and ascetics became open, Bishops, like lawyers, were concerned with uniformity of dogma, regularisation of dioceses and the administration of power, secular as well as spiritual. To the hermit such interests were nonsense. 'This is an old maxim of the Fathers,' wrote Cassian, 'a monk ought by all means to fly from women and bishops.'

The badge of ascetic life was Pelagian. There was no intermediary between the hermit and God, neither bishop nor grace. Grace was acknowledged, of course, as a gift from God but the hermits thought it curious and questioned its importance. They believed in themselves and trusted their own ways, living the heroic life of Moses.

Clochán, *Slea Head, Co. Kerry*

'Greeks go abroad and cross the sea to study letters,' said Antony. 'but we have no need to go abroad for the Kingdom of Heaven, nor to cross the sea to obtain virtue. The Lord has told us in advance: "The Kingdom of Heaven is within you." Virtue therefore has need only of our will, since it is within us and springs from us.' The Pelagian thrust was an affirmation of human strength, and sitting out here on this rocky spur my thoughts drift away from the pieties of so many pilgrims who have been here before, doing the same thing (with probably more nerve) than I. Instead what radiates throughout this wild and savage storm is the simplicity or naïveté, whichever you prefer, of ancient man — his confidence, all knowing and incontestable, that he was confronting God face to face. The rite of the Spit was not, I think, really a ceremony per se for the hermit. It was something more: an awesome conversation that somehow, through insufferable pride or fanaticism or complete insanity, was perceived as being between equals, or if not that, at least between friends speaking the same language. The Spit, at some point in time, evolved into ritual, of course, an experience even I can't duplicate as I bend over to kiss the wet and salty stone — I have too little faith. To go beyond even this simple step (merely a re-enactment) is almost unimaginable. 'I saw Satan like lightning falling from heaven,' Antony recalls, quoting Luke. Somehow, rocking back and forth on the Spit, wind blowing, rain beating and ocean breaking, I can well understand that he did. What I see here is not God — who of us today could — but the past: intimate, physical, almost visual. 'Memory is a root in the dark,' wrote the poet Octavio Paz, and dangling here one is drawn to his point.

Another dank evening in my cell. After washing with some water from the monastery's well, I decide that today is a good time to circle the island, to see if I can find the two other ancient landing spots and their stairs. The weather is dull and overcast, the mainland clearly visible, but without the sparkle of the sun the view provokes little enthusiasm. Both Skelligs are surrounded with broad haloes of grimy foam. As I walk along the north slope I am startled to see about fifty yards ahead two men on their hands and knees peering into a hole. I am within twenty feet of them before the smaller of the two notices me. His shock reveals a mixture of sheer surprise and embarrassment. Have I caught two poachers?

It takes a few minutes for the two of them to calm down. I learn they are keepers at the lighthouse and they learn who I am. It is evident they consider me a bit ghoulish, coming out in this weather to rummage around in old ruins. They ask repeatedly why I didn't wait until summer.

I inquire as to what it is they're doing and discover the makings of a Skellig blood sport. Years and years ago some unknown soul brought a pair of rabbits to the island. I have seen one or two myself. Along with puffins they are largely responsible for the rock slides I noticed my first day here. Both species burrow into the thin sea-pink to make nests, and thereby loosen the fabric of shale that keeps everything on the slopes intact. The rabbits especially have become a nuisance.

Puffins are scrappy little birds who enjoy fighting with each other in spring during mating season. Their appearance gives no indication of an aggressive character: they sport a handsome plumage of black and white feathers set off during mating by the brightest of orange beaks. Their tiny webbed feet are also that colour. For some reason their demeanour and antics remind me of penguins. They are the only cheerful thing about the Great Skellig.

Puffins are used to rabbits, moving into abandoned burrows when and where they find them. If none are available they will dig their own in steam shovel fashion, their beaks scooping up the dirt and depositing it by their feet, which then kick it out behind them. They can even work the rock itself if it is soft and flaky.

One of my new companions caught a puffin earlier this morning. He had simply stuck his hand in a tunnel and pulled one out. The puffin had pecked and fought all the

18

way, and the hands of his captor are covered with bruises and bleeding cuts. Then the two of them waited until they saw a rabbit, followed him to his den and stuck the puffin in after. They blocked the hole so neither could escape. This contest, I gather, represents one of their few amusements on this remote assignment. It is, they say, hardship duty. Because I am a novelty the sport is abandoned. The puffin takes off as soon as he is able. The rabbit stays motionless in his hole.

The bolder spirit, John, who had stuck his hand in the burrow, says this is tame stuff indeed. When he was growing up his father used to take him hunting for foxes. They would find a lair and crawl in if they could. With a stick in one hand his father would tantalise the fox, almost mesmerising it, until he could get close enough to grab the scruff of his neck with the other hand. He and his father would get a pound a fox from the local hunt. He shows us a missing inch from his right hand, the result of a quicker fox than he.

I find these fellow inmates agreeable and while they know nothing about the monastery (and care less about it), they seem well versed in animal lore. Puffins for example: most ocean birds such as the herring gull and guillemot accompany their offspring in its first flight to sea, but not so the puffin. When an infant puffin is about seven weeks old its parents fly away from the nest never to return, even to each other. The chick endures several days of anxious hunger before working up the courage to venture forth. He eventually waddles out of his burrow in the dead of night and throws himself over the cliff. In this dark and lonely fashion he faces the world by himself, instinctively flapping his wings to soften the landing on water below. In the course of a night he experiments on the ocean and learns to fly, swim and fish. He then heads out to sea.

'In the spring and the beginning of summer,' wrote Dr Smith, 'the country people resort hither in small boats, when the sea is calm, to catch these birds; they eat the flesh, which is filthy and rank; but the principal profit is made by the feathers. The birds are exceedingly fat, and the persons who take them carry on a kind of traffic with them, by exchanging two salted puffins for a peck of meal.

They eat them in Lent, and on their fast days as well as fish.' I ask if anyone hunts the birds these days, a question which provokes them to laughter. 'Who'd want them?' one cries. 'No one in Ireland is that poor any more.'

We clamber about the rocks and four other kinds of birds are loudly pointed out: the guillemot, kittiwake and two varieties of gull. The gannet, curiously enough, is never seen on the Great Skellig. We come around by the old lighthouse which is situated on the western corner of the island. It was built in 1826 but eventually abandoned because of its exposed position; the Atlantic proved too much for a nineteenth-century construction. I ask about the graves of two children that were dug in the old monastery, and find out they were the infant son and daughter of a keeper; both children starved to death one winter when the supply boat couldn't land for over two months because of stormy weather. I am asked down to the new lighthouse for some tea. Shivering with spring's chill we come off the slopes.

The new lighthouse was built just a few years ago. It is more sheltered than its predecessor and faces due south. There are three keepers on duty, each of whom stays six weeks on and then two off. There is someone awake checking the machinery at all times. The island is re-supplied with food every two weeks by helicopter. Radio reports — called 'weighing in' — are transmitted to the mainland each morning. Neighbouring ocean stations are the Tearaght Light to the west and two others to the east: the Bull and Fastnet Rock. Wives and children are no longer allowed on offshore lights. From talking with the men, two of whom are married, I gather the separation is welcomed. 'We're here 'cause we're queer,' says the bachelor. There is a television to help while away the time, and it is on constantly in the evening. None of the keepers have any hobbies or reading interests. As we are drinking tea the weather weighs in over the wireless. Gale warnings and stormy weather for the next two days. The threats of high winds and water alters nothing in the daily routine. A switch is thrown at dusk as usual. From what I can see this is all they have to do provided nothing breaks down.

I am invited to stay at the lighthouse. There are extra bunks and considering the weather everyone thinks it might be best. This is all against regulations but no one cares. Two nights on a saint's bed is enough for me so I agree, and trundle off to get my gear.

That evening I assimilate myself into the routine. I inspect the lighthouse from bottom to top, noting in particular an eccentric blend of old with new. Dinner is fresh fish and I am asked to join in. I enquire how the fishing is, expecting an enthusiastic reply. To my surprise I am told it is terrible. None of the three ever fish and they don't know any keeper who does. The fishermen throw a few up on the dock down at Blind Man's Cover every once in a while, and that's the only really fresh food they ever eat.

The conversation is animated. I am such a willing listener that many tall tales burst forth. The head keeper tells me about the Fastnet. In trade talk the Fastnet is a 'trap rock'. It is minuscule, like Lemon Rock, just a few feet above sea level. In brisk weather it is impossible to land. The lighthouse itself is a tall, slender cone of one hundred and fifty feet. He remembers a winter storm some years back when fourteen waves completely swamped the lighthouse — rollers over a hundred and fifty feet high! I cannot even imagine it. The light was flooded out and he and his fellow keepers huddled in the bottom of the shaft, expecting with every wave to be swept into the sea. It is a fine story. I don't even care whether it's true or not.[2]

In the course of the evening it becomes obvious that most of the keepers have nicknames, largely derogatory. Our head keeper summarises the more infamous, all of whom are neighbours: on the Bull reigns The General, on Fastnet lives The Senator and on Tearaght, The Bishop, so dubbed for his holiness — he fasts each Wednesday and Sunday. Everyone laughs and the head keeper leaves for bed. Behind his back I discover his tag, The Minister for Information, because he's a gossip and a snoop. I am asked not to tell him I was so informed.

Friday. On this stormy day I sleep until noon. I have run out of food and thus am dependent on these new found friends for tea and bread. John, who fancies himself a cook, baked a loaf during his night watch and he cuts off thick wedges for lunch. These he calls 'doorsteps'.

I laze about for the day and spend a couple of hours just sitting by the great light, listening to the rain batter against the glass. For dinner I have bread and tea. The Minister for Information opens a can of rice pudding for dessert.

Saturday. More of the same — rain and doorsteps. No boat will be out today.

Sunday. I might get off this afternoon everyone says, although I am certainly in no hurry. With an ancient spyglass under his arm the Minister for Information walks down to the copter pad and scans the horizon. He sees two boats coming our way, both fishermen. One of these is probably mine.

At about 2.00 I go down again, gear in hand, and sure enough my boat is about a mile off. I say goodbye to my friends, thanking them for putting me up. They seem sad to see me go, and throw my things across after I jump into the boat. As we back out the three wave to us and we, like children, wave in return.

The fisherman was worried about me, he said, especially when the weather turned rough and unfriendly. He said he hoped I wouldn't mind but he planned to check his pots off Valentia Island since he was out, even though it was a Sunday. It would add a couple of hours to our trip.

The northern coast of Valentia is wild and cliff-bound. The sun has disappeared and yet more storm clouds gather on the horizon. By the time we start pulling up traps it is raining hard, the Skelligs cannot be seen. I am drenched by the time we reach Knights Town and change into dry clothes at the fisherman's.

I feel like today is a Sunday as I set off again that evening. The rain has stopped but the dusk is wet and cold; few people are out on the lonely country roads. There is perfect stillness. I can recall a poem from a book of haiku that I generally take with me when I travel:

> Fresh spring!
> The world is only
> Nine days old —
> These fields and mountains!

20

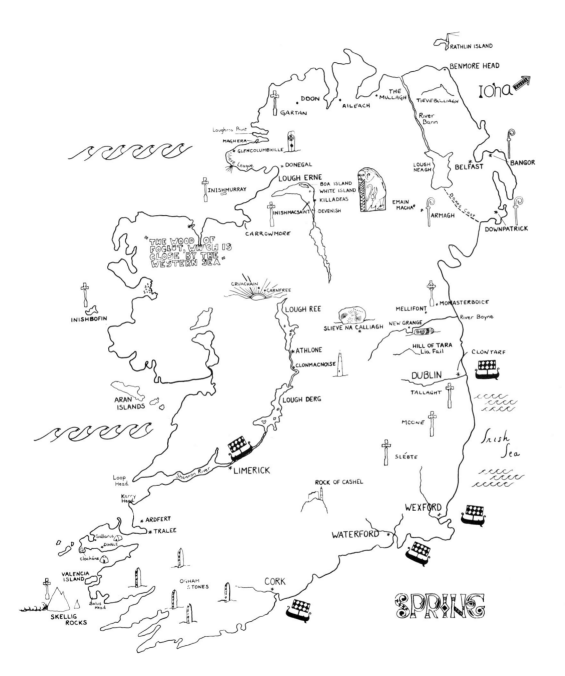

Map of Ireland

1 *Newgrange*

Raw and cold is icy spring, cold will arise in the wind; the ducks of the watery pool have raised a cry, passionately wailful is the harsh-shrieking crane which the wolves hear in the wilderness at the early rise of morning; birds awaken from meadows, many are the wild creatures from which they flee out of the wood, out of the green grasses.

The Four Seasons Irish, eleventh century

I HAVE been told by friends in Dublin to prepare myself for a shock. We all visited Newgrange together many years ago, when the spring winds were rolling in from the west, shaking the huge elms that grew around the mound on its throne of a ridge top, throwing rain and flying topsoil over the long, sloping, empty fields down to the river, dotted with their own smaller cairns and the occasional standing stone. The aged caretaker, emerging from his rickety wooden shed, dim flashlight in hand, led us, crouching, down the passageway to the interior of the great tomb itself, where we could finally stand upright to admire the abstruse yet strangely modern decorations of nameless prehistoric artisans, and the large stone basins lying empty at our feet, once full of the dust and debris of human remains. We remembered O'Faolain's warning that here 'we have no bridge on which to step across so many centuries. It is as if our minds had lost a dimension in the darkness of an interrupted civilisation.'

All this, I am told, has been lost. Transformed through restoration, Newgrange stands now as a gleaming, mechanistic marvel that has little in common with the waywardness of romantic imagination, but rather belongs to the cold, brash currency of a modern Ireland. 'If Neushwanstein is your idea of a medieval castle, then the Newgrange experience is fine,' someone said to me a

couple of nights ago. 'Otherwise, don't bother.' The heated talk, naturally enough, made me anxious to go.

Irish landscape, I think to myself as I drive north out of Dublin, depends more than most on the weather for effect. When it's raining hard, of course, a drab Irish gray wattles every feature of the view into glum uniformity. This is not, I find, as bad as it sounds; in fact, it is preferable to the reverse (and often pervasive) condition of gleaming haze, which dissolves the vibrancy out of colour and leaves what is left a washed-out, listless pastel. I lean to the damp, overcast, wet day when the land glistens and radiates a sheen, rather like freshly washed hair, making the fields and roads, the stone walls and buildings, dense and textured — there is nothing like it for impact, especially (as is many times the case) when alternated like piano keys with patches of clearing light, the threatening clouds creating layers of drama with rays of the sun. Nowhere is the sky more theatrical than in Ireland.

Today is such a day, and leaving Drogheda at the coast for the inland road that follows the river Boyne, I marvel at the valley's low hillocks and grooved farmlands ready for spring planting, at the same time soaked but sun drenched — the land serene, the daylight in turmoil.

I cross the Boyne to its southern bank at Oldbridge, known better as the heart of battle 1 July 1690, passing the stump where a victory obelisk to William of Orange once stood, since dynamited by offended patriots. My aim is to catch first sight of Newgrange from across the river. The Boyne begins a great protective arc at this point that will not finish its sweep until the town of Slane, five miles further along. Within this semicircular bend lie more than thirty-five monuments to the creative energies of prehistoric man, the most imposing of which are the enormous megalithic tombs — Newgrange, Knowth and Dowth.

As a collective description, scholars have dubbed this area the Boyne culture, even though the time span between early and later remains is frequently several centuries. Nothing has yet been found to suggest an actual village or settlement in the medieval sense. Instead the entire area seems to have been set aside as holy ground, a place for burial and worship, a vast and deserted necropolis.

It is probable that early bands of mesolithic peoples — the first inhabitants of Ireland — lived along the shores of the river prior to neolithic migrations that brought the builders of Newgrange to these shores. They were a more simple people who knew nothing of agriculture or the keeping of domestic animals. Their source of food was never certain. They hunted in coastal forests, fished in the sea and rivers and gathered what wild foods they could find. Where they came from and how is uncertain, but remains of their largest settlements are found clustered along the northern coast of Antrim. Among the immense basalt cliffs of this area they discovered lodes of flint, the soft, workable stone they preferred for tools and weapons.

As the more advanced neolithic tribes began coursing into Ireland c. 3500 BC we can follow the movements of these primitive fishermen and hunters as they turned in-land. Since Ireland was largely forested at the time the only avenues of escape were the river valleys, and not surprisingly it is along the river Bann in Ulster that most mesolithic remains have been discovered. The Bann from Coleraine to Lough Neagh is the main waterway to the interior from the northern coast. At scores of locations along its flow we find traces of mesolithic settlement. Most were probably semi-permanent camp sites, hastily erected and then deserted when newcomers came following along the river. These places are generally marked by their refuse, called 'middens' by archaeologists: huge piles of oyster shells, animal bones, broken flints and so forth, all indications of their dependencies in life.

The fate of the Boyne mesolithic peoples is largely conjecture. They undoubtedly had settlements at the mouth of the river and probably filtered inland at least as far as the great bend, which marks the high point of the Boyne's tidal reach. Whether they pushed on further or made an accommodation here with the newer peoples we cannot know. They disappear from our sight.

The neolithic arrivals came mostly, it seems, from Central Europe. They were farming peoples who appear to have shared a cultural if not a tribal unity: they planted alike, they herded alike, and they made stone tools and weapons alike. But essentially, in the words of one observer, 'we know almost nothing about them.'

In discussing the histories of this culture we are now, in our own times, at a turning point. The traditional explanation for structures in Western Europe as special as Newgrange, for instance, generally attributes their construction to a nameless group of adventurers somehow more gifted than their contemporaries — unique, distinct, often 'newly arrived'. In the case of Newgrange it has been assumed that this superior neolithic tribe originated somewhere in Eastern Europe, perhaps the Mediterranean area, from whence they supposedly travelled, over the course of several generations, to the Iberian peninsula and then north to Brittany, a later colonial offshoot finally making it to Ireland c. 3000 BC. In their wake they left clusters of impressive remains: temples in Malta, passage graves in southeast Spain and Portugal, great fields of standing stones and more graves in Brittany, climaxed by Newgrange and its satellites in Ireland. People who specialise in Irish prehistory tagged this ethnic group as a 'megalithic' people, the term derived from the simple definition of megalith which is 'huge stone'. It describes the ability of these newcomers to think and work in the most grandiose of terms imaginable. Their skill in organisation and construction techniques, together with ambition, set them apart from other neolithic tribes and made them masters of the Boyne and its surroundings for miles and miles.

I can remember from my childhood history classes hearing all this laid out in neat precision. It was rather like diagramming a sentence: a colony here, another there, the corroborating link being a stone arch or circle of 'similar' design, a spiral decoration 'held in common' and so forth. This progression was essentially marked by the devotion it paid to the formulative influence of Grecian culture over that of a more backward west. The spectacular citadel of Mycenae, for example — Agamemnon's capital with its famous list of ruins: the Treasury of Atreus, the Lion's Gate, the tomb of Clytemnestra and so forth — was a favourite parental clue, generally seen as a primal force in the development of 'later' monuments in Iberia, Brittany and the British Isles. Stonehenge is another illustration of this attitude, a historian of some repute insisting that its architect 'must almost certainly have been a man familiar with the buildings of the contemporary civilisations of the Mediterranean world.' The connecting link? Wandering tribesmen or traders.

In 1973, however, a book entitled *Before Civilization: The Radiocarbon Revolution and Prehistoric Europe*, written by a professor of archaeology at Southhampton University in Great Britain, by the name of Colin Renfrew, pretty well demolished the sequential or 'diffusionist' theory on the basis of data developed over a period of thirty years during laboratory research of the most arcane sort. Renfrew, who initially (he says) meant no harm to any of the cherished dogmas in his field, was primarily concerned with the technological processes of radiocarbon dating, the single most devastating tool in the history of archaeological science. A complicated verification procedure of the carbon-14 dating (involving comparison with the annual tree rings of bristlecone pines, some of which have been alive for over five thousand years) first warned him that several accepted theories of development were seemingly erroneous, that in fact many western monuments were centuries older than those at Mycenae and considerably more ancient than even the pyramids. The notion of Aegean colonists sailing westward to Iberia, with monumental designs and ideas of cultural advancement in mind, was absolutely shattered, and with it the 'chess game of migrations'. 'Movements of peoples', he wrote, 'are no longer acceptable as explanations for the changes seen in the archaeological record.'

Within Western Europe itself a few more established speculations, for many years sacrosanct, fell to the ground as well. According to Renfrew's new procedures for dating, the Brittany monuments within the triangle of Carnac, Locmariaquer and Auray were at least a thousand years older than their cousins in Spain, thus invalidating that migration too. Newgrange remained steady at *c.* 3000 BC but the usual arguments as to its builders — that 'new' tribe of neolithic immigrants — now became suspect. In Renfrew's opinion all of these monuments in the west were the result of a 'continuous evolutionary process', a 'local response to local factors'. In a summary that he wrote four years later, Renfrew concluded that 'the study of pre-history is in crisis'.[1]

A few minutes after crossing at Oldbridge I pull over to the side of the road and leave the car, starting up on foot to a ridge overlooking the Boyne and Newgrange itself, across the river and further north. After climbing over brambles and barbed-wire fences to an elevation of about three hundred feet, I finally turn round to pick out Newgrange from the landscape. It is a sight that startles me, a blend of both astonishment and something close to guilt. I am in love with it, but wonder whether I should be.

In the same spot, back in the early sixties when I saw this great burial mound for the first time, I can recall how it took a few moments to locate it, a small green hemispherical lump on a pasture lower than my own vantage point, covered with trees and scrub vegetation, neighboured on the terraces sloping down to the Boyne by other smaller mounds and a rather prominent standing stone. The tomb stood about two hundred feet above the river at its most symmetrical bend. By walking to and fro you could also locate Dowth off to the right, and continuing to the west the tumulus of Knowth would eventually come into view, two hundred and fifty feet above the river. I remember these as marvellous vistas — the excitement of discovery and appreciation with each tomb identified. But it did not take my breath away, as this apparition so many years later has.

Storm clouds passing, various shafts of streaking sunlight illuminating the entire northern bank of the Boyne, there at the apex of the ridge is a shimmering Newgrange. My first impression is that of stainless steel, something not exactly bright but rather glistening. This is obviously the famous (or infamous, depending on one's point of view) outer layer of brilliant white quartz stones that the tomb had been faced with, hundreds of which were discovered at the foot of its entrance during excavations, and which are alleged to have coated the mound as a final decorative step on the part of its builders. Accentuating their glow is the new sleek look of Newgrange itself, now bereft of trees and its hoary, gently rounded dome, restored to an original (it is believed) drumlike appearance that, again, brings to mind some odd comparisons. I am reminded here of Scandinavian dinnerware and Frank Lloyd Wright's furniture, a modernistic look of spare elegance. The rest of the valley seems outmatched and dowdy, the arena of fusty antiquarians in ill-fitting smock coats preaching conservatism and hesitation. Whoever did this to Newgrange, I thought, has surely made and deserved his enemies.

An hour or so later I am at the site itself and the marvel of it all has yet to dissipate, though aesthetically there is a let-down. The wonders of modern Newgrange are better felt from afar, I think, for a structure as old as this one should not appear to the eye as though it was built only yesterday. Up close, this is the feeling one has — not just that the place is tidy, but that it's germ free. The facing of quartz, for example, so striking two miles away, is a disappointment close at hand, particularly the insertion (with computer-like symmetry) of darker coloured gray granite stones that were found during digging intermixed with the quartz. The look, according to the excavator himself, is that of a 'currant cake', the gray boulders representing raisins in the mix. To say the effect is a curious one understates the matter. A car and bus park, the new paved entrance road, modern toilets, an exhibition kiosk — these additions to the Newgrange scene are regrettable but cannot, in all honesty, be argued with, for after entering the enclosure itself one's back is turned to the commotion. But the only way to escape from the quartz is to enter the tomb.

Of the three great mounds Newgrange seems by far the most satisfying visit. Knowth has been closed to the public for over ten years while an archaeological dig progresses, mostly during the summer months when inexpensive student workers are available. It is surrounded by a heavy security fence. Dowth, on the other hand, is the flea market of the three. It has suffered from the indiscriminate rummaging of countless looters and explorers, starting with the Vikings in 862, to say nothing of later barbarians. The most notorious of the many excavations was an 1847 Royal Irish Academy effort. Puzzled as to how they should enter, the committee decided that a central shaft be driven down the centre of its cone, which was carried out only after destroying a Chinese-style pagoda, built on top of the mound in the early 1800s by Viscount Netterville as a folly and tea house. With the dig completed only a portion of the earth was replaced, which leaves Dowth looking like a collapsed soufflé. This irritating cavity gives fine shelter for a picnic, however, and provides a dramatic view of Newgrange just a mile off. The interior is unfortunately a major disappointment, since many of the support pillars, called orthostats, have long since collapsed or disappeared. They were replaced by

Newgrange and the Boyne Terrace, with Satellite Mounds, Co. Meath

drab concrete columns which contribute a somewhat depressing aura to the place. Newgrange, at the present moment, is certainly the most rewarding of the three.

This stupendous monument was probably the most important of the three anyway. Aside from its formidable location in terms of both the Boyne itself and the other mounds (Newgrange being in the centre), two additional features make it unique. One is the great circle of standing stones that surround the mound. The second is a 'roof-box' that, incredibly, orients the entire structure towards the winter solstice. Both features were possibly related, and if so the common link would probably have been a clerical sect of some sort, perhaps dominated by a single high priest of exceptional vigour and scholarship.

We met the shadow of this man, or his sort, on the Great Skellig — in fact, the history of Ireland is dotted with his presence, for few societies in the world have been as obsessed with religious matters as this one. It is possible, I think, to imagine the arguments he must have used before tribal assemblies to initiate this project, so dear to himself and his cadre of disciples. They had studied the matter, they had figured it out, roaming about the hills for years, watching the heavens, noting its cycles, discussing among themselves mysteries in the sky. Their people below — clearing woods, growing crops, breeding stocks of cattle, sheep, pigs and dogs, making huts — were achieving a measure of real prosperity, a reflection, their priests would remind them, of God's pleasure. But some tribute was necessary, some monument of enduring strength that would stand forever, through which the dead might pass to the other world and their God speak to them in return. It would be an extraordinary structure, nothing like it had ever been undertaken. What chief in the world, what people, would shirk a duty so enormous and yet so prestigious? And so the project might have started.

For his site the priest has chosen the very centre of the great bend. Consulting with builders and architects he traces the outline of the passageway and central chamber, and orders trees in the vicinity cut down that this great work might be seen from miles away. The chieftains, for their part, mobilise the tribe and delegate responsibilities. Their people have succeeded in meeting the land on at least equal terms: there is enough food in the productive cycle to free a labour force from agricultural duty for most of the year. Teams will have to be formed, tasks assigned and quotas met. A bureaucratic machine, one of the earliest and most sophisticated in the annals of man's prehistory, takes form.

Sophisticated yet primitive, of course. As I look over the valley with its open fields and rounded hilltops, I remind myself what an enormous job just the clearance of forest must have been. This was a Stone Age endeavour: no tools of metal, no machinery, no efficient vehicles of transport, the most common implements being stone axes, stone mauls, stone hammers, stone chisels. It is amazine that any energy was left over after the ridge was stripped of its cover to proceed, for the next step — assembly of materials — was equally demanding. Quarries had to be found and stonecutters employed in working them. With tools made from porcellanite or other hard stone, large chunks of rock are either hacked loose from their bedding or incised with long and deep veins which are filled with water, allowed to freeze over, then heated with fires and gradually wedged off. These are probably dressed at the quarry, as workmen even and smooth off the surface by banging with crude hammers. When finished they are strapped to wooden sledges, and gangs of haulers or teams of 'bewildered bullocks' are gathered to drag the stones off, one by one. This work of transport was surely the most menial of the many tasks required at Newgrange and constituted the labour of the poorest classes. The stone-cutters were skilled workers by comparison, with plenty to occupy their time at either quarry or work site. Because the area immediately surrounding the Boyne is pock-marked with little valleys, the job cannot have been easy. As the wheel was unknown, sledges with rollers were certainly used. Rope was probably made from cattle skins

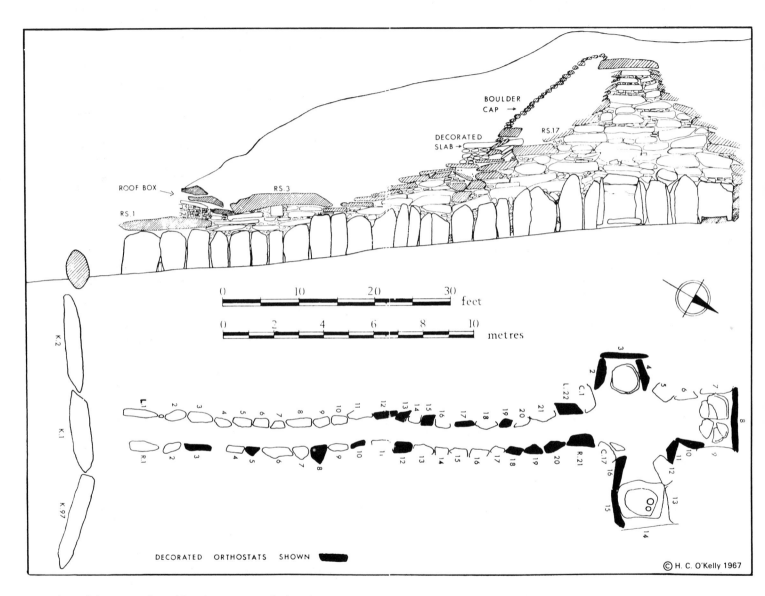

BOULDER CAP →

DECORATED SLAB →

RS.17

ROOF BOX →

RS.3

RS.1

0   10   20   30 feet

0   2   4   6   8   10 metres

K.2

K.1

K.97

L.1

2 3 4 5 6 7 8 9 10 11 12 13 14 15 16 17 18 19 20 21 L.22 C.1

R.1

2 3 4 5 6 7 8 9 10 11 12 13 14 15 16 17 18 19 20 R.21 C.17

3 2 4 5 6 7 8 9 10 11 12 13 14 15 16

DECORATED ORTHOSTATS SHOWN

© H. C. O'Kelly 1967

Plan and sectional profile of passage and chamber at Newgrange

twined together. What kind of daily progress was made we can only guess.

Meanwhile the ridge at the Boyne has been prepared for building. The passageway and central chamber have been carefully laid out, and with the arrival of the first great stones the digging begins. First the passageway is started. Forty-three standing stones are entrenched, twenty-two on one side, twenty-one on the other. These range from five to eight feet in height and are roofed with equally large slabs going crosswise. Corbel stones are wedged between supports and roof slabs at intervals, to help with the weight that soon will be stacked above the structure. The finished passage is sixty-two feet in length and the aisle approximately a yard in width. The priest would have been seen in frequent consultation with those in charge of construction, anxious that the upward slope of the passageway correspond exactly with his specifications.

As the work progresses artisans have been busy decorating various stones with ingenious designs of spirals, chevrons, diamonds, zigzags and suns. They are puzzled when the priest instructs labourers to place some of the decorated roof slabs face up. Dirt and stone, when piled high above the passageway, will cover all their craftsmanship. Much of their work is for God's eye only.

Next the main chamber is built. Here the visitor can stand erect after the confining sixty-two foot squirm from entrance to interior. The chamber is oval in plan, not unlike a *clochán*. Great stones are laid in corbel manner — that is, one on top of the other, slanting inward — until a single capstone completes the dome. From floor to ceiling is about nineteen feet. Off this central chamber in cruciform pattern are three smaller rooms or recesses. Pillar stones are set about at the edges of the chamber, and all have been decorated.

Completion of the inner mausoleum was marked, at the start of the tunnel, by the insertion of Newgrange's most astonishing feature. The 'roof-box' is a small, hollow, rectangular stone frame placed in a portion of the passageway ceiling cut especially for it, about eight feet in from the entrance. The lintel of this frame, overhanging the box on top, has been carefully decorated with a long row of half diamonds. It is a particular marvel through

which, according to stone age theology, God would speak.

This box represents the major discovery of recent excavations, as before 1962 only the decorated lintel of the structure had been visible to the eye. The antiquarian Sir William Wilde, father of Oscar, was the first to comment in print on what he considered to be a 'very curious' rock which was revealed *c.* 1699 at the same time as the entrance was discovered. 'This most exquisitely carved stone,' wrote Wilde in 1844, 'of which we can only perceive the edge, is five feet eight inches long; its sculpture, both in design and execution, far exceeds any of the rude carvings which are figured, apparently at random, upon the stones found within the cave; and as it never could have been intended to be concealed from view, it is probable that it decorates the entrance into some other chamber, which further examination may yet disclose.' Wilde, like so many of those infatuated with Irish megalithic remains, felt that Newgrange might preserve an inner arrangement similar to Egyptian pyramids, several of which had separate rooms built on top of, or adjacent to, the major burial vaults. At least Sir William curbed his curiosity to dig around the stone itself, a restraint not shared by an English visitor in 1874 who casually employed '2 men with crowbars' to see if they could work the stone loose. Later attempts were equally crude and luckless, for when the entire apparatus was professionally excavated it was found largely intact, though its purpose remained at first a complete mystery.

With the roof-box installed, builders turn to minor details. Small wedges are taken into the central chamber and jammed among the crevices of the larger slabs to tighten up the structure as much as possible. Any slippage on the part of these stones (the pressure of the walls and roof being inwards) would trigger a cave-in or partial collapse. And then stonecutters are instructed to chisel out small gutters on the roof slabs. Rainwater that penetrates into the mound will thus run off from the passageway.

For many months labour gangs have been busy transporting sea sand to the site from beaches at the mouth of the Boyne, ten miles away. Laden down with its weight, they let the tidal current push their rafts along, but many times they must pole in unison to make headway. The men who hauled the great stones await them when they arrive at the bend. With baskets made from twigs or wicker, they carry load after load up to the finished monument, pouring the sand over it. On top of this coating, gobs of burnt turf, mixed with water, are matted about the chamber as a caulking compound. A researcher would later tell me that experiments indicated such a mixture hardened 'to the consistency of cement'. The sand and turf, of course, are designed to protect the inner structure from water seeping in through outer layers of stones (for the most part hand-sized) which are now ready to be hauled from the riverbed below to the ridge.

In expectation of this final effort a great outer ring of curb stones has been built to form a collar, approximately two hundred and seventy feet in diameter and more than an acre in area. These stones, forty-seven of which are now exposed, are from five to fifteen feet in length and weigh between four and five tons each. They are meant to buttress and support the small stones and fill that soon will be piled over the tomb itself to a height of over fifty-five feet. The estimated weight of this mound, or cairn, is two hundred thousand tons. Artisans have decorated many of the curb stones with zigzags, chevrons and diamonds. They have spent considerable time on the most important of these, the entrance stone.

Streams of men now plod up and down the ridge, carrying water-rolled stones from the Boyne out of which the great mound will rise. Every so often courses of fresh turf are added.[2] Many months of hard work and hundreds of thousands of stones later, builders add final touches, the first a layer of bright quartz crystal, fixed in a revetment wall to the front of the tomb, intended without a doubt to serve as a beacon from great distances away. No supply of this stone exists near the Boyne, and search teams of prehistoric geologists must have worked for months if not years to find such a deposit, eventually mined from veins in the Dublin/Wicklow Mountains to the south. Once again rafts and canoes of dugout logs — perhaps even barges — set out and return, trip after trip, until enough of the stone is collected and arranged at Newgrange to absorb the sun's warmth and to reflect its brilliance. A standing pillar is then placed on the summit of the cairn (it disappeared sometime in the early 1700s), and a great ring of stones, possibly thirty-five in number, encircles the mound. The tomb is complete.

Joining the inevitable tour filing into the passageway, we all struggle down to the centre of the tomb. Its interior, remarkably, remained untouched from the day of its completion until the close of the seventeenth century, when workmen of a local landlord in search of building materials accidently uncovered the now famous entrance stone ('one of the most remarkable slabs not only in Newgrange itself but in the whole of megalithic art,' says the guide) with the main inner tunnel behind. Standing around the chamber, cold as an ice box and also dim, I make out through the crush of bodies some of the ceremonial basins. These are four in number, large stones shaped by hammering and hollowed out in the middle, rather like oversized salad bowls. The cremated remains of those who had died were placed here, some in leather bags and accompanied with goods deemed necessary for the after-life: stone tools, flint arrowheads, drinking vessels and sometimes even food. Burials were communal. Newgrange was not the tomb of one individual, but of many. There is a stone basin in each of the three recesses. On top of one of these sits a fourth of clearly superior quality. This basin might well have been reserved for tribal leaders and priests. It would have been placed in the centre of the chamber's floor. By turning off the lights we can see its position would be in line with the roof-box, a speck more than sixty feet away.

The winter solstice, the shortest day of the year, falls nowadays on 21 or 22 of December. On that day the sun rises in the southeast. The passageway, roof-box, main chamber and central basin were all aligned to greet its approach.

The sky in the southeast would brighten first, warning all who had gathered that God was on his way. The high priest and one or two tribal elders may already have entered the tomb and placed offerings in the holy basins. In the most elaborately worked of these, which sits at their feet, they might have arranged several bags of bone and ash, the remains of important leaders who had died during the preceding year. All are silent, everything is dark. At first break of dawn a tiny beam of light streaks from the heavens and settles on the basin stone. God has entered his temple through the roof-box, he has proceeded unobstructed through the passageway and now he collects the spirits of the faithful. For the next seventeen minutes the light expands into an oval, illuminating the entire chamber as if several torches were lit. In due course the oval shrinks and the brilliance subsides. Soon the shaft of light disappears as silently as it came. Another year has ended. By coming to them once again at this appointed time and place, God has confirmed his pleasure with the people. The priest leaves, ordering the greatest of the curb stones rolled back again to block the passageway for yet another year. He tells the people that omens are good for the coming cycles of the moon. God, by his sign that they all saw, had said as much. The people disperse, pleased that their temple has so delighted God that he chooses to live there, if only for a few minutes.

The ritual may well have been different. Perhaps God visited this chamber alone, perhaps no priest stood here to greet him. In a way it hardly matters. Enough can be pieced together from the signs they left us to determine that the sun came into this dark and chilly place once a year for no other reason than to connect, in some fashion, with those who worshipped its power. The impact of entry must have been overwhelming, the conversation intense and beyond description.

In leaving I cannot help wondering about the outer circle of stones. These ancient peoples understood the basics of heavenly movement, though the extent of their knowledge is a debatable topic at the moment. The controversial and highly publicised analysis of Stonehenge (a later monument than this) by Gerald Hawkins, an astronomer now teaching at Boston University, should probably have opened the way for a more thorough study within academic communities of the celestial implications inherent in remains such as this. Instead the debate has been rancorous, ill-mannered and stuffy. Yet the basics seem to be these: no other passage grave in Ireland is surrounded by a ring of standing stones. Hawkins believes he can prove first at Stonehenge and then at Callanish, a stone circle in Scotland, that such monoliths seem sure to have been erected with an eye to the heavens. Stonehenge not only clocks the seasons but apparently it predicts eclipses of the sun and moon as well. Callanish too appears to have been a fairly precise megalithic calendar. More convincing are the researches of Alexander Thom, a professor at the University of Oxford, undertaken in the Carnac region of Brittany and centring on a pillar of gigantic proportions known as the Grand Menhir Brisé, now a fallen shaft broken into four pieces, but when erect a three hundred and forty ton single piece of tapering rock standing seventy feet in height.[3] Thom, a retired engineer, after carefully measuring and surveying the standing stones, circles, outsize menhirs and alignments that abound in the region, concluded that what we might have here is an incredibly sophisticated lunar observatory. 'We must no longer assert', he wrote, 'that these people could not possibly have known this or done that.'

At the very least Newgrange was certainly an annual register. It recorded the passing of years by marking very precisely the winter solstice. It seems logical that the addition of a thirty-five stone circle — unknown anywhere else in Ireland — and the presence of one standing stone on the summit with at least two more in the fields below, might well be significant in terms of charting the movements of sun, moon or stars. Some interesting orientations involving other neolithic sites in the Boyne Valley have been charted, but few outlandish claims have yet been made, to the collective relief of the historical community. They have had enough of astronomical excesses. Has archaeology become 'a field of quacks?'

The dilemma has surely been a trying one for traditionalists. 'Let's face it,' an American student at University College, Dublin, said to me recently, 'these older professors have always felt superior to the very subject they've given their careers to studying. Certainly they're impressed with Stonehenge, Newgrange, Carnac, Callanish — with the *monuments*. But they retain this "savage in a loin cloth" image, sweating grunts pushing huge stones around from place to place, burying their people with childish offerings for the afterlife ahead. The very idea of any real scholarship behind these things is really quite alien to them — Stone Age peoples with Stone Age mentalities, that's what they think they're dealing with. The astronomy business frightens them thoroughly.'

As a generalisation it does seem true that astronomers who have become intrigued with the study of neolithic remains have usually displayed a rather infectious (and admiring) enthusiasm for the subject. 'We are now in the midst of a campaign,' a professor at the Massachusetts Institute of Technology has said, 'no doubt full of errors and misconstructions, which looks as though it will establish the origins of a quite sophisticated observational and theoretical astronomy, the birth of an abstract science...long before the dawn of writing.' These people, he continued, 'lacked the easy elegance of algebra and geometry of the last millenium or two, but one resource they had in plenty...They had time.'

'We seldom look at the sky on a starry night,' two of his colleagues have added. 'Indeed, some of us will never see it at all, (but) consider the slow eastward slippage, past a fixed and ancient horizon marker, of the familiar constellations marking solstices or equinoxes, clearly noticeable after but a few generations...All one needed to notice this was an old tree and faith in the veracity of one's grandfather. Obviously, a set of stone markers of the sort amply documented by Thom would have done even better...Naked-eye horizon phenomena.'

Conversely, the Old School remains bitterly convinced that the interdisciplinary intrusions into their field of specialty have been both garish and shallow — 'a refined academic version of astronaut archaeology' according to Glyn Daniel, Fellow of St John's College at Cambridge University. 'These are extravagant and unconvincing claims,' he noted not long ago in reference to the reputedly 'religious passion for astronomy' that some have claimed for stone age wizards. 'What the builders of megaliths had was a practical knowledge of laying out right-angled triangles.' He continued:

There has been much spoken and written recently about a revolution in our picture of the prehistoric past. Archaeologists are described as having thought of Neolithic peoples as savages, and so the new view of the past that shows them having great mathematical, geometrical and astronomical skills and knowledge dramatically changes our image of prehistoric man.
This thesis makes sense only to those who have never understood the archaeological record and who want to sensationalize prehistory. I have never had any doubt that the Neolithic peoples of Europe were good technicians and skilled engineers. They quarried large stones, transported them for considerable distances and erected them with consummate skill and artistry...We must never deny the greatness of the megalithic builders' achievements. Nor should we deny that from time to time, pausing from their labors at the harvest or at the construction of a monument, they looked as we all do to the sun, the moon and the stars.

Ill-feelings have certainly stifled creative interplay. Astronomers, exasperated by resistance to their speculations, seem to be looking to the unexplored, uncontaminated and relatively uninterpreted sites that seem more available (and more complex) in Central America. 'In concentrating on the Old World, we may be examining only the dullest part of the evidence.'

Besides the Boyne necropolis there are three other large megalithic passage grave cemeteries in Ireland:

Carrowmore outside the city of Sligo, Carrowkeel above Lough Arrow in that same county, and Slieve na Calliagh, about an hour's drive from here. The day is drawing to its end as I head further west into County Meath, where the countryside grows more irregular and hilly, a picturebook blend of field and forest. Beyond Slieve na Calliagh — the final barrier — is the great central plain of Ireland which stretches on to the Partry Mountains in County Mayo. Slieve na Calliagh is actually one peak among six in what is commonly called the Loughcrew Range, but it is the highest, reaching over nine hundred feet. On the summit and that of a neighbour, Carbane West, over seventeen passage graves were built. Scattered on the peaks and slopes of the other four, eleven more tombs still remain. The entire range runs about three miles, a vast, largely unvisited ghostland.

A single track runs up the narrow ravine between Slieve na Calliagh and Carbane West, and I follow it. My guidebook says that all of these graves have been rifled and partially destroyed, and perhaps their less imposing, approachable size has something to do with that fact. They certainly exude a ravaged look, these several miniature Newgranges, and their level of decoration is far inferior to that which I had seen earlier. In one tomb, however, a fine collection of spiral engravings catches my eye.

The view is immense as I wander about, the sun just setting, a mist spreading slowly among the smaller valleys below, dotted with Celtic raths and at least a couple of Norman mottes, one with the outline of its bailey plainly visible. The dying light, like blinking shards of glass, reflects from the wings of ravens flying by, the only movement in an otherwise still and frozen landscape. I keep thinking to myself on the many contrasts here, these utterly depopulated hilltops, of no contemporary importance at all aside from pasturage for sheep and cattle, yet at one time the utter pinnacle of significance for a people long vanished these thousands of years. Such graceful tombs for their dead — here at Slieve na Calliagh modest in scale, but at the Boyne immense, almost Cyclopean. Should we attribute these to mere craftsmanship, as some of the more traditional arguments suggest — the work of rude engineers, novice astronomers, peasant herders? Or

does that truly abused word, genius, apply instead?

Some weeks later I am at the source, so to say, a barren, disorganised office in the archaeology department of University College, Cork, talking with Professor M.J. O'Kelly, the man responsible for the excavations at Newgrange and its subsequent restoration, a thirteen-year effort completed in 1975. O'Kelly is forty-five minutes late for our interview: his secretary, a friendly but rather vacant student, 'hasn't a clue' as to our appointment and little hope that the Professor will remember it. Luckily for me a swirl of black robes and the worst smoker's cough that I have ever heard announce his arrival — 'I didn't forget, I didn't forget, come upstairs please,' and here we are. A handsome man in his sixties, O'Kelly needs little prompting to discuss his work, for just the hint of a question sets him in motion. I note rather quickly a detachment, however, a strictly professional approach to archaeology that seems incongruous given the eccentricity and hopelessness of the collegiate paraphernalia scattered about his quarters — tattered notebooks, freshmen essays, primitive filing systems, stray and battered pieces of neolithic pottery. perhaps I expected a madman, someone so buried in Newgrange that he has lost all perspective. Instead the Professor seems almost remote, even as he delivers opinions strongly believed in. I ask him first about the famous roof-box.

'This was first written about by Sir William Wilde, I believe?'

'Yes, but not as the roof-box per se. All that was known in the past of this part of the structure was the decorated front edge of the slab. That had been visible for a long time protruding through scrub vegetation, literally just above the entrance to the tomb. But it only revealed itself fully as a boxlike structure when we excavated the area to do some conservation on a number of stones that had moved out of position.'

'Was it the decoration that attracted him?'

'It was the decoration that everybody spoke about in that time, the middle of the last century or so.'

'Did they think it was just a pillar?'

'Well one of the ideas that was held rather strongly was that there may have been another storey to the passage,

Passage Grave, Slieve na Calliagh, Co. Meath

and that if you went in at this upper level you'd enter above the roof of the lower passage and perhaps find another chamber. The idea was quite current largely because you see precisely these arrangements in some of the Egyptian pyramids, and in fact one of the earlier excavators at the site, the late Professor Macalister, who was a teacher of archaeology at University College, Dublin, wanted to investigate this possibility of an upper storey for himself. In 1928, I think it was, he dug in under the decorated stone, found it wasn't a passage, got the stuff shovelled back again and left.'

'When did you first see Newgrange, as a student or in a professional capacity?'

'I saw it first as a student somewhere way back about 1939 or '40, when I was enrolled here at Cork. The war was on and one had very little means of travel, the few trains that still had coal to run on were scanty and uncertain, so I made my way to Newgrange on bicycle, my first look over the handle bar so to speak, not ever thinking that I would be involved in the excavation of it.'

'Do you remember remarking on this particular stone?'

'Oh yes. This was visible, and I and my wife — we weren't married at that time but we were there together — we contemplated the stone and speculated about it ourselves and so on. Of course I saw it at various times after that, but it wasn't until 1962 that I was asked to take charge of the excavation.'

'What theories developed as you started digging around the roof-box, I mean when you realised that it was more than a single pillar or lintel?'

'Well, we considered several possibilities. In some of the comparable Scandinavian tombs, for example, particularly in Denmark, excavation had revealed that people came over a period of time to the entrance area of a tomb and put a number of pottery vessels on top of the curb stones at the edge of the mound on each side of the entry, presumably containing some offering, perhaps flowers or God knows what, and when the next lot of people came they threw these pots down and put up their own.'

'You mean pushed them through the opening?'

'No, no, just pulled them down onto the ground. You must understand, this roof-box thing is known only at Newgrange, this feature doesn't occur in Scandinavia. No, they put up these pots, presumably containing an offering, on the support ring of curb stones and the next lot who came by threw these down, put up their own, and this went on and on so that at one particular site they were able to count out something like four thousand broken pottery vessels in a layer on each side of the entrance. Now it occurred to us that perhaps some similar thing might have been going on at Newgrange. Since we had already established that there was no broken pottery on the ground outside the tomb and wondered if perhaps, as this thing revealed itself, this wasn't the place where you made the offerings. But absolutely no evidence of that — broken bits of pottery and so on — was found when we had completed the excavation.

'Now the other thing was, there had been a tradition at Newgrange, the locals would tell you, and particularly a very nice old man called Bob Hickey, the official caretaker there but long since dead now, that on a certain day of the year the sun would shine into the tomb, and the time suggested, particularly by Bob, was midsummer. Now for me, I wondered if this slit — a deliberately made slit in the roof with this built structure around it and the ornamental lintel on top — wasn't the place where the sun would shine through. But for midsummer the sun is almost vertically overhead, there's no way it could shine either in the entrance to the tomb or through this slit, so the possibility then occurred to me that if we looked at this in midwinter, when the sun would be rising at its southernmost point on the local horizon, could it be then that sunlight would shine there? So I went, I think it was in 1969, to see for myself. I was there entirely alone, inside the tomb, looking down the passage towards the slit, gradually seeing the sky going from gray to pink, and finally the tip of the disk of the sun appeared above, over the horizon, which is a hill about three miles away, and then this shaft of light striking straight in right the length of the passage and into the centre of the tomb. First as a thin pencil of light, which gradually widened to a band about seventeen centimetres wide, and that slowly swung across the floor and gradually was reduced as the ray began to be cut off. Fifteen minutes after this whole process begins, it just disappears.'

'Does it hit on anything specifically as it comes down?' I asked.

'No, it strikes to the floor, and the reflection of light from the floor makes the whole interior quite visible.'

'What were your feelings? Did you feel you'd discovered a new continent?'

'Well I wondered, should I be there at all,' O'Kelly laughed. 'Would I hear a voice saying "Get the hell out of here," or feel a cold hand tapping me on the shoulder or whatever, you know? But it was certainly a very dramatic experience, the most exciting discovery you could imagine. When I came back and told people what I had seen they hardly believed that it could be so. Well then, of course, we had to do a lot of research. We had astronomy people working on it and very accurate surveys done to determine whether this had all happened by accident or whether, as we thought, they had specifically oriented the structure onto the sun for just this purpose. And the result of these investigations made it quite clear that the whole thing was a deliberate attempt to catch the sunlight at this particular time which, as you'll be aware, was the winter solstice, the end of the old year, the next day the new year begins, a time when right around the world there has always been a midwinter festival. We are still celebrating it as Christmas, with the day changed a little bit, the whole thing Christianised. It shows that at a significant time of the year these neolithic peoples must have been thinking about Newgrange itself, in and of itself, I should say, as an entity — that it wasn't just a tomb into which you got rid of dead people but a place where the spirits of the dead would live forever. They took these incredible precautions, for instance, to keep the inside dry, caulking the roof joints with burnt soil, putty, sea sand; cutting all these water channels on the upper sides of the roof stones so as to drain off the water from the mausoleum itself — no need to do any of this if it's only bones of dead people on the inside. I think they must have been thinking of Newgrange as an abode for the spirits of these dead people and that once a year, at this momentous time, winter solstice, they believed perhaps that the spirits of these important dead people should be woken up, as it were, and caused to join the general midwinter festivities,

or whatever. This is all, by the way, total speculation on my part. I'd hate to say categorically that all this is absolutely the way it was. No one will ever be able to do that.'

'What level of sophistication are we talking about here, in terms of this solstice orientation? Some people would think of this as an extraordinary achievement, and you yourself have indicated that its discovery was the highlight of your work at Newgrange. Yet others tend to downplay it, saying in effect that really, this is a very basic sort of thing.'

'Frankly, I don't believe the people of the times would have needed any abstruse knowledge of astronomy to create the whole apparatus of the roof-box. An agricultural people wherever you find them always spend a great deal of time in the open, dealing with their crops, seeds, animals and so on. They're very good observers. They can look at formations of clouds in the sky and tell you whether it's going to be pouring in half an hour's time or they'll tell you whether it's going to stay like this for the rest of the day — almost subconscious observations of the natural pehnomena around them. Now to an agricultural people there are a number of important points during the year that they have to be aware of, in this case the end of the old year, the beginning of the new year and the equinox that will come up in the springtime when you have to have your crops planted or be seriously thinking about it; and then the high point in summertime when the crops are ripening, followed by harvest and the autumn equinox, finally on to December. Now all that would have had to be done by these people to get this orientation right was for somebody to sit in the position which the centre of the tomb chamber would eventually occupy, and sit there morning after morning for a period of time watching the sun — its rising point, moving southward until it comes to a stop and begins to go back. Now when he has determined that, I think he would have to drive a line of timber pegs into the ground to give him the axis line for the whole construction, and then the designer, builder or whatever would set his plan symmetrically around that line. So that gives him the direction and the orientation that he needs. Now the monument is on the top of a hill, so the ground is

Dolmen, Carrowmore, Co. Sligo

sloping up, rising as you go towards the entrance. And it rises all the way into the tomb, so that when you're in the centre of the tomb chamber you're two metres higher than somebody standing at the entrance; so he had to take this slope of the ground into account as he figured the job so that when the tip of the sun appeared on the horizon, and as a horizontal ray of light comes towards the tomb, the slit is at the right height to catch it and direct it the full way in to hit the floor, which is two metres lower than the slit. It's an engineering problem and it wouldn't require anything other than a practical ability to do it — think it out, conceptualise the problem, and just do it. In the final stages, of course, there would have had to have been a bit of adjusting up and down to get the slit at the right horizon point.

'To get to the point of your question, though, I think we have real problems these days with people getting carried away by the various geometrical possibilities that some of these monuments present. The tendency in recent years has been to go too far with all this theorising. It's often very easy to make a theory that you've developed fit on the ground, easier than you might think, and some of these that have been promulgated — like much of the stuff about Stonehenge — is to my way of thinking rather fanciful.'

'Yes, but you can see the other point I'm sure,' I said. 'Here we have a monument, a structure, without equal in the world, and to what level of talent are you willing to grade its builders? You talk about skilful technicians, skilful engineers, but never about vision, exceptional vision, without which Newgrange, some feel, could never have been built. There's something more here than just building a mound.'

'I know that, of course, but the answer may not be to look at Newgrange in such isolation. You see, on the evidence that is gradually building up in Ireland it would appear that the earliest of these passage tombs, as they're called, were built in Sligo, on the northwest coast of Ireland. We have radiocarbon dates from recent excavations in a cemetery of tombs at a place called Carrowmore, very near to Sligo town, and these are of the order of 300 BC or before. Now they are rather basic

structures, built out of large boulders admittedly, but they are small and simple as compared to anything in the Boyne Valley. These are the earliest tombs we have, for remember that radiocarbon dates for the building of Newgrange are 2500 BC, so that Newgrange is 500 radiocarbon years at least later than the Sligo monuments. If you pursue these things across the country from Sligo, on to Carrowkeel over Lough Arrow, then to the east coast and the Boyne Valley, there's a gradual elaboration that seems to be going on. When you get to a place twenty miles west of Newgrange, Loughcrew, there's a cemetery of passage graves — something like twenty-five still survive from an original, bigger number — where the cairn structures have become noticeably more elaborate than the Sligo ones, and they begin to decorate them with these spirals and so on. And then you have the zenith of it all in the Boyne Valley where they're building lunatic structures, if you like, in the sense of taking up so much man time and effort. And putting up not just one but three great sites and several other quite large ones within the bend, and though these latter look small as compared to Newgrange or Knowth and Dowth, nevertheless they're big. Now I think what happened was that these farming types built up to a high level of wealth in animals and agriculture, were building these cathedral type things at the height of their careers, and in fact went so far there was an economic collapse and the whole thing died down.'

'What you're implying is that there's almost a diffusionist theory here in Ireland starting in the west and reaching its culmination in the Boyne?'

'Yes, you can argue that.'

'And as a matter of fact I did notice at Carrowkeel in the Bricklieve Mountains that none of those tombs were decorated.'

'No, absolutely not.'

'And you see the pattern of decoration getting more sophisticated going east?'

'Yes, in fact there is no evidence of decoration in the west at all. In the northeast and swinging as far as Wicklow is where you find the carvings we come to associate with megalithic art.'

'In other words, each little project added that much

Decorated slab, Slieve na Calliagh, Co. Meath

more to the general fund of knowledge. It wasn't a spark of lightning coming down and hitting someone, with Newgrange the sudden result?'

'Well, that's what I think. You see every one of these tombs is an individual effort. Now my sept, family, tribe, group, whatever set-up we had, if we built a fine one the next lot would say, we can damn well do better than that, and they do another little bit of elaboration until you finally get to the stage where the highest architects, craftsmen, whatever one is calling them, are able to design Newgrange and carry it into effect. Again, I'm not trying to belittle what they accomplished. If you think that the covering mound contains 200,000 tons of stone, which had to be brought at least a mile from one of the river terraces where we think they quarried them, the mere organisation required to deliver that much stone onto the site means these people must have been highly sophisticated in the way they could organise things. I think they couldn't have done this without using some of their older cattle as traction animals, and they may have had wheels — low pallets with wheels or rollers, maybe sled type carts — to help them get this stone up to the site.

'We have no evidence, absolutely none, for any of this you understand, but I can't see the project having been done without first, a very highly worked out social machine; second, a whole work pattern for the entire job; and third, having at their disposal traction animals, which would have been cattle, not horses, and perhaps some kind of wheeled vehicles. But going back to this 'genius' theory, I don't see a neolithic Galileo at work here.'

'You do seem to be saying that this might have been an exercise in megalomania, however,'

'I suppose one can look at it that way, just as you can look at some of the cathedral buildings of the Middle Ages, absolutely enormous structures, and even some that are being built at the present day for religious worship which are a hundred feet high when twenty would do, with all the elaborations of decoration and everything else. Now you can call that madness if you wish. In one sense it is mad when something much simpler would serve, and something very much simpler than Newgrange would have served likewise.'

'Is it possible to consider a building like Newgrange without thinking at the same moment of a priestly order of some sort?'

'Certainly not. You can't look at Newgrange or, indeed, any of these other monuments, as just a tomb into which you put your dead people and they're out of sight. It was something very much more than that. Was it a particular tribe that set up Newgrange and was it a special people of that tribe who were put inside? They needn't have been chieftains, they needn't have been kings, they could have been special in various ways, let's suppose somebody who was thought to have the gift of the evil eye or could foretell, or whatever, maybe they were the ones interred there. But you see we have found inside the remains of only four or five people. Now that may be because the thing has been open to visitors since 1699, and people have been coming and going, taking bits off in their pockets and so forth. In addition, the inside has been tidied up several times in the past by the State when they took it over into their care, and we don't know what they might have swept out. So we cannot estimate whether the full original complement of people inside was five or more.'

'Has Knowth been disturbed as well?' I interrupted.

'Knowth, this is being excavated at the moment, and they haven't really got to this part of it yet. But another tomb at a place called Fourknocks, near the village of Naul in County Meath and excavated some years ago, though a much smaller site than Newgrange, yielded the bones of sixty-seven people, mainly women and children of various ages, all of whom had been put in at one time. So it's difficult to speculate whether Newgrange was built for *all* the people or just a select few, which would enable us to guess more intelligently the extent to which a priestly order was involved, the boundaries of its power within the social order and so on. But as a generalisation you can't think of Newgrange without thinking of religion.'

'What about the origins of this entire passage grave tradition? The new radiocarbon techniques have pretty well dissolved the diffusionist theory of influence from Grecian culture, but did Ireland evolve completely untouched by Western Europe?'

'Again, to work on radiocarbon dates, the earliest tombs of this kind are now in Brittany, where the radiocarbon indicates they were being built as early as 3800 BC, back nearly to 4000 BC on the west coast of Brittany. Now is it not likely that the idea for this kind of structure, cult, whatever it was, spread out from Brittany southward into the Mediterranean, Spain, Portugal and so on, and also northward to France, Ireland, the west of England, Scotland, Scandinavia? I think so. I don't believe for a moment that it was a question of the movement of people. Many books will try to suggest that a great colonising group of people came into Ireland and brought these beliefs with them, settled the place and set up all these tombs. This is what a colleague of mine has called 'the archaeological Ellis Island' approach, and I really don't see it. I think it's the idea or the germ of an idea that spreads, and then in each place where it takes on the locals do their own thing with it. And so you can't get an exact parallel in Brittany or elsewhere for any of the Irish tombs. They all have in each area where you find them their own peculiarities, even though you can see an underlying thread of connection.

'Now the mesolithic period in Europe dates to around 9000 BC onwards, while in Ireland it begins at 7000 BC. In other words, the earliest date for the beginnings of man in Ireland that we have now is *c.* 7000 BC in round radio-carbon figures. Many of these people were living on the coasts, in Brittany, in Ireland, in Scandinavia, and it's now beginning to emerge and gain acceptance as a theory that it was these fishermen, hunters, foodgatherers . . . that it was these people who diffused the idea, began this cult. They were moving in their boats round all the coasts from Brittany north and south. They could have promulgated the idea in the west of Ireland. Now look — in excavations now going on in Sligo it is becoming quite clear that it wasn't a settled agricultural people who built these earliest, sort of primitive cemeteries, but rather still a food-gathering, semi-nomadic people. In the Carrowmore area you get a graphic idea of this. You're standing there with a kind of basin all around you within which these people would have been moving. They went down to the seacoast to fish for oysters and other fish, as indicated by findings within the tombs themselves of considerable deposits of shell fish, in many instances great quantities of mussels which were deposited as offerings fresh from the sea and unopened; they did some hunting, which we know by red deer bones that have been found; and they collected fruits, berries, whatever. The cemetery of tombs was the centre of their lives and probably the place they would come to for festivals, gatherings and for God knows what else. Now the Swedish team which has been studying this Carrowmore area are suggesting that these early tombs were in fact being built not by a settled agricultural people but by these food gatherers. And that as time goes on the knowledge of cattle herding and agriculture comes in *from Europe* as a result of these people travelling out on their fishing expeditions. Or else some people from the European mainland travelling out on *their* fishing expeditions might have hit on the coast at this particular point. You see, we know that cattle, sheep, goats and probably pigs had to be imported into Ireland, they were not indigenous. The same holds true for wheat and barley, these had to be introduced as well. So gradually there must have been a changeover from the food collecting way of life to the beginnings of food production where in the first instance they would have had a few cattle, then this cattle herding would gradually and slowly take on, possibly somewhat later in time the cultivation of wheat and barley, and a gradual transition from partially settled food collecting to a fully settled agricultural way of life. And as the agriculture prospers, there's a greater development in the storage of food, then surpluses of food, all of which can now be used to feed the people that you put to do the building of what are now becoming really grandiose tombs, or any other specialised activity.'

'Newgrange would have required that.'

'Absolutely.'

'You feel this cult, which seems to have started in Brittany, could have been circulated just by wanderers.'

'Yes, contacts of various kinds, simple contacts more than likely, and not by an invading or colonising force, great flotillas of boats coming up to the Irish coast, rushing ashore, starting to build these things all over the place. This has been the kind of idea that has been current for a long time, but I've never been able to accept it in that form.'

'If the Boyne tombs were not a sudden creation, then, in what order do you think they were built?'

'At the moment all we can do is guess because there isn't a sufficiency of radiocarbon dates. My hunch is that Newgrange was probably the first, and I would imagine that the mound at Dowth, at which no excavation has taken place since the middle of the last century — and that was savagery, by the way, not excavation — that came next, and Knowth would have been the last. Now the reason I'm saying this is, first of all, at Newgrange the quality of materials used is of the highest order. Every stone slab in the place was the best they could get. There's some deterioration at Dowth, where, in some instances, they're now using less good stones. But when you go to Knowth, the quality of material is bad. Several of the curb stones have shattered, the structural stones of the tomb have cracked, collapsed and so on, because the materials being used were not as good as the others. Furthermore, in the mound at Knowth there are considerable amounts of transported turfs. They dug up black shaly soft rock, put in layers of this, along with small quantities of stone and so on. In other words, they were literally scraping the bottom of the barrel to get enough fill to build the mound. Now look at the decorations, they're different in all three. There are similarities, of course, but there's real difference. Now except for the really good stones at Newgrange — the entrance stone, K52, K67, a few others — an awful lot of the Newgrange decoration is rather scrappy, some of it little more than doodling. Well, there seems to be an advance if you look at the material at Dowth, and when you go to Knowth the whole motif, the way of doing things, is completely different, a much larger scaled thing altogether, quite different in feeling and spirit, much more developed looking. I think we see in this a progression and a growing maturity, all indicative of a younger date for Knowth. Some radiocarbon dates from Knowth would be nice, naturally enough, and we have some though not from positions sufficiently significant to allow a positive date for the tomb structure itself. We were extremely lucky at Newgrange that this burnt soil they caulked the roof joints with gave us enough charcoal to provide a series of dates, which come out at the round figure of 2500 BC. This is material put in place by the very builders themselves, so our radiocarbon samples are tightly associated with the actual construction of the tomb. This is not so for Knowth.

'The other curious thing is this: Newgrange was not interfered with by later people. Visitors came to Newgrange all the time, of course, because we have bits and pieces that were dropped around by people from the building period right up to today. All these Roman coins and Roman gold work that we found, for example, these must have been votive offerings to the Gods of the place, given by Roman tourists crossing the Irish Sea, coming over here for lost weekends or whatever. But otherwise Newgrange remained inviolate until 1699 when the local landlord, looking for stone, dug in at the nearest point and this revealed the entrance to the tomb. But except for that, largely left alone. Now in the case of Knowth, soon after it was finished Bronze Age people fiddled around with it, were living on it and digging holes in it and various things; Iron Age people after them were sticking in burials here and there all over the place; and in the early Christian period, say around AD 400 to 1000 people were living and squatting on it, digging ditches and converting the mound into a kind of defensive structure; and finally the Anglo-Normans in the early thirteenth century built a tower on top of it. The same happened to Dowth: very much interfered with. Why is it that Newgrange, in contrast, remained untouched by all these people? I think it's because this mound was the first one built, and probably most special in the minds of people. For instance, if you look at the names for each of the mounds, Knowth comes from the Irish name *Cnogba* and Dowth from the term *Dubad*. So their old Irish names have persisted, now in anglicised form, to the present day. The original name of Newgrange, on the other hand, was *Brú na Bóinne*, which translates as 'The Fortress of the Boyne' or 'The Great Building of the Boyne'. It was a special abode of the great pagan gods, sometimes referred to as their palace, and it figured far more prominently in the old literature than the other two. And the votive offerings, this Roman stuff,

42

gold coins and the rest, this must mean that when these visitors came to Newgrange they were being told by the natives that this particular mound, and not the others, was where the gods lived, and for this reason the offerings that we've discovered were made around the edge. All of these things — quality of building materials, the progression of artistic maturity from site to site, the fact that Newgrange was not turned into a habitation spot but rather left alone, its name and these offerings that I just mentioned — seem to indicate that Newgrange was first.'

My allotted time coming to a close, I asked Professor O'Kelly to comment on the reception given to the renovated Newgrange. 'Naturally enough there has been controversy about it,' he replied, 'and not all of my colleagues agree with it. But we did an enormous amount of research on this and I went to investigage tombs all over Europe and all the ones here in Ireland, of course, as well. The thing that sticks in people's throats is the wall on top of the curb. There had always been the notion, and indeed it was the idea I had when we started, that a mound goes up as a kind of hemispherical thing from the top of the curb. But at an early stage when we were able to see the sectional profiles of the edge of the mound it became quite clear that this was impossible. The rounded, domelike appearance had been caused by slippage of the cairn material — it exerted enormous pressure, of course, on the outer curb, and eventually it just collapsed, slid over the edge and spread outward as far as the ring of standing stones. So when we realised this, we saw that a Newgrange restored to its original look, would present a strikingly different profile to what people were used to. Now secondly, there was the problem of this white quartz: what was its purpose, what did the builders want it for? We had always known there were quantities of this bright stone in the cairn. Ever since 1699 when people first began quarrying up on the mound they had remarked on it, and indeed, a great deal of it was taken away. Every garden around the Boyne has loads of quartz taken from Newgrange, it's very decorative. Excavation through the material outside the curb showed clearly that this quartz and another type of stone, rounded granite boulders the size of a rugby football, were in a layer at the very bottom, so it must have been the first material that fell down. Now if, as had been the idea, the surface of this hemispherical mound had been coated all over with a thin layer of quartz, the stratification as we found it could *not* have developed from *that* arrangement. It was gradually forced on us that there must have been a built revetment wall on top of the curb to hold the body of the mound in place, and that the whole front of this wall was decorated with the quartz, which was quarried somewhere in the Dublin/Wicklow Mountains. They used that on the important front, and for the rest of the way around, the revetment was in ordinary stone. Now when we began to research into this we found that in old accounts of the Loughcrew cemetery, for instance, the man who excavated many of these sites in the middle of the last century reported that there was a wall standing on the curb, or just immediately behind the tops of the curbstones, built of quartz, three feet high in one instance and nearly three feet thick, as he saw it then. It has all fallen down about the place since. Later excavations, done back in the late 1930s, of similar sites also reported these revetment walls. And in Brittany, at a place called Barnenez, a contractor taking away stones from this great mound discovered that it was a cairn covering eleven passage graves. When the destruction was stopped and excavation undertaken, they found that the edge of the mound was revetted with walls built of stone five metres high, *still standing!* Only the top parts had slid down. So there's a whole lot of evidence that at several sites revetment walls stood on the curb and that these monuments had a sort of drumlike appearance rather than a nicely rounded mound as had been thought in the past.

'The other problem, closely related, was that mixed in with the quartz were these rounded, rugby football shaped gray granite stones that I mentioned earlier. The ultimate origin of these was the Mourne Mountains, fifty or sixty miles north of Newgrange. Now these stones, originally from the rock of the mountains, were water-rolled or glacially-rolled, and ended up somewhere between the Mournes and the Boyne, perhaps along some of the beaches, we haven't been able to tie it down. As I said, these were intimately mixed with the quartz, so they had to have been part of the revetment wall that the quartz came from. In putting it back, all we could do was intersperse them with the quartz like crumbs in a cake, which I'm perfectly certain is not the right thing to have done. If I had had full freedom I would have put those stones back in great swirling spirals, zigzags and patterns similar to the carved decorations, using the gray stones for this, setting them off against the glistening white of the quartz. I can't imagine that they were just mixed higgly piggly or any other way with the quartz. You see they went to extraordinary trouble to get these stones. I think they said to themselves, we want a gray stone to contrast with the white, but we want this stone to have crystalline streaks in it that will glitter when the sun catches it. I can't imagine that they wouldn't have decorated the revetment wall along the front in that way. If I had done what I wanted, needless to say, I'm sure I would have had to go off sheep farming in Australia or something.'

'As it was,' I asked, 'how much blood was shed over the restoration?'

'There was endless argument and discussion, it went on all the time. But you see the trouble was that when the evidence was visible on the ground to be looked at — the stratification, in other words — many of my colleagues wouldn't come and talk it over, and then at the end of the day, so to speak, when the decision had been made and the work completed, then they'd say, "Well, what's been done is all wrong." But I had a consulting engineer whose life's work has been to deal with mounds and loose materials, and what happens when it slips — working in connection with rock-filled dams and all these things, where if you don't do your business right the dam is going to fall over and God knows what will happen. So I had him to study the stratification as it could be seen, and I gave him none of my ideas. I said, "Look, can you, from this layer structure, tell me what this must have been like originally?" And he came back with this: "The wall must have been approximately three meters high — roughly ten feet — it must have had a backwards slope of about a foot in a ten-foot height, it must have been there as a revetment, and when the pressures of the body of the cairn pushed the curb stones outward, which did happen, you sort of pull the mat out from under the wall and it comes down in a great collapse."'

'Well that shows that the revetment wall worked, if it was the curb stones that went first.'

'Exactly. The effect then was for the quartz and the rest of the revetment wall to come down in this first slide. The way the curbs fell, and what was or was not underneath them, proved this beyond a doubt. You see when they were setting up the curb stones they wanted to get the top line fairly smooth, so if the stone wasn't high enough they propped it up, built up a layer of stones underneath and stood it on top of this. Conversely, if the stone was too high they built a deeper socket or trench in order to sink the stone down so that the top lined up with its neighbour just right. Some of these socketed stones — and you know they're big, weighing anywhere up to and over five tons — some of these fell flat on their faces, with *no* quartz underneath them. So the quartz cannot have been laid as a carpet on the ground, as some of my colleagues have argued for.'

'You mean some of them thought the white quartz may have been a layer just on the ground outside?'

'Laid on the ground on the outside to make a nice white rug. But since it's not underneath the stones that fell over, that can't have been their position, and in fact the results of the engineering study just mentioned also showed that the only position from which the quartz could have come is from a revetment wall. Now when the engineer told us all this we excavated a two-metre trench, recording all the layers as we went downward, until we came to the quartz/granite at the bottom, and we used that quartz/granite to build a revetment wall of our own to his calculations in order to verify the findings. Our experimental revetment was constructed for a length of two meters, building it as high as the quartz and granite would go, filling behind it with loose stones as was the case originally. Then we caused this wall to collapse again, as it had hundreds of years ago, re-excavated the collapse to see if it would compare with the stratification we had found first, and it came out like a text book answer, exactly the same. This is the only time in archaeological

Tievebulliagh, Cushendall, Co. Antrim

history, by the way, that I have ever seen anything come out so perfectly.'

'That would seem to justify everything you did.'

'Well I think so.'

Our interview over, O'Kelly walks me down the stairs. 'You're probably one of the lucky ones,' he says. 'There will come a time soon when a decision will have to be made about access to the tomb. Seventy-five thousand people entered Newgrange last year, and inadvertently the damage they cause is unrepairable. Just the people rubbing against the orthostats, just the people tracing the carvings with their fingers is simply wearing the place down. It would be a shame to close it to the general public, but at some point it will happen. In a way the magic of the valley itself can make up for the loss. It's quite an experience to walk through the fields below the tomb, after they've been ploughed and after a rain. You should see the stuff that can be found — flint chips and flakes, animal bones, bits of pottery sometimes. I think a person can get the feel of Newgrange even if he never sees the inside.'

The ferry boat from Scotland, emerging through a fine hail of drizzle, beats through a choppy sea to its terminal in Larne. I am amazed at the ship's speed, as I sit eating lunch in my car on a slippery dock overlooking the harbour. In all my trips to Ireland I cannot recall the sea as aquamarine in hue as it is this afternoon, almost Caribbean, though the day itself is typical for an Irish spring, wet and cold. The ferry loses speed very smoothly, docks without effort, passengers disembark into the stiff offshore winds. I start up the car and continue north along coastline into County Antrim, the heart of Ulster.

As a final reminder to myself of what Newgrange and, indeed, the entire Stone Age represents, I have embarked on a sidetrip into obscurity. These sorts of expeditions appeal to me, which helps, but I find myself hopelessly dependent on specialist literature of a sometimes dated sort, in this case a learned paper delivered in 1906 by an antiquarian named W. J. Knowles, for whom neolithic axes had what appears to have been a religious fascination.

I am looking for a mountain called Tievebulliagh, some miles west of Cushendall, a village on the coast road facing the ocean. Tievebulliagh is clearly identified on my set of maps, but the exact approach is somewhat vague. Several inquiries in Cushendall are received rather coldly, and only the postman finally gives directions that seem trustworthy. I follow his advice as I turn inland to the glen nearest the main road, park the car and hike upwards into the mist.

Knowles had done much the same thing, visiting this glen on repeated occasions, stopping all the farmers he met and asking them if they had uncovered any stone tools or implements as they ploughed their fields or worked on ditches. More often than not they had, and Knowles would be invited into the house or out back to the barn, where an axe head or a pick, a knife blade or a skinner, a maul or chopper would be produced. Often he'd be led to a drainage channel, lined with stone cleared from field or pasture, and a trove of megalithic hardware. These he would buy whenever he could, and 'each time required the aid of the farmer's cart to convey my collection of manufactured objects to the railroad station' for the trip home. Gradually he worked his way up the valley, where word of his interest had spread, and the farmers produced what specimens they could. And eventually he reached Tievebulliagh:

One day in walking up the side of Tievebulliagh, a peak 1340 feet high and very noticeable from Cushendall, [my wife and I] came on sites near the top, from which the covering of peat had been removed by frost and rain, and here we saw everything as it was left by the manufacturers. In [the valley below], though the objects were all there, they had to be turned over by the plough and harrow in order that we might find them. We did not see them as they originally lay on the ground; but here on Tievebulliagh everything was visible and in its original position. An object-lesson in the process of axe-manufacture was there displayed before our eyes — hammerstones, halved, and quartered hammerstones that had been used again, axes, partially-made axes, broken axes, failures, worked flakes, and thousands of orindary flakes were all lying in the positions where they had been dropped thousands of years ago by the Stone Age folk.

'Tievebulliagh', he felt, 'would seem to have been the great centre of the industry which spread down into the valley.'

Modern scholarship has confirmed Knowles's suspicions. Here at Tievebulliagh a factory of enormous significance had indeed been established by neolithic entrepreneurs. Near the peak of the mountain, in an exposed outcropping of bluish porcellanite rock — harder by far than more brittle flint — prospectors quarried, produced, polished and exported the finest grade of stone tools available in Ireland, tools used to clear the ridges of the Boyne and countless other river valleys, tools to cut and shape the pillars of passage graves and standing stones, tools to chisel out the decorations of megalithic artisans. In the 1940s petrologists, after carving thin slices of stone from axes found in England and examining these under high intensity microscopes, were able to identify several specimens as clearly Irish ('characteristic Antrim porcellanite'), an indication both that commerical contacts routinely existed between the islands (a confirmation perhaps of O'Kelly's thesis that the passage grave cult may have been spread by neolithic tradesmen), and that Tievebulliagh axes must have been highly regarded for their quality to be found so far afield. In Knowles's case, fame proved his undoing, as farmers began glutting the antiquarian market with forgeries ('spurious articles are weathering in the valley,' Knowles warned). When, on behalf of a cheated friend, he angrily confronted one of these purveyors of fakes, the calm reply 'His eye was his merchant' came instead of a refund. Knowles soon removed himself from the arena, but not before he had assembled over four thousand stone implements, eighteen hundred of which were axe heads whose condition varied. It is said that even so, more await discovery on the slopes of Tievebulliagh.

Following a rocky pathway higher into the glen, I check with a young farmer to make sure of my bearings. He turns out to be something of a scholar. 'I'll put you on the right road,' he says, 'but first come see some flakes.' He himself has an impressive collection: some rough outs, or unfinished axeheads; a well defined specimen that had, in its final working, broken in half; several dozen flakes, useful for spear heads or knife points; and three maul-type hammers. 'It's fun to pick for them in the scree pile at the foot of the workings. It's just too bad that stone isn't worth anything. Or maybe,' he said a moment later, 'I don't mean that. It may just be better that there isn't any value here at all.'

The eastern face of Tievebulliagh is nearly perpendicular as I approach it, rising hundreds of feet over the barren bogland stretching up from the glen. Climbing up the face of the mountain is a little tricky in the wet, but soon I reach the quarry itself, a few dozen feet from the summit, the porcellanite glistening in the soft rain. Looking below the great scree chute broadens in its descent, a long trough really, where refuse and chips — the residue of mining the quarry — slid down the face of Tievebulliagh to its base. After coming down I sift through this debris, imagining that every stone I turn over is an implement of some sort. Frankly, they all look like axe heads to me.

The essence of Newgrange, in a way, is here. To think of stone as a tool only brings to mind the most primitive of societies. What a struggle just to fell a small tree (you wouldn't be cutting it down so much as battering it down). But on the other hand one is dealing here with complexities: the sophistication, for example, required to manufacture these axe heads to their final, highly polished form — items of real value in the neolithic world — and then to develop an export trade all over the British Isles. By extension to Newgrange, of course, these same contrasts apply. It is a tomb dedicated to the simple worship of the sun, as basic to early man as his use of stone hammers. But is Newgrange the work of truly simple men? The archaeological record would seem to indicate not. With the rain coming down harder, I retrace the track into the glen.

Axe quarry,
Tievebulliagh, Co. Antrim

Tievebulliagh axe head, National Museum, Dublin

2 *The National Museum*

BY current standards the National Museum in Dublin, like its neighbour across the courtyard, the National Library, must be considered something of a folly. In both cases the antiquity of collection is matched by antiquity of style, whether caused by attitude or financial shortages no one seems to know, but two more obsolete institutions would be hard to find. Which is, of course, their charm.

Several years ago I remember walking up the stairs to the Library's antiquated reading room noting, as usual, the dozens of tin boxes that were stacked along the steps and adjoining corridors. Curiosity provoked me to open one of these (a typically American thing to do) and I found myself looking at scores of old and faded medieval manuscripts, the first I had ever seen outside a display case. It was something of a shock, I must admit. I even asked myself what could prevent me from stealing half a dozen, even as clerks and uninterested librarians shuffled by, oblivious to this stranger opening boxes full of parchments with long, dangling seals of red wax.

The Museum next door, while somewhat more secure, was in those days equally haphazard with its treasure. Though guards did make a point of ambling by now and then, all organisation seemed to stop there. Crammed into every corner of the building the heritage of this island culture was scattered like so much dust. An assistant curator told me the difficulty was having so much to show but so little room in which to spread it out. They were even thinking of setting up displays in the bathrooms. 'A perfect metaphor for Irish history,' he said, 'confused, hopelessly disjointed, tragi-comic.' Still, on a sunny day with light streaming in through a huge transom above, the National Museum was a lovely place to spend some time.

It helped, of course, to know what you were looking for.

The right display cases, in the right order, are all one needs to speed the centuries by. This may be a ridiculous way of thinking about history, to say nothing of developing the feel for a country's past, but the immense and often empty reaches of prehistoric generations — nameless, unknown, trackless — force upon us the use of summaries and the great, sweeping encapsulations so prevalent in textbooks and museum catalogues. Five hundred years in a sentence or two, thousands of lives and individual sagas dismissed in a page, but what else can they write? In the National Museum, at any rate, the confusion of display at least conveyed the right idea, for there was no way of reaching neat and definitive conclusions from the assembly of these collections. This was an age of chaos, we were told, and milling about from exhibit to unrelated exhibit that seemed an appropriate verdict though, in retrospect, a misleading one. Our understanding of these eras may be chaotic, that much is granted, but ironically enough the times themselves may well have been stable. Unfortunately, after three or four visits I had mastered the place and knew my way around. 'That's very bad,' a friend of mine warned me, 'pretty soon you'll think of yourself as an expert.'

With the realisation that times have changed I went again to the Museum during my last visit to Dublin, and was not surprised to see a pruning touch at work. A sense of order has finally been achieved, to the relief of most visitors I'm sure, though large doses of nineteenth century eccentricity still remain. The current arrangement does manage to reflect a more current perception, a modern confidence that in a general sort of way we are beginning

Burial Cist, Carrowkeel, Co. Sligo

to understand the progressions that prehistoric man undertook, over countless decades, one step of knowledge at a time.

The Metal Age appears to have commenced in Ireland *c.* 2000 BC when the working of copper was first introduced here. The old diffusionist theory had stated that skills in metallurgy progressed westward from Asia Minor in successive waves: first copper, followed by bronze, then gold. But modern scholars like Renfrew have identified separate and indigenous European metal industries that developed in complete isolation from the East, some as early as 5400 BC (in the Balkans and Spain). No doubt we may depend here on the role of the itinerant prospector or daring soldier of fortune in search of ore and mineral deposits, astounding the local Stone Age peoples with the magic that metal 'lives' in rock. It is interesting to note that in early Christian times metal workers were held in great fear as men in league with pagan sorcerers, given to wizardry and diabolic charms, as St Patrick understood when he called God's protection 'against the spells of women and smiths, and druids'. In Ireland's case it is believed that the gradual emergence of pastoralism as the primary means of raising food (the keeping of herds as opposed to growing crops) liberated many men from agricultural work and spurred them into the hills, where copper deposits were found in plenty, mostly along the coasts of Wicklow and Wexford. Crude but relatively effective means of mining the ore were devised, and certainly the technique of smelting was an early lesson. At some point, unknown at present, more news was assimilated, again almost surely the product of commercial contacts with Britain: that copper, when mixed with another kind of metal also found in rock, called tin, produced a harder alloy, yet one that was easier to work — bronze. The result must have been more trade: Ireland had copper deposits, Cornwall the tin. And then came gold, the precious metal, far more decorative yet difficult to find. Once again intensive exploration and once again success, this time in the streams and rivers of the Wicklow Mountains where sizeable amounts were discovered. Metal, like gunpowder later on, changed everything, altering prehistoric society more completely than any tribal migration, plague or natural disaster ever could. The megalithic order simply disappeared as a cultural entity, in much the same way as feudalism in Japan after World War II. Newgrange, long deserted, had become even then a folkloric remnant, though in general terms the Irish predilection for piles of rock and stone circles (more properly called today stone 'rings') was never forgotten. Most examples in Ireland today, such as Ballynoe and Drombeg, are generally dated to the Bronze Age.

Trade with Britain, the Continent and Scandinavia began in earnest *c.* 1750 BC, the traditionally accepted start for the Bronze Age. The progression of styles and techniques from early to later periods is easily noted at the Museum. The first metal objects made from bronze were simple axe heads, knives and other single mould utensils. Gold was mostly fashioned into the famous lunulae, broad crescent-shaped ornaments worn about the neck like a gorget. As the years pass by (and in the right display cases) a noticeable advance in design and execution can be traced. Flat axes and short daggers give way to longer swords, trumpets, cauldrons — all requiring two or more moulds and sophisticated assembly techniques. The simple lunula develops into a heavy collar of gold, frequently embellished with raised, alternating ridges. Vanity items such as bracelets and decorated brooches simply spew forth, everywhere foretelling the more famous Celtic designs that were to come.

There is no Bronze Age Slieve na Calliagh in Ireland, nor a Newgrange nor other revealing remains, which is why the National Museum finds a place in this itinerary. Bronze Age burials, for example, were generally modest, a simple undecorated cist as opposed to elaborate passage graves. A cist is no more than a rectangular box of stone slabs within which the body or its cremated remains was placed along with offerings. These were either buried in the ground or else placed on hilltops and covered with

Cairn, Heapstown, Co. Sligo

cairns of loose chips. Few mountains in Ireland fail to show a trace of at least one or two such mounds, and many times a year one hears of a farmer ploughing up old pasturage and finding a centuries-old cist.

But the mood of the Bronze Age is only partially found on lonely foggy mountain tops. Cairns of stone have not the secrets to tell that Newgrange did. They say little of trade, power, beauty or prosperity. Surprised as I am to admit it, here in the halls and passageways of this anachronistic building the Bronze Age is best understood. There is life here: an artistic tradition was born in Ireland during the second millennium before Christ that would not die until the 1660s, and even then it struggled to survive. These metal trinkets and golden bracelets explain to us the basics of this society: the authority derived from possession of metals; prestige and wealth acquired through shrewd and forceful barter; ambition served by daring travel to far-away lands for commercial profit, some as distant as Spain and the Mediterranean; affluence proclaimed by jewellery and precious ornament, with status defined by degree of decoration; and, lest we forget the life and toil of the average man, his burdens displayed by hoe and arrowhead. Strolling through nineteenth century confusion — now reformed and well intentioned — one can find a hole to peer through at this little known age.

> Bronze is the best of all metals
> though it go astray it will not take rust.

Advice to a Prince   Irish, eighth century

3 *Tara*

Pinnacle of a hundred kings, a second Rome.

Irish, eleventh century

THE Hill of Tara remains even now one of the more popular day excursions from Dublin. The bus tour companies rate it very highly as a prime attraction (after Glendalough) but for most visitors the trip is disappointing. After all the old talk and all the old songs there isn't much to see here except a few mounds and ditches, a weathered statue of St Patrick and an ice cream shop at the foot of the hill. This little enterprise profits most from the Tara experience, both legend and letdown. On most summer days there are more people milling around down here than up on the royal pastures, wondering no doubt why they ever came out and complaining of the fifty minutes wait (out of sixty, altogether) before the bus leaves. Most buy something, a modest cup of tea, a box of 'Tara' brand chocolates, maybe a dish towel with a recipe written on it, Irish stew or Irish coffee. The most unhappy of all just wait in the bus.

No one is here today, a chilly springtime afternoon. The ice cream shop is empty save for two of the owner's children. They sit in the window watching me pass by, mechanically shoving candy from grimy hands to grimy mouths. Following a very worn pathway to the summit of the hill, I am amazed by the breadth of view since Tara is an easy walk up and little more than a low plateau. The vast interior plain of central Ireland, unbroken really until the Partry Mountains in County Mayo, stretches westward for miles and miles. In terms of enjoyment this is the best thing here.

Tara is a place of almost supernatural confusion — not physically, in terms of the site itself or the few battered earthworks that remain there to explore (the most unfortunate of which was destroyed in the 1880s during a remarkably disjointed search for the Ark of the Covenant) — but factually, historically. For centuries this hill has been a pawn, a usable force, a convenient quarry for special interests and not a few deranged clergymen, both Protestant and Catholic. The end result in this era of promotional excess has been a final hardening of fable into fact. For an age that should know better we seem to be losing, on a large scale, our ability to sort through fiction and arrive at some bearing that approximates reality. People come to Tara in a littering wedge (the place is filthy with debris and trash) to speculate over the glories of days gone by, glories that in truth hardly existed. Few spots in the world have been, in popular imagination, more abused.

The single overwhelming force in Tara's case has been the famous legend of Patrick, Ireland's patron saint. I suppose, if you wanted, it would be a simple thing to imagine St Patrick as he approached the Royal Palace of

55

Tara from the nearby Hill of Slane on a fifth-century Easter Sunday (pinned down to a specific 8 April 456 by one Irish scholar) to do battle with the druids and chanting a beautiful hymn called the *Breastplate*:

Today I buckle on a mighty strength.
  The power of the birth of Christ, with His baptism,
  The power of the crucifixion, with His burial,
  The power of His resurrection, with His Ascension,
  The power of His coming to the judgment of Doom.

Most visitors who come here couldn't escape this vision if they tried, so firmly and persistently has the tale been repeated. The sequel, in fact, is rigorously maintained throughout the Republic in every school, church and tourist bus that one can see: how Laoghaire, High King of all Ireland, son of the immortal Niall of the Nine Hostages, himself remained pagan but allowed his followers to convert. A Christian tidal wave ensued with Patrick in control, divinely inspired, coordinating attacks on the druids and on every vestige of heathenism, sweeping all before him. In the span of just thirty years his mission stood complete, the island won for Christ or, in the words of an old poem,

Yea the very nails that nail Him
Nail us also to the tree.

But did Christ ever really walk on water? Did Patrick ever really come to Tara? It depends, I suppose, on how you were brought up.

Grave sites, which yield most of what we know about the Bronze Age, are the calendars by which centuries are clocked. Archaeologists have various means of dating what they find in these graves. Pottery classification is one, the variety and complexity of bronze and gold remains is another. In some cases radiocarbon dating is possible. Whatever the means we find that *c.* 900 BC an evolutionary development took place in Irish society. The Age of the Warrior came into being.

This is no surprise. As primitive societies alter, this sort of occurrence is part of the natural progression. Trade reaches a point where wealth as a concept is understood and desired, and gradually those with superior skills and ambitions consolidate through force the several pockets of power into the few. Grave goods reveal the fixtures of war for the first time: shields, large spearheads, unusually elaborate swords, equipage for horses and so on — all attesting the emergence of a militant aristocracy.

Some scholars believe many of these warriors were immigrants from the Continent, armed with iron weapons and knowledgeable of mainland trade links. Some go so far as to say they were Celts. Whoever they were we do know that by 350 BC a final series of pre-historic migrations did flood the island, and that these settlers were Celts. The Bronze Age gave way to Iron.

Aristotle was openly contemptuous of the Celts. 'It is not bravery to withstand fearful things through ignorance,' he wrote, 'it is not bravery to withstand them through high-spiritedness as when the Celts take up arms to attack the waves.' To him, the Celts were little more than savages.

A fuller picture of these Celtic tribesmen derives mainly from the later travels of Posidonius, the famous stoic, who seems to have spent considerable time among their tribes *c.* 100 BC. His works have mostly disappeared but fragments of observation and comment find their way into the writings of subsequent historians and travellers, most notably those of the Greek Strabo (*c.* 63 BC — *c.* 24 AD) and Julius Caesar. Some of these men acknowledged Posidonius as their source, others (notably Caesar) did not.

Interestingly, it is Aristotle's impression of the Celt as a man/child that is echoed most forcefully in their writings. Strabo comments that the 'whole race is madly fond of war, high-spirited and quick to battle, but otherwise straightforward and not of evil character. To the frankness and high-spiritedness of their temperament must be added the traits of childish boastfulness and love of decoration. They wear ornaments of gold, torques on their necks, and bracelets on their arms and wrists, while people of high rank wear dyed garments besprinkled with gold. It is this vanity which makes them unbearable in victory and so completely downcast in defeat.' His most lasting characterisation of the Celts was 'their witlessness'.

Diodorus Siculus went further by noting a symptomatic lack of restraint in the Celtic diet. 'They are exceedingly fond of wine,' he wrote, and 'desire makes them drink it greedily, and when they become drunk they fall into a stupor or into a maniacal disposition. At dinner they are wont to be moved by chance remarks to wordy disputes, and, after a challenge, to fight in single combat, regarding their lives as naught.' They are 'terrifying in appearance,' he continued, 'with deep-sounding and very harsh voices. In conversation they speak in riddles, for the most part hinting at things and leaving a great deal to be understood. They frequently exaggerate with the aim of extolling themselves and diminishing the status of others. They are boasters and threateners and given to bombastic self-dramatisation.'

The Celts were enormously vigorous people. They led what many writers have called the Heroic life, disdaining death and caring only for the glory of never-ending fame. The boundaries of their original homeland, modern day Bavaria and western Czechoslovakia, could not contain them and wandering bands of Celts rummaged through Europe from one end to the other: from Greece and Italy to Spain and France, Britain and Ireland. By 350 BC they were the most powerful people in the western world, but this is an almost meaningless phrase. The Celts were unorganised, they lived from day to day. The idea of creating an empire along Roman lines was unthinkable, utterly beyond their powers of conception. They could never see further than the next battle, the joy of the sword was too much their undoing:

When the armies are drawn up in battle array they are wont to advance before the battle line and to challenge the bravest of their opponents to single combat, at the same time brandishing before them their arms so as to terrify their foe. And when someone accepts their challenge to battle, they loudly recite the deeds of valour of their ancestors and proclaim their own valorous qualities, at the same time abusing and making little of their opponent, and generally attempting to rob him beforehand of his fighting spirit. They cut off the heads of enemies slain in battle and attach them to the necks of their horses. The bloodstained spoils they hand over to their attendants and carry off as booty, while striking up a paean and singing a song of victory, and they nail up these first fruits on their houses just as do those who lay low wild animals in certain kinds of hunting.

'Posidonius says he saw this sight in many places,' wrote Strabo, 'and was at first disgusted by it, but afterwards, becoming used to it, could bear it with equanimity.'

When bands of ferocious Celts reached Ireland they overwhelmed the petty nobles who ruled here. The struggle may have been piecemeal, small bits of countryside being wrested loose every few years by determined warrior bands. However long the conquest took and by how many diverse tribal units we will never know. But one conclusion is certainly definite, that in the course of a relatively short length of time Ireland became thoroughly Celtic. No other ethnic group survived.

The Celts may well have thought this island haunted at first, being, as Caesar noted, 'exceedingly given to religious superstition'. Along the river Boyne they found huge mounds with great stone circles and pillars standing nearby. On every hilltop and plateau, even on the highest mountains, smaller cairns beyond counting observed their movements through the countryside below, giving their travels an eerie flavour at best. On the tip of Tara Hill, searching for home and fortress sites, they discovered just such a mound and here, around this elder statesman, one of the earliest Celtic settlements took shape.

For many centuries this cairn has been known as the Mound of Hostages and identified with the legendary

Cairn, Knocknarea, Co. Sligo

Cormac mac Airt, a Celtic king who supposedly ruled from Tara in the third century AD and was regarded by several important tribal septs as a founding father. The association, though misplaced,[1] indicates that later generations of Celts had begun to associate these mysterious cairns with ancestor figures. This accumulation of myth tended to intensify the sanctity of these mounds even more, and many were gradually adapted as ceremonial fixtures. On the Mound of Hostages lay the *Lia Fáil*, or Stone of Destiny. It was the coronation stone that screamed approval when a man worthy of Tara's crown stepped upon it.

The function of *Lia Fáil* in early rites at Tara is open to considerable dispute. Originally it seems to have been a stone of oracle or witness, a judge of those selected for Tara's kingship. Set upright in the ground like a standing stone (as it is today) the *Lia Fáil* was apparently positioned at the far end of a chariot course on the summit of the hill. Harnessed to 'a king's chariot' were two wild, unbroken horses. A man chosen for the crown had first to drive these steeds at two crossed stones which, if he was worthy of Tara, opened before him allowing his chariot to pass. Then he would dash for the *Lia Fáil* and should he be acceptable it would 'screech against his chariot axle, so that all might hear'. Inability to control his team or negotiate the course meant failure, as did silence on the part of *Lia Fáil*.

At some point in time *Lia Fáil* was removed from the Mound of Hostages and placed atop Cormac's House, the major rath in Tara's complex, about six hundred feet away to the south. Some say this transferral took place in 1798 to mark the ditch where hundreds of Irish peasants were buried after a disastrous battle here against the British in May of that year. For whatever reason it now shares the spot with a more recent memorial to these men erected by the IRA in 1938, and a statue of St Patrick surrounded by a somewhat decrepit iron fence. None of these artifacts are particularly interesting from a visual point of view, the notable exception being the rath itself.

There are literally hundreds of similar earthworks all over Ireland and aerial photographs can pick out the tracings of thousands more. They were the simple everyday homes of the Celts, usually little more than a rounded trench with single entrance. Inside a wooden hut and sheds were built, generally circular in design and patterned after the *clocháns* of neolithic and early Christian times. Despite the ditches or moats that surround most of these raths they were not regarded as forts but rather as pens for livestock. When a site became cramped or run-down it was deserted without hesitation for another. Many raths, especially those in the central plains, may well have been seasonal cattle stations. A rath is more a statement of everyday Celtic rural life from the time of Christ into the later medieval ages than any other Irish remains, yet only fifty have been professionally excavated of their enormous number. Each year the plough destroys countless more.

We can assume, I think, that the raths here at Royal Tara — meaning the wooden structures within a rath — were more important and perhaps more ornate than the average rath of the common herdsman. Nevertheless there is no denying the relative simplicity of the architectural concept. Some examples such as these at Tara are complicated by the addition of half-moons or complete second circles, and others by two or more extra trenches, but essentially there seems little to justify the hyperboles of epic literature — the sumptuous palace, the mighty fortress, the unspeakable magnificence and so on. But they do have charm.

The most intriguing features of a rath are the ditches that surround it, for these emphasise the primary values of Celtic society. A king or noble was required to encircle his home with the number of trenches equivalent to his rank. Honour required every man's worth to be fully displayed, and indeed the accumulation and advertisement of honour was the goal of every aristocratic heart. The Irish word for honour is *enech*, the literal translation of which is 'face'. Loss of face through insult or humiliation was a savage indignity seldom endured. Most of the petty wars and quarrels which consume Irish history until the seventeenth century were the direct result of slights or derision.

The entire social chain, both political and commercial, required and maintained this system of values. Status for a nobleman was determined entirely by the number of

Cormac's House, The Hill of Tara, Co. Meath

Rath, Tullaghoe, Co. Tyrone

dependent clients he had economically under his control — in the modern sense, by how many people were renting apartments in his building. The binding factor was cattle. The more cattle a man had the more he could lease out to lesser herdsmen, who in turn owed him a percentage of their annual yield. In addition to the basic arithmetic of these arrangements the noble was required by honour to protect his clients. Livestock being the commodity of wealth, warfare took the form of cattle raids. A warrior who lost cattle and was unable to recover them, lost status. His major concern would be for revenge, a retaliatory attack for the same prize. And so it would go, back and forth. Minor nobles contracted to larger ones, larger nobles contracted to minor kings, minor kings to major kings, major kings to provincial kings and so on. The political context for all this manoeuvering was the *tuath* or petty kingdom.

This intensity of emphasis on honour largely explains the bombastic postures that classical writers observed as normal Celtic behaviour. Boasting and pride in the valour of past battles gave courage and the will to fight in more. Gradually a lineage of historic behaviour evolved with a special class of guardians to maintain and embellish it. In Irish society these were the famous *filid*.

Strabo mentions three professional classes among the Continental Celts: druids, bards and vates. The druids were concerned with religious duties, the study of nature and philosophic speculation. The bards were poets and singers, the vates interpreters of sacrifice and minor seers. Translated into Irish terms the breakdown is less precise. The druids, of course, were priests and wise men, yet also judges and counsellors. Classical literature frequently recounts their intervention between warring armies and their settlement of legal cases brought before them. They held so many powers that people feared to disobey them. The vates (in Irish the *filid*) seem a later development, and it is reasonable to think of them as originally a lower druidic order. Their attendance and participation in religious functions and, like the druids, their oral training speak of a clerical discipline. In Irish society a definite split between the two occurred. The druids became more absorbed in religious and magical duties as the *filid* took

over secular affairs. Perhaps a church and state controversy erupted in early Celtic society that we know nothing about, but whatever the reason their duties emerge fairly clearly.

More than simple bard, the *filid* was the custodian of tribal tradition. He preserved the noble genealogies and remembered the great deeds of former times. He created ceremonial poems of official praise and recalled for all the ancient standards of honour. He kept in his mind the literary works of his own predecessors and trained younger disciples to follow in his steps. He maintained in order the laws of his people and explained for judge and plaintiff alike the intricacies of its interpretation. His most startling power lay in satire. Celtic society honoured scholarship and the *fili* achieved the peak of learning. A warrior belittled or a king ridiculed lost immediate face and suffered dishonour, most particularly if the slights contained truth. Old stories tell of sores and blisters that satire could raise on the face of those humiliated, a blemish being impossible to hide away. As one ancient manuscript defined the *filid*, 'Poison is his satire, beauty is his praise.'

Celtic society is often described as conservative, a misleading adjective in a way. Lack of sexual standards, continual warfare, social vanity with its respect for flamboyance, hardly concur with our modern conception of the word. By conservative is meant rigid, however. Celtic mores, once set, were seldom if ever altered, and rarely did the Gaels adopt progressive notions not their own. The *filid*, as a powerful special interest group, were prominent in the effort to maintain traditional ways, prompting their opponents from Caesar on up to the Renaissance Elizabethans to share the usual complaint: that the Celts were barbarians because they refused to adopt the more enlightened standards that civilisation offered them. The only solution was a purge by the sword, and since the Celts understood nothing else anyway, this was the procedure adopted, both in 52 BC and in the 1500s, to say nothing of later.

One lesson of history, presumably, is that people who think themselves civilised very often are not. The surprising thing about Celtic society is that beneath the din of cattle raids and noisy boastings a genuine affection for the essence of honour existed. Celtic law was based on fair dealings and the truth. Its reach was originally confined to the single *tuath*, as no higher authority existed over that of the petty king.[2] A man's honour was his word. To guarantee his word, let us say on a loan, he provided a bond as well as an independent third party of superior status to stand as guarantor. Should he default, this witness — in order to preserve his own honour — was required to search out the culprit and force him to comply with the provisions of the bargain. 'A promise made', according to an old poem, 'is a debt incurred.' When a man was wronged, moreover, the law decreed he be compensated by the offending party to the degree stipulated by the victim's status. Compensation and the power of the truth, not to mention social rank, were literally everything. In the words of an eighth-century law tract, 'There are three periods at which the world dies: the period of plague, of general war, of the dissolution of verbal contracts.'

Crimes of passion and criminal trespass were frequent, of course, but the development of the relatively specialised *filid* is an indication that most people turned to the law for redress of grievance in some expectation that it could work. The *filid* were scholars of the law. They alone had rights outside their own *tuath* and their rise must logically correspond with the growing complexity of law, responding, itself, to mounting litigation.[3] The Gaelic name for one of ancient Ireland's best known legal codes was *Senchas Mór*, its literal translation being 'the old road to knowledge'. Celtic life may have been volcanic but it recognised restraint with values that were just and humane: 'As the house protects a person against cold and inclement weather, so the law and knowledge of the *Senchas* protect a person against injustice and against ignorance of each contract.'

This is quite a bit to extract from just a few old trenches, and as a caution it is best, especially here at Tara, to remain wary of idealising too much the Celtic point of view. Life in these years, and right on through the 'Golden Age' of the emerging Irish Church, was essentially violent and destabilised. We can retrieve a fragment of early truth in the confession of an old warrior that 'it was the custom of his country to kill men'. What should impress us is the birth and progression and intent of Celtic thought. How enforceable the *Senchas Mór* and other Irish legal codes really were in those distracted and, to us, obscure times is truly guesswork.

In 58 BC Julius Caesar began his famous drive into Gaul. By then Celtic fortunes on the Continent had already declined: Germanic tribes to the north had pushed them across the Rhine, Roman pressures from the south and east had overwhelmed their settlements in Italy and along the Black Sea, their influence in Spain just disappeared. Only in Gaul and the British Isles had a Celtic presence survived, and 58 BC saw the beginning of a final struggle.

Roman civilisation proved catastrophic for Celtic tradition. Caesar's campaign lasted eight years, and because the advancement of his career (to say nothing of his finances) depended on quick, stunning success, the drive was dramatic and exceedingly brutal. Caesar never spared the sword, perhaps overcompensating for the legends of Celtic prowess, which proved less awesome than expected. The Celts were stubborn and prone to revolt even when conquered, but their disarray and genetic distrust of each other enabled the Romans to deal with them in piecemeal fashion. The resistance of Vercingetorix in 52 BC is the only example of a Celtic defence that was even remotely organised, and in the end it too collapsed amid the quarrels of Celtic chieftains.

The conquest of Gaul signalled an end to the Celtic penchant for wandering at will. The rigid bureaucracy of metropolitan government meant the encouragement of town life with its regulations and structured behaviour. Taxes were imposed, duties and tribute laid down that only a settled way of life could meet. Roman policy sought to tie vassal peoples to the land and thus bind them more closely to their masters. Education was an important means to this end. Reading and writing, books and letters, would undermine native consciousness and make every man a citizen, or so was the intent; for according to Caesar, 'it is normal experience that the help of the written word causes a loss of diligence in memorising by heart'. The victim was oral learning.

The professional classes of Celtic society, in particular the druids and vates (the *filid*), relied completely on the mind as a warehouse for tradition, lore, genealogy and law. 'They consider it improper to entrust their studies to writing,' Caesar observed, and instead 'commit to memory immense amounts of poetry'. The poetry was in fact a vast compendium of verse composition, structured in such a way as to facilitate memorisation and then retention. The literary value, from our point of view, would seem absolutely nil since the handle to verse — the key to its recall — is metre, or the organisation of syllables to a word or line according to stress, pitch and length ... meaning rhythm. The mode of learning and delivery was the drone or chant. Harmony and rhyme were relatively unimportant, form and content were everything. Our current perception of ancient Celtic poetry as lyrical and freewheeling is thus confined to the comparatively minor works of the bardic singers. The more serious poetical business was the learning, retention and transmission of tribal tradition by word of mouth, and the fragility of Celtic culture in the face of Roman efforts to supplant it derives solely from this ancient methodology. The withering of Celtic professional classes and subsequent decay, as one ancient jurist called it, of 'the tradition of one ear to another,' meant the almost instant evaporation of roots and continuity. The competition of books and the necessity of Latin, the universal language, created within two or three generations an irretrievable gap between past and present. Without a past the Celts were absorbed into a Roman orientation, since even the conquerors saw them as 'quick of mind and with good natural ability for learning'. Starting with Caesar's raid of 55 BC the Roman legions went even further afield into Celtic Britain, and eventually began the same process there. The Roman general and governor Agricola even dreamed of crossing to Ireland in AD 80, saying that with a single legion he

could win her, ensuring thereby that 'Roman troops would be everywhere and liberty would sink, so to speak, below the horizon,' but turbulence in Britain kept him where he was. When the Roman Empire finally did fall apart in the 400s much of Celtic life had disappeared, in Gaul completely so: its language was no more, its myths and culture permanently lost.[4] Of the Celtic life, only in Ireland did a branch remain untouched, and with it Celtic idiosyncrasies.

It is difficult, as a twentieth-century visitor, to stand here on Tara with a full comprehension of something as intangible as oral culture — if the knowledge of letters decreases the capacities of memory, what of radio, television or the cinema? Likewise it is equally difficult to be overwhelmed by a fragment from such an ethereal world as the *Lia Fáil*, especially with the presence of a question mark appended to the sign identifying it. Like everything else involving Tara there is controversy about where *Lia Fáil* actually resides, here on this hill or, of all places, in the centre of London beneath a throne where the kings and queens of England are crowned. The alleged travels of the stone from Ireland to Scotland, and then as a piece of booty from the Highlands to Westminster Abbey, are entertaining but probably inventions, leaving us as before with little to look at other than a plain piece of rock, unsculptured, undecorated, unglorified in the familiar histories. Which is part of its perverse pleasure.

The *Lia Fáil* is out of our orbit, uninteresting in its own physical sense yet seething, all the same, with an immence mythological drive that we can today only imagine. This reflects how lost and far away these stretches of the Celtic past must be, though even with the murk of ancient times as an obstacle certain connections can be made. Consider, for a moment, the Western world of *c*. AD 350. If a brush stroke were drawn from the North Sea down to Spain, turning east from there across the

Lia Fáil,
Hill of Tara,
Co. Meath

Mediterranean to Mesopotamia, we would have the Roman barrier: physical, psychological, undeniably real. Its very existence, according to one scholar, forces us 'to think in terms of peripheral survival', to look around the edges where the influence of Rome never penetrated. And there can be found, in the primal scream of the *Lia Fáil*, a thread so fragile, on the face of it, as to seem farfetched. But the tie-in to India is real.

The word Indo-European is mostly used today for linguistic reasons. It designates the family of languages which share in common various philological characteristics and includes most of those spoken in Europe as well as Armenian, Iranian and (most importantly) the Indic tongues. In a cultural sense the term is more restrictive, thanks to Rome, reserving itself to the 'lowest common denominator of custom' which the various ethnic groups speaking these dialects share. Latin civilisation effectively destroyed the greater part of this heritage and substituted its own. Only on the outer fringes do we find on the one hand the immense lode of India, and on the other tiny Ireland.

The druid of Celtic Ireland is more than just a cousin to the brahman of India — blood brother is more appropriate. The two depart from the same source and the same custom, hard as they may seem to reconcile, wandering about over Tara's soggy pastures. For the brahman, like the druid and *fili*, relied exclusively on the powers of his memory. It made whatever he said additionally more important to his listeners, who heard the learned man speak forth his wisdom without any aids whatever. The evolutionary result was a belief in the power of the spoken truth or Word. The Word was holy and magical because it never changed. The wise men who chanted sacred Vedas were singing psalms and truths that were timeless, without variation, demanding of awe. The brahmanic caste enjoyed the same monopoly as the druids — only they knew God's Word.

The power of the Word was very real in Celtic society. Its codes of law show this plainly, Indo-European in origin and not Roman. It accounts for the joy men felt when praised by the ceremonial verse of the *filid*, and their shame if satire came instead, satire so malignant that a blemish could rise for all to see. The Word was powerful enough to cause physical damage.

The *Lia Fáil* represents an Indo-European concept as well — the mighty scream of truth when a deserving man touched it. But more than that: the *Lia Fáil* was cultic in a fertility sense. The noted antiquarian George Petrie reported in 1837 that Gaelic speaking peasants in the neighbourhood of Tara referred to the stone as 'the penis of Fergus', and its role in the coronation ceremonies of Tara's kings harks back to the Indo-European notion of royal sperm.

A king who is worthy of his crown is faithful to the Word. He is without blemish and his virtue finds expression in the peace and prosperity of the kingdom. If crops and herds thrive, and the yield is bountiful, the people can see for themselves the righteousness of their king. But food cannot grow without seed nor children be born without union, and so the king upon assumption of power must mate with the Sovereignty of his *tuath* to ensure the continuance of fertility. As the rain sows the fields, so the semen of the king brings forth the fruits of Earth Mother.

Ritual in both Ireland and India emphasised the union of king with country. In the most primitive of rites intercourse was frequently enacted between the king and a representative of Sovereignty, usually an animal. The most infamous example of such a practice was recorded by Giraldus Cambrensis, a Norman cleric of Welsh descent who visited Ireland in 1185 as secretary to Prince John. He completed his *Topography of Ireland* in 1187 and has been vilified ever since by nationalistic historians who see in his book no end to a rather rampant prejudice, an accusation of some justice as Giraldus made little effort to conceal his contempt for the Irish, 'a most filthy race, a race sunk in vice'. Nevertheless his narrative of the rite in question, though based on the reports of others, is in all probability accurate though outdated in terms of the twelfth century. 'There is in the northern and most remote part of Ulster,' he wrote,

a nation which practises a most barbarous and abominable rite in creating their king. The whole people of that country

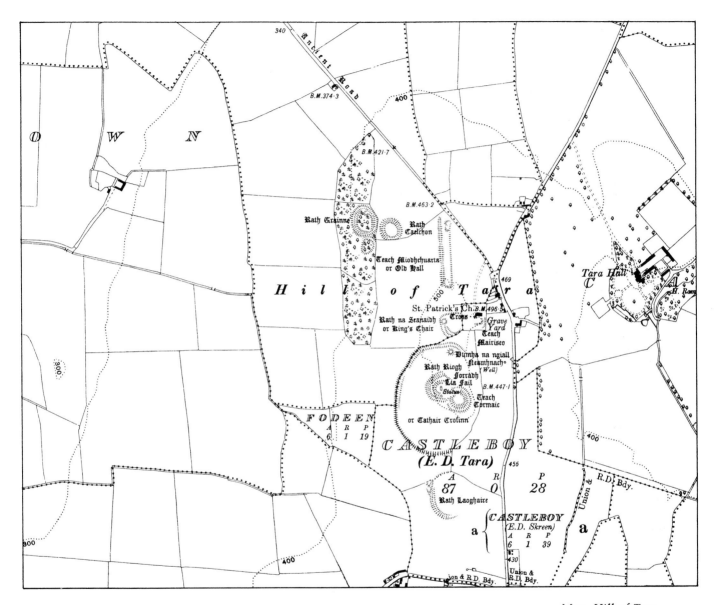

Map, Hill of Tara

Based on the Ordnance Survey by permission of the Government (Permit No. 4563)

being gathered in one place, a white mare is led into the midst of them. He who is to be inaugurated, not as a chief, but as a beast, not as a king, but as an outlaw, embraces the animal before all, professing himself to be a beast also. The mare is then killed immediately, cut up in pieces and boiled in water. A bath is prepared for the man afterwards in the same manner. He sits in the bath surrounded by all his people, and all, he and they, eat of the meat of the mare which is brought to them. He quaffs and drinks of the broth in which he is bathed, not in any cup, or using his hand, but just dipping his mouth into it round about him. When this unrighteous rite has been carried out, his kingship and dominion has been conferred.

Indian literature records similar episodes, again mostly with horses.

In later cases the mating just described by Giraldus certainly gave way to a more symbolic intercourse, the most controversial of them all being the *Feis Temro*, or Feast of Tara. The dispute, as is usual with Tara, revolves around St Patrick and his famous confrontation with Laoghaire. Briefly it is alleged that Laoghaire in his capacity as High King of Ireland was accustomed to call the Feast every three years to discuss and formulate new laws and policies. The Feast was a regularised calendar event and marked by a special prohibition of hearth fires or open flames anywhere in the kingdom until the great fire on Tara Hill had been lit. Patrick, with Easter approaching, builds a huge fire of his own on the Hill of Slane in defiance of the king, who sees the forbidden blaze from Tara and rushes off with his troops and druids to seize the apostle:

The wizard Lochru went angrily and noisily, with contention and questions, against Patrick; and then did he go astray into blaspheming the Trinity and the catholic faith. Patrick thereafter looked wrathfully upon him, and cried with a great voice unto God, and this he said: ' Lord, who canst do all things, and on whose power dependeth all that exists, and who has sent us hither to preach thy name to the heathen, let this ungodly man, who blasphemeth thy name, be lifted up, and let him forthwith die!' When he said this, the wizard was raised into the air and forthwith again cast down, and his brains were scattered on the stone, and he was broken in pieces, and died in their presence. The heathen were adread at that . . .

The story continues in like manner. The point to bear in mind is that Patrick's biographers felt it necessary to create a pagan fire festival which the saint's Easter flame could vanquish. The Feast of Tara was seized upon as just that and so portrayed.

In actual fact the *Feis Temro* was a fertility rite of Indo-European character, enacted but once in any king's reign. Linguistic scholars were the first to point this out by their refinement of the usual translation of *feis* as 'feast'. 'Etymologically it is the verbal noun from Old Irish *fo-aid* "to spend the night, to sleep with".' Other examples of such ceremonies were often called *banfeis* ('marriage-union') or *banais rige* ('royal wedding'), another emphasis on the sexual nature of this type of ritual. From a Christian point of view *Feis Temro* was certainly a pagan practice as were those connected with the *Lia Fáil*. In both cases a symbolic expression of manhood was required. What elevates our interest in this procedure was that proof of manhood generally came first, with ceremony second.

From the annals it appears that many kings did not perform their union with Sovereignty until honour allowed them to do so. For the petty king this generally meant the suppression of rival claimants to the throne. For the more important king, and later for the high king, it meant the seizure of hostages from vassal clients and *tuaths*. In the words of an old poem, 'The King who has not hostages in keeping is as ale in a leaky vessel.' Like the ditch outside his rath hostages were the visible sign of a king's status, and because of that few were ever given him without a struggle.

The circuit of a king for the purpose of securing tribute and hostages is the most intriguing of all the Indo-European customs shared by the ancient Indic and Irish peoples. The circuit was a final test. The king had weathered the factions and infighting, had won his crown. But unless he could display his might, the status of kingship was empty, the union with Sovereignty delayed or meaningless. Like the sun he had to seem bright yet be warm. One without the other was useless.

The sun, greatest of the megalithic gods — it is no surprise that ancient man patterned his thinking after the mood and personality of its style. The sun rules supreme in the sky, as the king rules supreme in his *tuath*. As the sun governs life on earth, so also the king. When the sun leads across the sky for all to follow, so must the king in similar fashion.

The ancient diurnal circuit of a king is basically man's attempt to emulate the sun, and the rigidity of custom in this matter is almost impossible to overstate. A king followed the movement of the sun because no king worthy of the name could do otherwise. He set out from his rath with the sun to his face and followed it from east to west. When it set he stopped. In practical terms for an Irish king this meant the circuit was undertaken sun-wise from east to south to west to north — the sea to his left and the plains to his right. Ill fortune, blemish, perhaps death awaited those who did otherwise.

An example from Indian literature portrays the norm, 'The Great king of Glory' who follows the 'heavenly Treasure of the Wheel, with its nave, its tire, and all its thousand spokes complete' — the sun.

Then the wondrous Wheel rolled onwards towards the region of the East, and after it went the Great King of Glory, and with him his army, horses, and chariots, and elephants, and men. And in whatever place the Wheel stopped, there the Great King of Glory took up his abode, and with him his army, horses, and chariots, and elephants, and men.

Then all the rival kings in the region of the East came to the Great King of Glory and said: 'Come, O mighty king! All is thine, O mighty king! Do thou, O mighty king, be a Teacher to us!'

Thus spake the Great King of Glory: 'Ye shall slay no living thing. Ye shall not take that which has not been given. Ye shall not act wrongly touching the bodily desires. Ye shall speak no lie. Ye shall drink no maddening drink. Ye shall eat as ye have eaten.'

Then all the rival kings in the region of the East became subject unto the Great King of Glory.

But the wondrous Wheel, having plunged down into the great waters of the East, rose up out again, and rolled onward to the region of the South (and there all happened as had happened in the region of the East. And in like manner the wondrous Wheel rolled onward to the extremest boundry of the West and of the North; and there, too, all happened as had happened in the region of the East).

Now when the wondrous Wheel had gone forth conquering and to conquer o'er the whole earth to its very ocean boundary, it returned back again to the royal city of Kusavata and remained fixed on the open terrace in front of the entrance to the inner appartments of the Great King of Glory, as a glorious adornment to the inner apartments of the Great King of Glory.

Such, Ananda, was the wondrous Wheel which appeared to the Great King of Glory.

Our finest Irish account of a circuit is found in a poem written by Cormacan Eigeas *c.* AD 942 describing the journey of his patron Muircheartach of the Leather Cloaks, a famous warrior king of the Northern Uí Néill who set out in the dead of winter from the mountain top fortress of Aileach to secure recognition as the high king of Tara. The prize he would demand from the men of Ireland was hostages, he would prove his worth by forcing his enemies to submit:

O Muircheartach, son of valiant Niall!
  Thou hast taken the hostages of Inis Fail;
  Thou hast brought them all into Aileach,
  Into the stone built palace of steeds

Thou didst go forth from us with a thousand heroes
  Of the race of Eoghan or red weapons,
  To make the circuit of all Erin,
  O Muircheartach of the yellow hair!

If Curoi of the oars were living,
  (O good son! O mariner!)
  He would become subject to thee, with his house
  Even Curoi mac Daire of the fair hands.

The day that thou didst set out from us eastwards,
  Into the fair province of Conchobhar,
  Many were the tears down beauteous cheeks
  Among the fair-haired women of Aileach.

One of their many stops is the Viking town of Dublin:

We were a night at fair Ath-cliath;
  (It was not pleasing to the Danes).

Aileach, Co. Donegal

A plentiful supply from an abundant store was given by the
Danes,
    To Muircheartach, the son of Niall,
    Of bacon, of fine good wheat,
    Together with penalties for bloodshed in red gold.

Joints of meat, and fine cheese, were given
    By the very good, the beautiful Queen;
    And there was given with liberality
    A coloured mantle for every chieftain.

We carried off with us Sitric of the Jewels,*
    To me was assigned the duty of keeping him;
    And there was not put upon him a manacle,
    Nor polished tight fetter.
*as a hostage.

Many months of travel later — through Ulster, Meath,
Munster and Connaught, in order — Muircheartach's
band approaches home:

From the green Lochan na n-each
    A page was despatched to Aileach
    To tell Dubhdaire of the black hair,
    To send women to cut rushes.

'Rise up O Dubhdaire,' spake the page,
    'Here is company coming to thy house,
    Attend each man of them
    As a monarch should be attended.'

'Tell to me,' she answered, 'what company comes hither,
    To the lordly Aileach-Rigreann,
    Tell me, O fair page,
    That I may attend them.'

'The Kings of Ireland in fetters,' he replies.

Even as late as the middle decades of the twentieth century
the holy rounds of pietistic practice personified in this same
fashion the movement of the sun. A nineteenth-century
observer wrote of this 'curious remnant of paganism'
where a 'peasant always approached a holy location from
the north side, and he must move from east to west, in
imitation' of the sun.

Eoin Macneill, like Douglas Hyde a prominent figure in
the revival of Gaelic studies, once wrote that the five
Cóiceda (or 'fifths') of Ireland remains the earliest reliable
fact of Irish history. While scholars disagree at times on
the actual alignment it seems fair to say that the geographical and political division of the country in the
fourth century AD was as follows: the Kingdom of
Munster, ruled from its fortress the Rock of Cashel; the
Kingdom of Connaught, ruled from the city of the plains,
Cruachain; the Kingdom of Ulster, governed by the Ulaid
Kings from the mountain rath of Emain Macha; and two
kingdoms of the men of Leinster, the more important
ruled from Dun Aillinne, a hilltop fort, the other from Tara.

Tara is the bone of contention. The literature is always
talking of five kingdoms but mentions specifically only
four. Tara is regarded as the final fifth for only two good
reasons, one of which reflects the simple process of
elimination — we know of no other really viable
candidate. The second explanation, like that of St
Patrick's raison d'être, is better seen in a seventh-century
context when history was rearranged for political
purposes, and that awaits us. For the moment we can only
say that Tara never shared the prominence these other
four kingdoms enjoyed. Her kings were certainly influential on a local scale, though as significant factors in
national politics we have no real evidence. The notion of a
single, all-powerful High King of Ireland who ruled from
Tara is entirely mythical. By the time Tara's High
Kingship did become viable around the 800s — both in
concept and fact — the site itself had long been
abandoned.

Tara did maintain a cultic position that none of the four
kingdoms could match, however. A king who ruled from
Tara enjoyed a symbolic prestige that somehow overshadowed that of any other. Perhaps the site itself, from
some association unknown to us, was extraordinarily
sacred and remained so throughout prehistory. The only
suitable mythological analogy is Camelot in its declining
years, when the great halls were empty save for the aged
king, his knights all departed on their quest for the Grail.
Tara's impact, like that of faded Camelot, lay in the
weight of its name, not its arm, a distinction the fables of

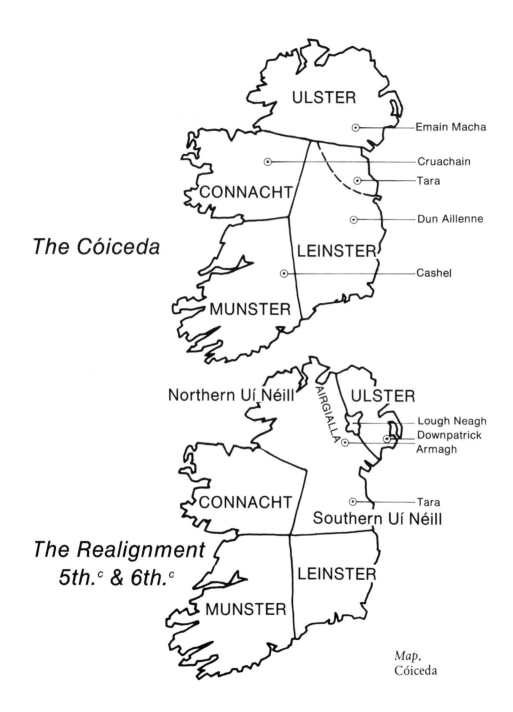

The Cóiceda

- Emain Macha
- Cruachain
- Tara
- Dun Aillenne
- Cashel

ULSTER
CONNACHT
LEINSTER
MUNSTER

The Realignment
5th.ᶜ & 6th.ᶜ

Northern Uí Néill
AIRGIALLA
ULSTER
- Lough Neagh
- Downpatrick
- Armagh
CONNACHT
- Tara
Southern Uí Néill
LEINSTER
MUNSTER

Map,
Cóiceda

Irish history have never recognised. Daniel O'Connell, the Great Liberator, held the largest of his monster rallies here in 1843 because he, like the Young Irelanders who surrounded him, knew no better. To them Tara had always been a mighty power, something irresistible with which to associate their cause. They did not understand the subtlety of its role in the Ireland of many centuries before. They had no idea of who or what the Uí Néill were about.

Going back to the car park I count to myself all the threads that Tara combines and, ultimately, confuses. The picture is never clear because more is involved than just this hill. Its story entangles many sites further away in both distance and time. But all roads lead from here. This is a fact well kept in mind.

Starting up I drive down to the level plains of the interior, heading west, looking back occasionally to the hills behind — *Brega* the Kingdom of the Heights. Later in the afternoon, after miles of bog and cheerless scenery, I stop and pitch a tent alongside a dreary lake, Lough Owel, which nevertheless features prominently in the mythical lore of Celtic Ireland. The patrons of a grimy country bar watch in silence as I eat a cold dinner of bread and cheese. A few times the old front door opens and a man walks in or out with a nod of the head and a mumbled salutation. Deep sighs, the cracked and filthy concrete floor, every now and then a huddled conversation up at the bar. A wet wind blows from the west raising a chill and a cough, memories of better days or days no different to this, the endless rhythm of a life without change. What a contrast to the violent emotionalism of warrior kings long, long forgotton. What a quiet place in which to think of sudden death and nameless, buried places far from any beaten track. The Heroic life seems a fair distance away, but echoes from those times can still be heard.

Three shouts of victory for a king, because of the excellence of warriorship in his land, are a shout of triumph after a stiff victory, a shout of high commendation, a shout at a feast.

Three shouts of discomfiture for a prince are the shout of satires to wound him, be it far off or near, the cry of his womenfolk in the grasp of enemies, the cry of his household when he has been defeated in battle.

Advice to a Prince Irish, eighth century

4 *Cruachain*

THE *Táin Bó Cuailgne*, or 'Cattle Raid of Cooley,' is but one tale of many from what is commonly called the Ulster Cycle of stories. Like the *cóiceda* it reflects one of the earliest historical realities that we have of Celtic Ireland — the continual warfare between two of the tribal Fifths, the Connachta from Cruachain and the Ulaid from Emain Macha in Ulster. The outcome of their rivalry marked the end of the Heroic Age, though certainly not of Heroic tradition, the spirit of which survived for hundreds of years. With the destruction of Emain Macha, however, and the rearrangement of so many boundaries, the balance of power altered fundamentally. The men of Ulster gave way to the men of Connaught, who in turn found themselves beleaguered from within by one of their own, the Uí Néill. The ramifications bleed into the historical period where dates and people become real to us for the first time.

The *Táin* specifically relates none of this, the characters and events it portrays being largely ficticious. But the essence of political manoeuvring is nevertheless unmistakably announced as the real centres of power — Cruachain and Emain Macha — occupy centre stage. Tara, significantly, is virtually unmentioned whereas levies from Leinster and Munster are briefly described as allies of the Connachta. The milieux of the fifth-century *Táin*, therefore, when Laoghaire the High King supposedly ruled the island from Tara, paints a largely different picture than later legends suggest. We approach the true Berlin of ancient Ireland, the city of Cruachain.

Cruachain is located round a country crossroads known as Rathcroghan, these days the collective name most often used for this place. It lies about three miles from the tiny village of Tulsk in County Roscommon. Touristically speaking the entire area is utterly obscure. Instead of candy wrappers and coke bottles, worn dirt paths and the footsteps of many who have come before, I wade through beautiful tall grass and peaceful, lush pastures. There are no signs and no directions. Cruachain hasn't been crowded for centuries.

Unlike Tara, Cruachain is a genuine city, a far-reaching complex of raths, many small and overgrown, others large and majestic. The most famous of all is Maeve's Hill, a perfect mound about fifteen feet high and two hundred in diameter. From the top, one can see many raths scattered here and there among the lonely farmhouses and grazing herds of cattle. The flat plains stretch on endlessly, and silence is unbroken.

Maeve, the Amazon Queen of Irish saga. is commonly thought to have built her palace on this particular rath, for no good reason other than it happens to be the largest. It sets the stage for the opening scene of *Táin Bó Cuailgne* when the plot is first hatched to make a raid into Ulster.

One linguist has called the *Táin* a 'window on the Iron Age' and despite the mythical nature of the personalities involved, this is so. The *Táin* is very accurate in describing the life itself (both the everyday and the extraordinary) of Heroic society. We have here, with feeling, an Irish *Gallic Wars*, a living verification of the classical reporters and history in a real and dramatic sense.

The story line is among the best known in Irish literature. Maeve, Queen of Connaught, is envious that her husband Ailill owns a finer breeding bull than she. Rebuffed when asking for the loan of neighbouring Ulster's

Maeve's Hill, Cruachain, Co. Roscommon

fine stud, the brown bull of Cuailgne, she decides to make off with it and assembles an army headed by her lover Fergus, a former king of Ulster. They depart from Cruachain and travel northeast.

A peculiar spell has meantime worked to their advantage, lulling the men of Ulster to sleep. Only the hero Cú Chulainn is available to thwart the theft, and in a lengthy series of individual combats at the ford of Ardee he defeats the champions of Connaught who come to do battle, often dashing them 'to pieces and morsels'.

After the demise of several Connaught heroes Maeve decides that only Ferdiad — 'the great and valiant warrior, the irresistible force, the battle rock of destruction' — has a chance of defeating Cú Chulainn. But Ferdiad is the foster brother of Cú Chulainn, a complication that must have moved (and, in a way, delighted) generations of Celtic audiences for the tragedy it promised would come. For as a means of cementing a political alliance or treaty, or sometimes owing to traditional ties going back over the years, important kings and nobles generally sent their children into fosterage with other families of rank, who in effect served as parents. For males the duration usually lasted from seven to seventeen years of age, the net result being to complicate an already intricate social situation. Warriors in particular were burdened with conflicting obligations: they served not only their own blood but that of a foster family as well. Curiously, the ties of affection were many times stronger for the latter than the former, and whereas a brother might kill a brother without much remorse, to slay a foster parent or brother was considered a fratricidal act of unusual disgrace.

The heroes of the *Táin* are deeply troubled on this particular point. Fergus, the former king of Ulster but now aligned with the Connachta, is Cú Chulainn's foster father and the affection of one for the other is intense. So too with Ferdiad, who grew up with Cú Chulainn as his foster brother. The thought of combat is abhorrent and he refuses.

Maeve, however, is shrewd, demanding, pitiless. She creates what amounts to a classic confrontation between Heroic values: honour and status on the one hand versus filial duty on the other. In a conflict worthy of any *kabuki*

drama she forces Ferdiad to choose one of two dishonours, for 'then did Maeve despatch the druids and the poets of the camp, the lampoonists and hard-attackers for Ferdiad, to the end that they might make three satires to stay him and three scoffing speeches against him, to mock at him and revile him and disgrace him, that they might raise three blisters on his face, Blame, Blemish and Disgrace, that he might not find a place in the world to lay his head, if he came not with them to the tent of Maeve. Ferdiad came with them for the sake of his own honour and for fear of their bringing shame on him, forasmuch as he deemed it better to fall by the shafts of valour and bravery and skill, than to fall by the shafts of satire, abuse and reproach.'

Cú Chulainn and Ferdiad meet at the ford. Although friends and loving even now they abuse each other traditionally before combat. A sort of antique formality marks the development of the duel which lasts for three days as they progress from weapon to weapon and one form of struggle to another: Cú Chulainn guarding the way north into Ulster, Ferdiad seeking to enter over the body of his kin. At length after epic battling Ferdiad falls, to the grief of Cú Chulainn, who 'hastened towards Ferdiad and clasped his two arms about him, and bore him with all his arms and armour and his dress northwards over the ford, so that it should be with his face to the north' in triumph.

Distracted by the endless duels Cú Chulainn cannot prevent the eventual theft of the bull Cuailgne. The King of Ulster is finally awakened from his sleep and warned of perils by the severed head of Sualtain: 'Men are slain, women stolen, cattle lifted, ye men of Ulster!' Off go the Ulaid, a battle is fought and the Connachta are defeated. The *Táin* ends with a great encounter between the bulls of Ulster and Connaught in which the brown bull of Cuailgne is triumphant. But significantly the exertion proves too much for the victor, who bursts apart from the enormous strain of battle.

The death of Cuailgne is a rather sinister omen considering the historical outcome of the Ulster-Connaught rivalry. That the *Táin* and its companion stories mirror the fact of continual raiding and episodic warfare between the two is indisputable. As Heroic sagas created by and for a Heroic audience, their subject matter was certainly accurate in essence, just as the boast, in order to have effect, must contain the glimmer of truth. But as the stories are Ulster stories they fail to give an ending. Indeed, by the Heroic definition of life no ending was possible, the idea of 'foray' being a liquid, self-perpetuating notion. If you crushed the enemy for good, after all, who would there be left to fight? The destruction of this society was not so much the result of the warrior values these heroes espoused, but of economic conditions that drove those with ambition to ends they never dreamed possible. The difference between Cú Chulainn and Niall of the Nine Hostages was slight but real, enough to account for the sack of Emain Macha, an event so sad the Ulster Cycle ignored it completely.[1]

Niall of the Nine Hostages is a shadowy figure. Some say he never existed, others that he did, still more that they can't be sure but think he may have, a reasonable conclusion in the light of what we know of fifth-century Ireland. There is enough, at least, to sketch in a reasonable plot. It proceeds from the premise that Cruachain and Emain Macha, as the Ulster Cycle suggests, were the two most important centres of power in the country.

'Sword-land', a brutal though fascinating concept (as ugly in its way as mercenary, as romantic in its way as pirate) is a term largely medieval in its application, and describes a territory won by predators or wandering warlords. Such was the end of Ulster. The immediate urge for expansion among the Connachta was neither greed nor the desire for new dominions per se, but apparently a response to overcrowding and overpopulation — too many people on too little land. The usual recourse of Celtic peoples in similar difficulties had been to gather up their herds and travel west, but nothing lay beyond Ireland save the Otherworld, a 'Land Under the Wave'. In Connaught the eyes of those deprived of power but desirous of it turned northwards to the traditional enemy, the men of the Ulaid. The most energetic of these were led by a single family, the Uí Néill.

Later ancestor legends of the Uí Néill, while fabulous and mythological, do suggest a sequence of events: an expedition into Sligo and Donegal, and another east towards Tara, both emanating (as in the *Táin*) from Cruachain. These efforts were different in character from raids or casual expeditions in search of plunder, the type of warfare most evident in the Heroic sagas. They aimed instead at seizing land to hold it, and the first plunge north was a fairly immediate success. One theory suggests that the Ulaid, encrusted in the old mould of Heroic combat ('trusting in their horses and chariots') were unprepared for the savagery of utilitarian warfare; that they could not cope with opponents who were hungry, who fought for something more than glory; and that they collapsed fairly quickly in a state of shock. Given the enormous success of Uí Néill colonisations in the northwest corner of the island, the imprint of which remained virtually unchanged until the seventeenth century, the plausibility of this theory is substantial.

A defeat of the mighty and prestigious Ulaid in even this, the remotest corner of their domain, had enormous repercussions. Momentum clearly lay with the Connachta who saw the chance to overwhelm their enemy completely and help themselves in the process to vast parcels of new territory. The mysterious betrayal of Ulster by the Airgialla, a vassal people whose land lay as a buffer between the Connachta and the Ulaid (Airgialla translates as 'those who give hostages') was apparently the final disaster. Emain Macha was stormed and destroyed, a magic spell lay broken. Sparta, Troy, Atlantis, Athens — all these and more was Emain Macha to Heroic Ireland. Its fall was momentous, and to the song of Connaught's victory add the dirge of Ulster's sorrow as the Ulaid retreated east to what remained of their kingdom, the northeast coast from Coleraine to Newry. Among the baggage they pulled along, stragglers and civilians, people whose fortunes lay with the Ulaid and thus with whom the exile must be shared, walked Patrick, their bishop.

Who led the assault on Emain Macha is unknown but circumstantial evidence points to Niall. The Airgialla, a confederation of nine *tuaths*, began submitting their pledges to the Uí Néill from whence, it is claimed, derived the accolade — Niall of the Nine Hostages. It is significant that these hostages were not sent to Cruachain, our first sign of conflict within the victor's camp.

Uí Néill origin legends of the seventh and eighth centuries indicate that Niall's sons spent most of their lives colonising not only the northwest of Ireland (Sligo, Donegal, Tyrone) but the central plains between Cruachain and Tara as well. For Niall himself there are fantastic stories which relate his adventures in Scotland and Britain, even as far away as the Alps. His career in Ireland, however, is largely ignored although his position as the first High King of the entire country, ruling from Tara, is simply stated and taken for granted. We hear very little in the way of details to describe his possession of the site, merely that Tara — not Cruachain, Dun Aillinne, Cashel or Emain Macha — is now the ancient capital of Ireland, its master duly recognised as high king. Tara is the magnet which lures the bishop Patrick from far away, and Laoghaire son of Niall (a mighty high king in his own right) is the man he seeks to convert. Every other *tuath* and *cóiceda* fades away as Tara becomes the star.

In point of fact none of this happened, largely because the men of Leinster proved a hardier breed than the Ulaid of Emain Macha. Niall of the Nine Hostages did indeed lead a second expedition from Cruachain with the same idea in mind as before, to carve out another strip of sword-land, this time the fertile plains that stretch beneath Tara's Hill. But despite the legends which tell of his death raiding in Britain, the facts seem to indicate that Niall was slain in combat by a king of Leinster. He never made it to Tara.

This is the crux of the problem. The Uí Néill by now appear to have felt constrained by their ties with Cruachain. They were the family that had engineered and carried out the expeditions into Ulster, and they were the driving force that fought with Leinster. Why should they be subject to kings in far away Connaught? The Celtic clamour of self-esteem evidently had its day among the Uí Néill who gradually drew apart from their cousins. What they needed was a jewel of their own, something to rival the mighty Cruachain in honour and prestige, something to replace the ruined Emain Macha. They needed Tara. But the men of Leinster for whom Tara was a royal site of some importance (but secondary nonetheless to their principal seat of Dun Aillinne), refused to give it up on anything like a permanent basis. For over a hundred years the struggle for this hill surged back and forth, neither side gaining a clear-cut, decisive victory, Tara itself changing hands several times. Hatred between the two became intense, maniacal. When Laoghaire died, for example, he was buried upright on the Hill of Tara fully armed with shield, spear and sword facing south to meet the 'new' traditional foe, the men of Leinster, that he might watch them flee for all generations before the might of Uí Néill to come. But Tara was never truly won, a high kingship never fully established. The passing of an age intervened first.

This is not to say, of course, that during the 500s the Uí Néill did not come close; or more accurately, that they didn't feel they were close, for mythological trades between Cruachain and Tara (in the persons of Maeve and Fergus) reveal otherwise. The goddess Maeve, a key figure in the *Táin Bó Cuailgne* and the personification of Connachta Sovereignty, was a motif the Uí Néill understood, something they apparently considered essential to a dynasty of their own. Her jurisdiction was accordingly extended to encompass Tara as well. Not so much an Aphrodite as a Mars, Maeve was an expression of militant sexuality in its most pungent Indo-European sense: she was fertility and Earth Mother. No man could be king of Tara unless (as at Cruachain) he slept with Maeve, 'the

Misgaun Medb *("Maeve's Cairn"),*
reputed burial mound of Queen Maeve, Knocknarea, Co. Sligo

Intoxicating One', 'She who is the nature of mead'. The antiquarian George Petrie's notation in 1837 of *Lia Fáil's* Gaelic nickname — 'the penis of Fergus' — illustrates this tradition at its ancient best, the *banais rige* or 'royal wedding'. *Lia Fáil*, the stone of coronation and witness that screamed should a man be worthy of Tara, doubled as a sexual member, expressing the demand of Maeve for a virile monarch whose penis must rival that of her finest lover, the royal Fergus, once a king himself. Without exaggerating too much, the scream of *Lia Fáil* can easily be recognised for what it was, the ultimate ejaculation.

We see in this exchange a basic Uí Néill dependence on their Connachta origins. It seems at first a rather tentative step on their part, an acknowledgment of the roots they grew up with. It also reflects the long duration of their struggle with Leinster, the uncertainty of possession (in terms of Tara itself) preventing the development of a uniquely Uí Néill tradition. It is not until late in the sixth century when Niall of the Nine Hostages was ritualistically canonised in legend and song as their official ancestor figure (with semi-mystical powers all his own) that a separate and distinct Uí Néill dynastic entity was established, thus at long last formalising their split with Connaught. Yet paradoxically, about the time they began calling themselves Kings of Tara, the Uí Néill deserted the site altogether. And not only was it Tara: Cruachain and Dun Aillinne, not to mention Emain Macha, surrendered their majesty to weeds and lonely herdsmen. The tribes had gone, only to return for an odd ceremony or hosting now and then. Only the kingship remained, to puzzle historians and travellers ever since.

The Heroic Age had simply run its course. Niall's great victory over Ulster, so shattering in its finality, had signalled the end. The antique values of saga lore had been replaced by the realities of sword-land. Niall and his followers could have looted Ulster in time-honoured fashion and simply returned home, but plunder of gold and silver no longer could feed a growing population. Neither could hill forts or the tales of *filid*. Land became all important. A warrior society based on combat gave way to a pastoral society, again well versed in combat, but not to the same degree. Kings and nobles were herdsmen first,

warriors second, a distinct evolution from the Heroic Age. The only trapping left over, at least as far as the Uí Néill were concerned, was the Kingship of Tara which now existed symbolically outside the body of Tara Hill. The Kingship meant control of the pastures, not of the mountains, ownership of herds in preference to chariots. In theory the men of Leinster could have the Hill of Tara now, it wasn't that important any more. Farmland and domestic wealth were all that mattered.

In these years the Kingship was never meant to include jurisdiction over all of Ireland. Instead its scope was restricted to control over the family itself, a task beset with considerable danger. Unity within the Uí Néill had cracked apart as the generations passed by, splitting the family into two septs, the Northern and Southern Uí Néill, who eventually began warring with each other. The famous Diarmait, for instance, Uí Néill king of Tara *c.* 560, suffered his worst defeat at the hands of his northern cousins at the Battle of Cúl Dreimne outside of Sligo, a campaign he had sandwiched between more traditional forays into Leinster. The prize of these internecine conflicts soon came to be the ceremonial title, King of Tara, symbolising as it did supremacy over both branches of the family. In the course of time the title was alternated between the kings of the Northern and Southern Uí Néill as a matter of course, but frequently the jealousies of the excluded monarch were enough to lead to war.

The riddle of Tara — its cultic personality as detached from the hill itself — has long been a mental block in Ireland. The schools perpetuate it, of course, as do the myths and nursery rhymes that bring so many tourists to the country. It would be too complicated to point out that the Uí Néill kings of Tara, from the sixth century on, never really lived in the royal palace of Tara, in fact might well have ruled from the highlands of Donegal. And to explain how the monks of Armagh became involved would confuse the matter even further. Cruachain, in a sense the father of Tara, has little to say that a traveller can hear or see for himself on all these thorny problems. The virtue of this purely Celtic place, in fact, lies in the busy silence of its fields and hillocks — the gentle rustle of the grass, the mournful cries of the western Atlantic winds and passing birds, the chatter of grazing livestock. In the hollow of one of the more derelict raths, I pitch my tent.

At 3.30 in the morning my alarm goes off. Early spring cold and pitch black outside, so instead of setting off cross-crountry as originally planned I head for a nearby lane, following it to the village of Tulsk, about two miles. From there I keep to the main road for another mile or so before turning off onto a farm track. Gradually the ascent begins to stiffen. There is not a breath in the air nor a sound.

As the road winds upward I find myself emerging from mist I hadn't realised was about. The hill I am climbing is not of any great height (according to my map about 400 feet above sea level) but the lower plains, flat and spreading, make it seem far higher. As I reach a vantage point I look back and see nothing, just miles of heavy cloud lying motionless on the floor of the countryside below. Not a single feature is visible.

I have come to Carnfree to view a sunrise, but in the pre-dawn light I doubt very much that I'll catch one. Everything is overcast and grey, wet and distant. The road stretching on before me is awash with moisture, the road behind faintly rippled with the tracing of my own foot-prints. Just a few yards to my left an immense standing stone peers at my approach. The statues of Easter Island could be no more impressive than this.

Carnfree is a rather level hill shaped like a loaf of bread. Its summit is a plateau of pasture and stone walls, sheep and cattle. A mound about ten feet high and fifteen in diameter stands at the highest point: the ancient coronation mound of Connaught.

On its top there used to be a block of stone, which was removed in 1840 to a nearby farmhouse where it lies split in two at the middle of a lawn. On it you can still see the imprints of two feet.[2] Upon this stone the king or 'captain' stood, as the poet Spenser describes:

It is the custom amongst all the Irish that presently after the death of any their chief Lords or Captains, they do presently assemble themselves to a place generally appointed and known unto them, to choose another in his stead. They use to place him that shall be their Captain upon a stone, always reserved for that purpose, and placed commonly on a hill, in many of the which I have seen the foot of a man formed and graven which they say was the measure of their first Captain's foot, whereon he standing receiveth an oath to preserve all the former ancient customs of the country inviolable, and to deliver up the succession peaceably to his Tanist, and then hath a wand delivered onto him by some whose proper office that is, after which descending from the stone he turneth himself round thrice forward and thrice backward.

'All barbarous nations', he concludes, 'are commonly great observers of ceremonies and superstitious rites.' Climbing the mound and facing north, hearing the cries and shouts of hundreds as the wand of Sovereignty is placed in his hands,

Fedhlimidh son of Aedh son of Eoghan was proclaimed in a state as royal, as lordly and as public as any of his race from the time of Brión son of Eochu Mugmedón till that day. And when Fedhlimidh son of Aedh son of Eoghan had married the province of Connaught, his foster-father waited upon him in the manner remembered by old men and recorded in old books; and this was the most splendid kingship-marriage ever celebrated in Connaught down to that day.

Amid the silence I look east now into the murk, for a tip of red can be seen, and soon more and more and more. The cloak of mist has brushed away its brilliance, for the sun is heatless, not even glowing, just a soft and mellow red, and I look at it without squinting at all. In about four minutes it climbs away into denser fog and disappears. I climb down from the mound and in the growing light of day head northeast for Rathcrogan across the fields. In about an hour I can see my tent, the flaps waving quickly in the early morning wind. The mist burns away as I approach, today will be sunny. I crawl inside, take off my boots, and go back to sleep.

> To Cruachain of the purple-berried trees
> Proceed in the track of thy ancestors,
> Pass thy time in the fort of Maeve,
> Remove from that fort its dejection.
>
> Irish, fifteenth century

St Columb's Rock,
Coronation Stone of the O'Dohertys,
Belmont, Co. Londonderry

5 *Downpatrick*

THIS morning's copy of *The Irish Times*, sitting open next to me on the passenger's seat, announces that the death toll in Northern Ireland since the latest troubles began has now passed two thousand. Considering the size of this country, and more especially that of the six counties which constitute Northern Ireland, these are indeed frightening statistics and I have been warned by friends to be careful on my trip north, more so now than ever before.

During my last stay in Ireland several years ago crossing the Border back and forth (many times) had never struck me as a perilous or even adventuresome experience. But I was impressed this time over that the situation has obviously deteriorated. I noticed this, or rather felt it, during the course of being stopped four times within the span of only two hours by impromptu rural road blocks set up by the British Army. To those of us unused to war, unused to weaponry, it's a startling experience (but in Irish terms, purely historical) turning the corner on a lonely country road, at 30 or 35 mph, watching the scenery pass by, suddenly to find yourself glaring down the barrels of several machine guns. Who is more startled, you or the collection of camouflaged soldiers, heavily equipped with blackened faces, gripping their arms with such a ferocious. menacing air? The result, for several innocent civilians, has been totally unexpected death. A safety catch inadvertently left off, squeezing the trigger automatically at an approaching car just coming into view, the accidental shot. Three days ago a mother of two, sitting in the back seat of the family car, had her forehead shattered by a bullet in circumstances in no way different from these.

The far from sophisticated Irish Republican Army can probably outlast these British with their enormous manpower, armaments, electronic wizardry, for reasons beyond the power of mere soldiers to control. Certainly dumping my camping gear along the road and turning bags upside down in a ditch seem futile gestures at best.

Other changes, less solemn: in the old days, especially on back country roads, one never knew the exact point of entry from the Republic into the North, yet somehow you could always tell. Everything seemed more tidy, calculated, purposeful. The ruins of old mills and micro factories from the nineteenth century with their single tall lean brick smokestacks signalled a thrift and resolution somehow lacking in the Republican landscape just left behind. Farms especially seemed modern and up-to-date, and even the roadways (for political contrast I'm sure) appeared determinedly superior, particularly for the first ten or fifteen miles into the North. All this has changed. The Republic's entry into the European Economic Community, where it has become the fastest growing member (it had a long way to catch up, after all) has more radically affected the twenty-six counties than any single event in this century — even the struggle for independence. I have never seen such a jump in prosperity anywhere else, though many of the benefits seem dubious. In terms of materialism, at any rate, I now find it hard to distinguish the tractor or new car or new house or new television antenna belonging to the Republican farmer from those of his Northern Irish counterpart, whereas before the former had none of these, nor even the decent prospects. The incredibly sudden, inflated value of farm goods — meat, poultry, dairy produce — generally forced the Southern farmer (with government encouragement, and a heavy

Cathedral Hill, Downpatrick, Co. Down

reliance of borrowing) to make his holding an efficient one. The contrast between poverty and plenty no longer really holds in this island, at least to the extent it once did. If the next twenty or thirty years are peaceful ones, and present trends continue, the Ireland of the sixties and seventies — to say nothing of generations ago — will be hard to recognise.

Downpatrick was originally known by the name *Dún Dá Lethglas*, or the Fort of the Two Broken Fetters, an apparent allusion to the huge mound that stands north of the town. It rises to a height of over fifty feet and is surrounded by three tiers of earthworks, but its antiquity seems less assured than that of the lower cathedral hill in the middle of the village. Excavations there have verified its habitation since the late Iron Age, and in all probability it is the *Dún* (Irish for fort) of pre-Christian fame. In ancient times the tidal reach of the river Quoile flooded the marshlands at the foot of this hill, making the rock a three-sided island. When the Ulaid retreated east after the fall of Emain Macha they chose it as their new capital. To Patrick they gave a plot on the hill and there he founded a church.

The present Cathedral is not an old building. The original structure, a huge abbey built *c.* 1180 by the Norman, John de Courcy, for Benedictine monks brought over from England, was slowly whittled away by the ravages of war and countless hostings. In the sixteenth century it was burnt for the last time by Leonard Grey, a Lord Deputy of the usual stripe, and left in ruins. For over two centuries the building served as a local quarry. People from the town in need of a wall or shed would come up with carts and carry off great loads of stone worked loose from the church. By 1790 when restoration was begun, only the choir was structurally sound, and the new Protestant Cathedral occupies its shell. Ironically the cost of rebuilding became the burden of the Catholic peasantry,

as funds were allocated from the yearly collection of tithes.

The building itself is of slight interest to me but the view is fine, especially off to the south and the Mourne Mountains. In the graveyard a huge block of granite with a Celtic cross and the single word 'Patric' carved upon it marks the legendary site of the apostle's remains. There is very little proof in support of the legend, this no doubt empty tomb bringing to mind Rose Macaulay's caution to be wary of 'a ruin's devious career'. What better advice for the thorniest of Irish controversies, the life and mission of St Patrick.

The most important questions to ask about Patrick are the simple ones: who was he, when did he live, when did he come to Ireland, how successful was his mission, how truthful are the later legends? More complicated inquiries centre on the identity of a deacon, later bishop, known to us only as Palladius and the extent to which Ireland was already Christianised in the early 400s. As a frame of reference, however, it is probably best to keep in mind what is commonly called the orthodox point of view, or the traditional tale as it has been handed down by Church and State for years, the highlights of which are best summarised by a monument erected to St Patrick just a few miles outside Downpatrick on a mountain top near Saul. A huge bronze statue of the Saint, which to my mind makes him look something like an Egyptian pharaoh, was erected in 1932 to mark the 1500th anniversary of the linchpin date for orthodox theory — AD 432, the alleged year that Patrick landed here, in this village, to begin his work among the Irish. One of three bronze panels arranged at the base of this memorial depicts these first few moments as Patrick meets the local chieftain. The second illustrates another vital feature of orthodoxy, Patrick's famous paschal fire, lit on the Hill of Slane and designed to initiate his confrontation with Laoghaire, the supposedly High King of Tara, while the third records his death, again here in Saul, AD 461. These are important dates and events to remember; they have been fought over for so many years that one cannot ignore them.

In general terms, the sequence of the legend goes something like this: Patrick born AD *c.* 389 on a small farm in

Britain close to the Irish Sea, is kidnapped by roving Celtic pirates and sold into slavery. After six years of captivity in Ireland during which, like Joan of Arc, he begins hearing voices from God, Patrick escapes and takes ship, presumably to Britain, but eventually on through to Gaul. After many adventures, and abetted by several instances of divine intervention, we come to a twenty-one year gap until his return to the Irish in 432 as a missionary. Reconstructions differ as to what exactly happened in his life during this period but most agree that Patrick remained cloistered in various European monasteries, studying and fortifying his character with prayer until some great challenge should present itself. Among the famous monasteries he is said to have visited were Lérins, an island retreat off the coast of southern France, and Auxerre, an important Gaulish community under the leadership of Bishop Germanus, a noted scholar, who accepted the earnest youth as his protegé. At some point in these wanderings, Patrick travels home for a brief visit with his parents. There he hears the 'Voice of the Irish' calling him to return: 'We entreat thee, holy youth, that thou come, and henceforth walk among us.'

In 429 the Pelagian controversy erupts in Britain. Pope Celestine, at the urging of a deacon by the name of Palladius, orders Germanus to cross the channel and deal with the situation. Germanus, 'the hammer of heretics', complies and succeeds quickly in his task. Pelagianism disappears, orthodoxy is maintained. Three years later the Pope decides upon a mission to the Irish. The same Palladius is ordained a bishop and in 431 arrives in Ireland. He immediately proves unequal to the task of dealing with 'these wild and harsh men', however, and, soon discouraged, he quits the place within a year. On his way home he even dies. Germanus, according to popular narration, acts quickly:

To Patrick and his bishop, Germanus, the news must have come as a blow. They had looked upon Palladius and his little band as the vanguard of the army of the Lord; and now the leader was dead and his followers in retreat. Honour and policy alike demanded that the breach should be filled, and filled immediately. The memory of the voice of the Irish and the voice of Christ himself which had never ceased to haunt the mind of Patrick must have immediately suggested that now the hour had struck, and that he was the man to carry forward once again the retreating standard of the Cross. The moment called for definite and immediate decision, and Germanus and Patrick rose to the occasion. They determined that Patrick should set forth at once to the work for which God had so manifestly called him and for which he had been for so long endeavouring to prepare himself. Without delay Germanus consecrated him a bishop, and sent him forth with his blessing to the task of evangelising the Irish people.

Patrick arrives in the year AD 432 to work 'unaided and alone'. His first church is a barn granted him by an early convert at the spot where he lands, present-day Saul,[1] just two miles from Downpatrick. There he plots his master stroke, the capture for Christ on Easter Sunday of Tara, the 'capital of the realm of the Irish'. In the words of a seventh-century biographer,

It seemed good to St Patrick, inspired by God as he was, that this great feast of the Lord which is the chief of all feasts, should be celebrated in the great plain where was the greatest kingdom of those tribes, which was the head of all heathenism and idolatry; there, in the words of the Psalmist, he would smash the head of the dragon, and for the first time an irresistible wedge would be driven into the head of all idolatry with the hammer of brave action joined to faith by the spiritual hand of holy Patrick.

Patrick, lighting his fire on the Hill of Slane and chanting the *Breastplate*, confronts the druids and Laoghaire, 'High King' of Ireland. The druids, we are told, 'could not fail to have heard of the religion of Christ which was sweeping the whole civilised world, nor could they have failed to have heard that a Christian Bishop had already landed on their shores,' and are consequently determined to destroy him. They inevitably fail as Patrick wins the permission of Laoghaire to proceed, and the conversion of Ireland begins.

Through the course of his almost thirty years in Ireland Patrick sweeps through the Provinces — Ulster, Connaught, Munster and Leinster. Eventually he founds a

Church in Armagh to be the chief establishment for the entire island, an Irish Rome. From here he directs the continuation of his work until finally, burdened with the infirmities of advancing age he retires to Saul. There he lives for a few years when, sensing that the end is near, he thinks of Armagh, 'which he loved beyond all other places,' and orders that he be carried to that town to die. But death intervenes, Patrick passing away on Easter Sunday 461. His place of burial, like that of Moses, is uncertain. Tradition says Downpatrick but Saul is generally regarded as more likely. On this solitary note of uncertainty, the story ends.

Patrick's own writings — the *Confession*, apparently compiled on the eve of his death some time in the fifth century AD, and a shorter work known as the *Epistle to Coroticus*, a letter addressed to a tribal chieftain from either Wales or Britain — are not in themselves the source material for most of the legend's embellishments. The great highlights of Patrick's story derive mostly from later commentaries, one being a *Memoir* of Patrick's life and career written by a bishop named Tírechán about 675. This is a sporadic work, more catalogue than narrative, Tírechán's intention being to list the many churches Patrick founded (or more precisely, churches which claimed Patrick as their founder) as well as the priests and bishops he reputedly ordained. Tírechán apparently wrote most of his *Memoir* from local traditions that were largely oral.

The *Life of Patrick* by Muirchú, another exceedingly important work of this genre, was written at about the same time as Tírechán's *Memoir* but in a far more biographical manner. Muirchú was a monk, probably of Armagh, who wrote his book at the urging of a bishop, Áed of Slébte, as he informs us in a most revealing introduction:

Forasmuch as, my lord Áed, many have taken in hand to set forth in order a narration according to what has been delivered to them by their fathers and those who at the beginning were ministers of the word, but because of the difficulty of the narrative and the different opinions and many doubts of many people, never arrived at one definite line of history; so, unless I deceive myself, I — to use that proverb of ours, 'as boys are led into the amphitheatre,' — have led my boyish skiff with its unskilled oar into this deep and dangerous gulf of sacred narrative, with its mounds of waves surging wildly amidst the sharpest rocks fixed in uncharted waters, a gulf hitherto entered and occupied by no boats.

Muirchú's work is a pious reconstruction of Patrick's career in Ireland, with the usual injection of miracles and timely assistance from heavenly allies that mark most of the *vitae* common to the age. He in effect fleshed out the skeleton that Tírechán merely began, but on his own admission the terrain was slippery to begin with, being already two centuries old.

Tírechán and Muirchú were both familiar with Patrick's writings. In *c*. 806 a scribe of Armagh copied the *Memoir* and *Life*, as well as Patrick's *Confession*, into the famous *Liber Ardmachanus* — the Book of Armagh. Additional entries ranged from the New Testament in its entirety to a life of St Martin of Tours, as well as the fascinating Book of the Angel. All together this single volume represented the most prestigious and concentrated edition of Patrician lore in all of Ireland. Veracity was gradually confirmed by the growing age of its content, to say nothing of its holiness, the Book being a fixture on the high altar of Armagh and daily used in the singing of mass. Aside from Patrick's staff (given to him by an angel, and the same used by Jesus in the Holy Land) there was no holier relic in that city.

Finally there is the *Tripartite Life*, compiled *c*. 900 and written mostly in Irish. It is a purely fantastical interpretation of Patrick's life, little more than a corruption of the Book of Armagh and contemporary ninth-century myth. This *Life* is divided into three parts and consists of material from which sermons and homilies were meant to be composed, specifically for an important Patrician feast held annually in the spring for three days. In some ways it is the perfect union of Tírechán and Muirchú: it spreads Patrick out to cover the whole country (in terms of churches founded) and hallows every step in glory. After the *Tripartite Life* there are few really serious additions to Patrick's legend.

Reputed Grave of Patrick, Cathedral Hill, Downpatrick, Co. Down

Ogham stones are rare in the North, only nine in number. In Connaught there are eighteen, in Leinster thirty-eight. Scattered throughout Munster, mostly in Counties Kerry and Cork, are two hundred and fifty-one.

These are pillar stones, generally cut and shaped from larger rocks and anything from three to six feet high. They continue the Irish affection for standing stones that characterises Newgrange and other circular monuments. The interesting thing about them is the linear notches of varying lengths that were carved up and down along the edge of each stone (called a stemline) in groupings of from one to five. It is the earliest form of writing that we have evidence of in Ireland. During the nineteenth century the ogham 'alphabet' was a favourite intellectual mystery for amateur archaeologists, each of whom sought to break its code. The Irish equivalent of the Rosetta Stone was finally discovered in a manuscript compilation of AD *c.*1400 called the Book of Ballymote, which set out the appropriate letter for each of the various symbolic combinations. Once the key was found, however, all the excitement simply disappeared. Everyone had expected the stones to yield secret messages and mystic oaths because of the many episodes in ancient literature where druids or wizards would carve each other notes and signals on wooden posts, trees, and (by implication at least) pillar stones. But the inscriptions now deciphered proved disappointingly mundane, mostly proper names that either marked the ownership of property or else were simple epitaphs. The more explosive implications of ogham stones lay undiscussed for years.

Caesar observed that the Celts in Gaul were familiar with alphabets and letters, using Greek when they desired to put 'their public and private accounts' into writing. Roman education transferred the emphasis to Latin, and the invasion of Britain spread its use among the Celtic peoples there as well. But the Roman general Agricola didn't cross the Irish Sea with his single legion, and knowledge of writing never thundered into Irish heads as it did in Gaul and Britain. Instead the use of letters barely trickled over the sea, leaving few signs and only the faintest of scents to follow. The ogham stone is really our only clue.

The alphabet itself appears to have been a spin-off from druidic sign language. Most scholars, for example, see a definite correlation between the five notches with their many variants and the fingers of a hand. The premise is that in order to appear profound the druidic caste resorted to the riddles of a 'gesture alphabet' that only they understood, communicating from one to the other in a secret language while bystanders looked on, having no idea of what was being 'said'. When the knowledge of Latin letters became widespread it was a simple thing to pair gesture with letter and come up with a secret hieroglyphics. It seems fair to conclude that our earliest ogham inscriptions were druidically inspired, a caste response (devious and complicated) to the pressures of something new which threatened their monopoly of the educative process, hitherto transmitted orally — namely, writing. The ogham code was their way of salvaging some prestige and a semblance of magical aura from an otherwise unpromising evolution. The artificiality of its mode of expression pretty well confirms this theory: the script was ceremonial and never conceived as utilitarian. Its interest to us, however, is not so much involved with druidic idiosyncrasies as it is with the Latin. The implications as far as Patrick is concerned are significant.

Counter migrations reversed the flow of Celtic peoples as early as the AD 300s when Irish colonies were established in Wales and southern portions of England. Tradition and origin legends single out two tribes in particular which settled in southwest Wales and Cornwall — the Déisi and the Uí Liatháin, each from Munster. Close ties with the parent tribe were apparently preserved by both. Evidence of similar activities in Britain by tribes from Leinster is also on record.

These colonists, whether by trade or war, came into frequent contact with their British cousins, now Citizens not Celts. From them they learned the rudiments of the

Latin alphabet, as 'linkage' stones in the area of their settlements attest. These bear dual inscriptions for the most part, one in Latin, the other in Irish, and the ogham code came along in natural consequence. Over fifty-seven ogham stones survive in Britain today, forty in Wales alone. From their example derive the many scores we find in Ireland, where the pattern of their distribution resembles beacons flickering in the night alongside an airport runway. Rome trickled in by way of Munster, and with it Christ, right through a crack in the door.

In his chronicle *The Ruin of Britain* the monk Gildas (an individual of somewhat cantankerous disposition) records under the year 410 the following calamity: 'The Romans declare to our country that they could not be troubled too frequently by arduous expeditions. They urge the Britons, rather, to accustom themselves to arms, and fight bravely, so as to save with all their might their land, property, wives, children, and what is greater than these, their liberty and life. They then bid them farewell, as men who never intended to return.' The withdrawal of the Roman legions left Britain an easy prey to warlike Irish pirates (called Scots) and wandering Picts from the north of England. Britain had been guarded so long by professional standing armies that it took many shocks to galvanise her now peace-loving inhabitants to anything near resembling a warlike response, and in the meantime a reign of terror ruled. For as the Romans 'were returning home, the terrible hordes of Scots and Picts eagerly come forth out of their tiny craft[2] in which they sailed across the sea valley, as on the Ocean's deep, just as when the sun is high and the heat increasing, dark swarms of worms emerge from the narrow crevices of their holes. As lambs by butchers, so the unhappy citizens are torn to pieces by the enemy.'

These raids were to prove a constant nuisance in British life for most of the fifth century, and many people including Patrick saw their continual recurrence as a sign of divine displeasure. At some point in the 430s he himself was carried away as he tells us in his *Confession*. His father 'had a small farm hard by the place where I was taken captive. I was then nearly sixteen years of age. I did not know the true God;[3] and I was taken to Ireland in captivity with so many thousand men, in accordance with our deserts, because we departed from God, and kept not His precepts, and were not obedient to our priests, who admonished us for our salvation.'

The locale of Patrick's captivity is thought by many to have been Slemish, a mountain near Ballymena in County Antrim. Modern scholars dispute this tradition and lean towards Foghill in County Mayo,[4] but agree that it was somewhere in the northern portion of the island. Patrick states that among the heathen he experienced a spiritual reawakening, becoming a Christian in fact as well as in name. From his own words we gather this conversion had no effect on the pagan beliefs of his master.

As a solitary example this is interesting because it helps to contradict a theory that many historians hold true, namely that Christians carried off in raids somehow had a salutary effect on their nonbelieving captors, thus initiating in a modest sort of way the spread of Christianity throughout the country and creating that nucleus of converts to whom Palladius (in 431) and then Patrick in the following year were sent to minister. This seems unlikely. Patrick's experience only confirms an earlier observation by Caesar that the common people were completely ignored in day-to-day Celtic life, their views 'never invited on any questions'. The beliefs of a foreign slave were no doubt received in similar fashion. The only way a person in Patrick's set of difficulties could possibly influence the thinking of his superiors would be if one or two were Christian to begin with. Without any sort of common bond between captor and captive there existed no alternative means of communication given the strictures of Celtic society. For a master to converse with his slave in any mode other than command entailed a substantial loss of status. The key, presumably, lay at the top.

Yet we know that Christian communities did exist in Ireland when Palladius was appointed their bishop in 431.

Were they mostly British slaves with a few Irish converts sprinkled in among them, as some historians suggest? The answer is certainly no.

The overwhelming preponderance of ogham stones in the southern portions of the country indicates a sudden, fairly substantial intrusion of a new and dominant cultural order on the local scene. The initial point of impact was probably County Kerry in Munster where the greatest concentration of these memorials remain. They are not the result of an interflow of ideas established through trade links between Britain and Ireland. Ogham stones represent a single attitude and a single tribe for the most part; they witness a homecoming, the return from Britain of Irish colonists whose forefathers had emigrated generations before. In their baggage were two items that couldn't help but impress their new neighbours: the secret language based on letters that everyone save the Irish was familiar with (Latin), and a new faith. Thus set apart, and automatically endowed with considerable status, these people set about their rise to power. They come down to us today as the Eóganacht. As a dynastic power they were the contemporary equivalent of the Uí Néill in the North. By the seventh century their kings would rule all of Munster and small portions of Connaught and Leinster as well.

The establishment of the Eóganacht as a force in Irish politics took many generations. Their return to Ireland is vaguely dated AD *c.* 380 even though some historians are loth to accept this at all, given the absence of hard, legalistic substantiation. The accumulation of circumstantial evidence, however, is convincing. Tradition and myth as compiled by the *filid* of the Eóganacht single out a Niall-like figure of their own as a founding father, Conall Corc, who supposedly discovered the famous Rock of Cashel in a blinding snowstorm with the help of angels, and subsequently settled it as the seat of his dynasty. Conall's mother, 'a female satirist', is conspicuously a Briton, but even more intriguing is that he gains Cashel without a fight. There are no lengthy contests between Conall and hordes of pagan wizards, no displays of matching prowess or magical feats. Unlike Tara ('their Babylon', according to Muirchú), Cashel through legend is unstained with heathen or druidic associations. A semi-Christian aura pervades it instead. Its very name is civilised, a derivation from the Latin *castellum*. And finally, of course, we have the ogham stones.

The ogham stones were a colonial invention, the result of a cultural interflow between Roman and Irish ideas *in Britain*. In the process of exchange came Christianity, since the British had been receptive to the faith since the second century AD and the new religion, unlike the old, was consumed by the drive to gain conversions. Pagan creeds with their many gods and diverse traditions were generally passive and disunited in the face of determined, monotheistic missionaries. The only restraints that slowed the process were the vested interests of the pagan priesthood and the even more powerful force of habit, which in a conservative society could prove enormous. But when the forebears of the Eóganacht returned home to Ireland many were certainly Christian. The ecclesiastical nature of Cashel's medieval kingship (whereby many of its monarchs were bishops as well) reflects the long Eóganachta tradition of orthodoxy.

Even though Christian to a certain degree, the Eóganachta were nonetheless warlike and ambitious. As much as Celtic society admired learning and erudition, it respected the sword even more. When the Romans left Britain in 410 the Eóganacht were among the first to climb into their curraghs and cross the sea, to augment their power with deeds of valour and spoils of war. The difference for a Christian between being carried off by the Eóganacht as opposed to the Uí Néill is best understood by Patrick's experience. With the Eóganacht that essential link of a common religion (which preached, after all, peace on earth and similar homilies) was such that evangelising one's captor became at least a possibility. An evolutionary pattern of this sort did occur in Munster, with its long traditions of pre-Patrician, native Irish saints, but nowhere else in Ireland. St Ailbe of Emly, for instance, is said to have been born of Christian parents carried off from Britain. The milieu was such, however, that his own lifetime was not spent in slavery but rather in teaching the gospels of Christ. If Patrick, far to the north, had never escaped he would have ended his days in Ireland just as he began them — herding cattle.

Ogham stone, Dunmore Head, Dingle Peninsula, Co. Kerry

Prosper of Aquitaine was a Gaulish theologian and savant, a lay brother for many years in a monastery at Mersailles. In 436, however, he travelled to Rome and served as a secretary to Pope Leo I. He is best remembered for his extremely accurate *Chronicle* and his defence of Augustine, whose writings were frequently attacked by those then called (after the disgrace and condemnation of Pelagius) semi-Pelagians. In 429 he recorded the triumph of his friend Germanus in Britain. He had been sent by the Pope 'at the instigation of the deacon Palladius' according to the *Chronicle*, which understates in a way the probable chronology of events.

It is impossible to overestimate the effect of this heresy on the intellectuals of the Western Church. There were few if any scholars who were indifferent to its implications, but among those who supported the Church and opposed Pelagius the controversy was seen as especially satanic, an appeal to pride. Germanus, as a leading bishop and man of affairs was, like Augustine, greatly alarmed at the spread of this most pernicious error. We do not know, unfortunately, through what channels he first heard of its outbreak in Britain, but he believed the danger grave enough to pause before leaping into the fray. It is evident that he felt most concerned over the extent to which heresy had penetrated upper echelons of the British hierarchy. An authority greater than his own personal title would be required to coerce them into submission, which explains the mission of Palladius to the Pope. Palladius was the personal emissary of Germanus, his deacon and trusted subordinate, his task to inform the Pope that Germanus was willing, indeed eager, to travel into Britain and to do what he could to destroy those who had fallen into the sin of Pelagianism. He feared, however, that without the prestige of papal authorisation he would be unable to command the attention or respect of either the ringleaders or the more impressionable of the lower clergy who followed them. Palladius returned to Auxerre

with a commission and Germanus set out at the head of a deputation to Britain, where Prosper records that he 'overthrows the heretics and guides the Britons to the Catholic faith'.

It would seem likely that while in Britain Germanus heard stories about Christians in Ireland, poorly organised and inadequately served by the Church, located mostly in the south of the country. Perhaps he feared that Pelagianism, having some special attraction to the Celtic mind, might spread even further to the faithful there. Pelagius himself, after all, was one of their own. For whatever reason, the idea of a mission to Ireland was probably his. As an intellectual himself and a firm believer in episcopal rule, the notion of Christian communities existing outside the orbit of proper controls was troublesome. On his return to Auxerre the next year he evidently singled out his deacon as a man forceful enough to guide such a mission with vigour. Armed with letters from his bishop, Palladius departed again for Rome and Prosper of Aquitaine records his commission under the year 431: 'To the Irish believing in Christ Palladius, having been ordained by Pope Celestine, is sent as first bishop.' His mission appears to have lasted some thirty years.

The orthodox imagination, as we noted previously, draws a somewhat different picture. Palladius proves immediately unfit for the task, giving in to despair from the moment he lands. A grave is quickly dug, Palladius conveniently dies, the body is interred and that is the last we hear of him, the 'unfortunate' Palladius. More likely, however, is the situation where Palladius is welcomed in Munster by many who have already embraced the faith. It is commonly held that not a single martyr died for Christ in Ireland during the fourth, fifth or sixth centuries. 'No one was found in those parts', wrote a Norman cleric many years later in a neat twist of the truth, 'to cement the foundations of the Rising Church by shedding his blood', for the simple reason that such a sacrifice was unnecessary in Éoganachta territories. Palladius came at a time and place in Ireland where the civilising effects of Roman influence had some degree of foothold. Opposition from the druids and *filid* may have been significant, but apparently the thought of a purge or exter-

The Book of Armagh, Trinity College Library, Dublin

Pointer indicates controversial sentence:
'Palladius the first bishop sent here, was also called Patrick.'

mination of Christians in their midst just never occurred to those in power. Munster was already showing itself of different character from the more remote and pagan provinces of the island. The annals record that in 439 three additional bishops were sent from Auxerre to assist the mission — Secundinus, Auxilius and Iserninus — reinforcing the links between Gaul and southern Ireland. Local traditions, though faint in our own day, indicate the work of native saints as well: Ciaran of Seirkieran in Offaly and Declan of Ardmore, on the sea in County Waterford, are but two. These men began the arduous work of converting the majority of Munster to faith in Christ. It was time consuming, difficult labour, but the ground had been broken long before.

Hagiographical literature of the ninth and tenth centuries sought to organise the bewildering multitude of Irish saints into something like military formation. In the First Order stood Patrick, 'Most Holy'. Coming next, in the Second Order, were those who founded the famous monasteries, the 'Very Holy' — Columcille, Columbanus, Brendan of Clonfert, Brendan of Birr, Molaise, Ciarán of Clonmacnoise and so on. In the Third Order were 'those who dwell in desert places and live on herbs, and water, and alms, and have nothing of their own,' the 'Holy' hermits of Skellig Michael, Inishmurray and countless island oratories. All in all a carefully planned pyramid, logical and precise, but a serious misrepresentation of the facts just the same, both in content and chronology.

The conversion of Ireland was not the neat affair so many writers have claimed. The housekeeping charts of the early hagiographers represent a sweep of the broom for several of the first missionaries to this island, about whom next to nothing is now known. In fact, we might always have been in the dark about Palladius had not a few simple words survived the many revisions. How they managed to do so is a mystery, since they strike at the very heart of a conspiracy over eleven centuries old.

The annalists instruct us that Palladius died in 432. That same year Patrick was rushed from Auxerre to fill the gap and remained until his death in 461. One problem with these dates, as so many experts have pointed out, is that people with whom Patrick was supposedly in contact — kings, princes, druids and so on — all seem to have existed (or 'flourished') in the latter half of the century, that is from roughly 450 to 510. Muirchú, writing c. 675, solved the discrepancy by stretching out Patrick to cover both ends of the century. Like Moses, Patrick enjoyed a long and very full life, reaching the age of 120. More modernistic orthodoxy, while in sympathy with Muirchú's intention, tends to dismiss all the annalistic obituaries as misleading and unworthy of trust — excepting, of course, the single obit of 461 for Patrick.[5]

In the Book of Armagh, however, there runs a disturbing sentence following Tírechán's *Memoir* which reads as follows: 'Paladius episcopus primo mittitur qui Patricius alio nomine appellabatur.' Translation: 'Palladius the first bishop sent here, was also called Patrick.' Irish material of later centuries often referred to Palladius as 'Sen-Phátric' or the 'Older Patrick,' and an Irish poem of c. 750 would seem to bear out this idea of Two Patricks:

When Patrick went aloft, he fared (first) to the other Patrick; together they ascended to Jesus the Son of Mary.

According to D. A. Binchy, the most thorough of the modern Patrician scholars, these words 'simply reflect a contemporary belief that there was an older Patrick who in somewhat unorthodox fasion declined to go to heaven until he could be accompanied by his junior namesake.' Whether through confusion or design (probably the latter), Palladius was made to disappear and Patrick transplanted in his stead. In point of fact Palladius/Sen-Phátric lived until 461 and upon his death or some time thereabouts Patrick the National Apostle first set foot in Ireland. The two events were not, it appears, related as

95

nearly every circumstance of Patrick's mission differed markedly from that of Palladius. They seem to have existed on widely separate levels.

Palladius, for example, was an educated man. He, not Patrick, was a protégé of Germanus and he, not Patrick, studied and travelled about from the great centres of Gaulish learning to Rome and back again. His commission and consecration were from the hands of the Pope himself, and his presence in Ireland represented both Gaulish and papal authority. The legends of Patrick's sojourn on the mainland are an obvious distortion of Sen-Phátric's background, as even the most cursory examination of the *Confession* reveals.

I have camped this evening near the ruins of Inch Abbey, on the banks of the Quoile just a mile upstream from Downpatrick. In the Republic I rarely ask permission to spend the night in a farm field, but with the situation as tense as it is here it seems best to introduce myself to whoever is master. As a result, after a trip to the nearest farmhouse, I pick a beautiful, open spot above the river, with Inch Abbey below to my left in a slight hollow, and the Cathedral hill and tower of Downpatrick before me. I read for a few minutes from the *Confession* before returning to town for some groceries.

The thin, battered copy of Patrick's writings that I happen to own is without monetary value, but as with many books that I have it possesses a special worth and special memories. It reminds me primarily of my first visit to Downpatrick in 1969 when, browsing through a Protestant bookshop full of argumentative, sectarian religious literature from the late 1880s, I uncovered an old second-hand edition of the *Writings of Patrick*. I can still remember the amusement I felt standing in the aisle of that musty, Dickensian place skimming the translator's Introduction, where the argument seemed to be that if Patrick were alive today he would certainly be a Protestant

and most probably the Archbishop of Canterbury. Carefully listed in a rather archaic hand on the frontispiece of the book, originally owned by a Harry Beckford, 'No. 7 Company, 55th Regiment', was a list of ten popes from 402 to 492; the dates of Bede, Columba, Aquinas; and separate from these, some for Patrick himself, birth and death. On the end sheet, in a more hurried script, was an inventory of possessions ('3 shirts, knife & fork, comb, button brush, marking') and what appears to have been Harry Beckford's laundry list. If my recollection is correct, I paid pennies for the volume. As I walked through town this morning, I noted the shop had disappeared.

More personal, however, than just a memento from a visit several years ago — read quickly, then shelved away — this book became instead a symbol, as striking in its own way as Patrick's empty tomb in the Cathedral graveyard less than a mile away. For it too has led the merry chase, has followed the dictates of a 'devious career'. It too is not everything it seems.

My own realisation came after two or three readings of the *Confession* (these writings are very short) when I began paying more attention to the hundreds of footnotes, annotations, symbols and explanations both learned and ridiculous with which nineteenth century Irish scholars indulged themselves whenever dealing with the intricacies of their obscure and tortured history. I remember noting the continual use of brackets, for example, that were often inserted for no apparent reason in the middle of paragraphs, even sentences. Looking about for some rationale I caught sight of a larger picture altogether: brackets enclosed material 'omitted from the Book of Armagh'.

My reaction to that disclosure was not the type one associates with great discoveries (which this was not, of course, in the widest sense). Rather it was, initially, just a pause; then a re-reading; finally the comprehension that this was something out of the ordinary. Further rummaging about brought another interesting note, that the transcript of Patrick's *Confession* in the Book of Armagh, 'considerably shorter than that presented in other manuscripts ... bears many internal evidences of an abridgement.'

What did this mean? Specifically that the translator of this little antiquarian oddity had been forced to look further than the famous Book of Armagh, the official repository of Patrician lore, for a complete and unedited version of the *Confession* and the *Epistle*; in fact, had had to consult Continental manuscripts once in the possession of Irish monasteries established on the European mainland. Four of these, I later learned, are in the collections of Oxford University and the British Museum in England, with three others preserved in France (Arras, Rouen, Paris). No other early copies are known to exist. Thus of the eight versions that remain today, one — the *Confession* as transcribed in the Book of Armagh — is demonstrably false in its purpose, a conclusion easily reached after I carefully went through and marked those passages enclosed in brackets, i.e. the "Continental" material. The results, for want of a better description, were startling. Almost half of Patrick's *Confession* had been edited and thrown away, his *Epistle to Coroticus* completely so. As a Catholic, I certainly knew where the truly offending material would turn up — in what had been cast aside — yet here I was with edited and unedited side by side, the opportunity to watch and note, as though over the shoulder, just what it was that had worried the scribes so gravely, had caused them to censor a man regarded by all of them as a saint. It was no surprise then, and isn't now, that the fuller picture of Patrick reveals more of the man and less of the legend.

As a result, reading Patrick is something of a curious experience, especially for someone familiar with the more political and sophisticated of the early Church fathers: Augustine, Bernard, Aquinas, Abelard. These are men whose lives and work are larger than life, we study them as though from afar. Patrick, by contrast, is supremely simple. We do not hear in these writings a forceful, dynamic champion, the erstwhile National Apostle toppling all before his might, but rather a poor stuttering fool, a simple Lear-like figure almost too exhausted by his mission to keep going, wishing instead that God might, in some fashion, whisk him away to a well-deserved rest. The picture of an all-conquering hero evaporates in front of our eyes: Tírechán's invincible Patrick, setting out on a circuit of Ireland like a high king becomes a grotesque parody. We have instead a defeated man whom glory, honour, fame have all passed by. Sin for him, like the hermits of Egypt and the Holy Land was real and painful. Christ was joy, though hard to come by. I am Patrick, he writes, 'a sinner, the rudest and the least of all the faithful, and most contemptible to many. Let him who will, laugh and insult.'

The *Confession* was written 'in my old age,' Patrick says, and the wandering, often incoherent sequence of his thoughts might reflect this fact. It is more likely, however, that we witness in these brief works a distinctly agitated state of mind, an impulse to clear the record, answer the charges, to refute — before death — those who have sought to discredit him. The *Confession* is, quite simply, an apologia, and reluctantly undertaken at that, 'for I blush today, and greatly fear to expose my unskilfulness because, not being eloquent, I cannot express myself with clearness and brevity, nor even as the spirit moves.'

Sentences like this, constant throughout the *Confession*, certainly do profess the humility, deference and modesty that commentators, especially those of the clergy, enjoy emphasising in their discussion of the Apostle's saintly disposition; but more than that they undercut with devastating effect one of the primary dogmas in Patrick's legend, the notion of a Gaulish education. For the *Confession* is written in a style of Latin that even the most generous of Patrick's defenders can label no better than 'quaint'. More realistic appraisals range from 'bad, ungrammatical, rude' to a decidedly insufficient command of Latin. Patrick was writing under 'a real linguistic handicap,' says one scholar, 'the difficulty of formulating his thoughts in Latin,' for a man supposedly versed in the cosmopolitan ways of Bishop Germanus and his sophisticated Auxerre community. In addition, a passage from the censored version of the *Confession* (while ambiguous) does imply that Patrick never set foot in Gaul, that he thought of that country as a far away Mecca, as later pilgrims would feel about Jerusalem. 'Though I could wish to leave them,' he says in despair of the Irish, 'and had been most willingly prepared to proceed to the Britains, to my country and parents; and not that only, but even to go as far

St Patrick flanked by Saints Francis and Dominic,
Dean Odo's Doorway, 15th century, Clonmacnoise, Co. Offaly

as the Gauls, to visit the brethren and to see the face of the saints of my lord. God knows that I greatly desired it. But I am "bound in the Spirit" who "witnesseth to me" that if I should do this, He would hold me guilty; and I fear to lose the labour which I have commenced.'

When Patrick the slave sneaked away from his master in Ireland and travelled on foot to the coast, taking there passage on a vessel just setting sail, he landed in Britain not Gaul. The voice of God who had encouraged him to escape had said after all, 'Thou shalt soon go to thy country.' Once there, having determined on a religious life, he may have joined a monastic community or lived apart as a hermit. His statements of faith remind us of Antony and the Desert Fathers; so too his descriptions of accidie and the temptations of the flesh, 'for strong is he who daily tried to subvert me from the chastity of religion. The flesh, which is in enmity, always leads to death.' One night, he recalls, 'while I was sleeping, Satan greatly tempted me, in a way which I shall remember as long as I am in this body. And he fell on me like a huge rock, and I had no power in my limbs, save that I should call out "My God". And in that moment I saw the sun rise in Heaven; and while I was crying out "My God" with all my might, behold the splendour of that sun fell upon me, and at once removed the weight from me.'

This intensity of Patrick's emotionalism recalls that of the earliest Egyptian hermits: mystic and somewhat anti-intellectual, its primary style that of arduous prayer and fervent recourse to the Bible. In Patrick's writings both these traits predominate. His *Confession* and *Epistle* reveal 'no traces of quotation or borrowings from any other book than the Bible,' an echo of Antony's warning that 'The scriptures are sufficient for our instruction.' Likewise Patrick's account of his routines as a young man at prayer which stress the number and hardship of his devotions instead of their content or meaning. The picture we see is a man afire with faith but backward in learning. His surroundings and companions in Britain were probably crude and ignorant, their studies unenlightened by Continental glosses or commentaries. Their inspirations were the Fathers of the Old Testament, the wisdom of the Psalms. Germanus might well have thought them children. 'How I have been instructed and learned in diction', writes Patrick, 'can easily be proved from the drivel[6] of my writing.' Another passage deleted from the Book of Armagh.

Tírechán's *Memoir* states that Patrick lived sixty years among the Irish, but the Saint himself said 'I did not of my own accord go to Ireland until I was almost worn out.' His immediate goal, or that of his superiors, seems to have been the conversion of the north, untouched as yet by any mission. The Continental effort under Palladius had progressed satisfactorily in the south, and possibly reached the midlands, though tribes in Munster were in most respects an easier mark. The presence there to begin with of Christians had made the work simpler if no less tedious. But in the north the ground lay untouched, the warlike reputation of its peoples perhaps a daunting factor. Its tribes had rarely mingled with the more civilised Celts from Britain or Wales, as the lack of ogham stones attests. Any seepage of Roman culture was strictly the brutal product of war — booty and slaves taken in battle. These were the heathens Patrick was sent to convert, his scope of operations totally confined to them. It was to be a strictly local effort on the part of the British hierarchy, and funded accordingly. No commission from Rome, no special message from the pope, no Gaulish bishops for support. Just Patrick and a few followers.

From the description he gives of later difficulties, Patrick's selection apparently left behind him a residue of rancour and jealousy. His lack of education, his 'rustic' and uncouth ways, seemed inappropriate to the rank bestowed upon him of bishop. But Patrick's superiors, whom he calls 'seniores' in the *Confession*, apparently felt that his zeal for 'work so pious and so wonderful' better suited the challenges ahead than knowledge of Latin. Who among the northern Celts, after all, knew Latin anyway? And so Patrick set off, no doubt with high hopes and honest faith in his Lord. Who could foresee that by the end of his life a degree of bitterness would set in, so intense that he could write:

And ye rhetoricians, who did not know the Lord, hear and examine: Who aroused me, a fool, from the midst of those who appear to be wise, and skilled in the laws, and powerful in speech and in every matter? And me — who am detested by the world — He has inspired beyond others (if indeed I be such), but on condition that with fear and reverence, and without complaining, I should faithfully serve the nation — to which the love of Christ has transferred me, and given me for my life, if I should be worthy.

I pray to Him to grant me that I may pour out my blood for His name's sake, even though I myself may be deprived of burial, and my corpse most miserably be torn limb from limb by dogs, or wild beasts, or that the fowls of heaven should devour it.

One of the few realities about Patrick's work in Ireland that we can decipher from the hagiographical cloud of legend is the Saint's association with the See of Armagh. He never mentions the place in his writings but tradition is extraordinarily persistent in matching the two together and for once logic seems to confirm myth.

Palladius and Patrick considered themselves, at least attitudinally, as citizens of Rome. The Empire had finally failed the British, of course, and would disintegrate completely on the Continent during the later years of the fifth century. Intellectuals like Cassiodorus and Boethius would spend their lives trying to maintain the essence of Roman values in the face of barbarian invasions and the restructuring of society, but in general terms this era is known best as the Dark Ages. Even so, for both Palladius and Patrick, Rome and what it once stood for remained the ideal.

In ecclesiastical terms such an outlook necessarily involved a preference for episcopal organisation. The bureaucratic and political framework of the Empire had consisted of towns and municipalities; the Church simply laid its gridwork over that already in existence. Power lay with a bishop, and his seat (like that of a civil governor) was always a town. His diocese copied the municipality, his tax collectors were parish priests and even much of his influence was secular. Sometimes the bishop was at the same time governor. Many were married or kept mis-tresses. His control ostensibly included jurisdiction over monks who settled in monasteries outside of towns. These monks elected abbots as their superiors, but they were, at least theoretically, obliged to obey the commands of the bishop within whose diocese their abbey lay. Friction between abbots and the more worldly bishops, however, was more often the norm than cooperation.

Patrick set foot in Ireland as a bishop. The exercise of his authority required a town and a diocesan system which of course were non-existent. Even six centuries later a Norman traveller would call the place 'truly a desert land, without roads,' to say nothing of a proper town life. The Irish lived in their scattered raths with no conception at all of what villages, with their commerce, markets, coins and taxes, were all about. To them barter and theft were commerce, and the rath of a petty king their town. They gathered together only on special occasions, for a ceremony or hosting, and more often than not these occurred on hill-tops far from life or in sacred groves. Patrick had no choice but to feel for himself where the source of power truly lay and in effect follow it about, for how else could he slip into the almost episodic stream of Celtic life? And it is fascinating to note that the hill of Armagh where Patrick established the nub of his mission is nowhere near the brow of Tara, seat of the legendary high kings of Ireland. Power and prestige in the northern half of the country lay with the Ulaid and the stronghold of Ulster was the rath of Emain Macha, less than two miles from Patrick's church. As Binchy notes, the notion of a high kingship for the entire island does not even exist in the earliest law tracts. 'The highest "grade" of king is the king of a province,' and so for Patrick at least the *Cóiceda* or Fifths of Ireland was the existing political reality, and of all the Fifths Ulster was by far the dominant. Patrick's association with Tara, Laoghaire, the druid Lochru, the *Breastplate* — is fiction.

Patrick's ultimate misfortune was being caught in the tumult of a major political realignment. The collapse of the Ulaid probably occurred in the latter half of Patrick's thirty odd years of labour amongst the Irish, by which time his prestige and social standing were irrevocably tied up with that of the Ulaid kings. It would have required more tact and intuition than he possessed to switch from

The Dane's Cast,
Scarva,
Co. Down

their patronage to that of the Uí Néill who, behind Niall of the Nine Hostages, stormed Emain Macha and became its master *c. 475.* Instead he retreated east to the sea and along with the ousted chieftains of the Ulaid, he settled in *Dún Dá Lethglas,* present-day Downpatrick. From there he continued his work, albeit in somewhat reduced circumstances. The Ulster kings would build a great earthen bank from Lough Neagh to Newry — called today the Dane's Cast — to mark their new border in the south.[7] The river Coleraine in the north, flowing from the lake to the sea, formed the line there. No longer was Patrick a bishop 'of Ireland'. Instead he presided over a shrunken remnant of Ulster.

This enormous reverse, which surely caught Patrick looking the other way, was probably the signal for his opponents at home. What better illustration of this man's incredible stupidity then to have been taken so flat-footed? Had he no sense of how the winds were blowing? Could he make no better arrangements than these? What good can our mission be (not to mention our money) stuck in this corner with, of all people, the losers? The man is incompetent, recall him. 'I offended against my wish,' the apostle records, 'certain of my *seniores,*' and later he notes 'many were hindering this mission''.

It appears that specific accusations of misconduct were levelled against Patrick in order to oust him from his position. Bad luck, after all, was not Patrick's fault and if they wanted to get rid of him something more damaging was necessary. Misuse of funds was the first allegation, it seems, and lack of moral fitness the other. Discussion of either one is missing from the book of Armagh.

In the early days of his work in Ireland Patrick evidently did a good deal of travelling. It did not take long for him to realise that among the Celts appearance meant more than substance at times, boasts more than deeds and vanity more than humility. Kings and powerful chieftains moved about in style with predetermined numbers of retainers. Hospitality and generosity with gifts were likewise indispensable components of their society. For Patrick to ignore these customs would have provoked their ridicule. What kind of God did he preach, who allowed His messenger to wander about alone and unaccompanied, without any sign of rank? So Patrick hired himself a retinue and even so, was often in trouble. 'I spend for you,' he writes to the *seniores,* 'that they might receive me,'

and among you, and everywhere, I travelled for your sake, amid many perils, even to remote places, where there was no one beyond, and where no one else had ever penetrated — to baptise or ordain clergy, or to confirm the people. The Lord granting it, I diligently and most cheerfully, for your salvation, defrayed all things. During this time I gave presents to the kings; besides which I gave pay to their sons who escorted me; and nevertheless they seized me, together with my companions. And on that day they eagerly desired to kill me; but the time had not yet come. And they seized all things that they found with us, and they also bound me with iron. And on the fourteenth day the Lord set me free from their power, and whatever was ours was restored to us, for God's sake, and the attached friends whom we had before provided.

Many times he was forced to pay brehons as well, to ensure the safe-conduct of his party through dangerous areas, But nowhere, he states, did he himself charge any fee for clerical services (as was the custom in Britain for burials, marriages and so forth) nor did he accept any money for his own enrichment:

For though I am unskilful in words, yet I have endeavoured in some respects to serve even my Christian brethren, and the virgins of Christ, and religious women, who have given to me small voluntary gifts, and have cast off some of their ornaments upon the altar; and I used to return these to them; although they were offended with me because I did so. But I did it for the hope of eternal life, in order to keep myself prudently in everything, so that the unbelieving may not catch me on any pretext, or the ministry of my service; and that, even in the smallest point, I might not give the unbelievers the occasion to defame or depreciate me. But perhaps, since I have baptised so many thousand men, I might have expected half a screpall from some of them? Tell it to me, and I will restore it to you. Or when the Lord ordained everywhere clergy, through my humble ministry, I dispensed the rite gratuitiously. If I asked any of them even the price of my shoe, tell it against me, and I will restore you more.

In the end he dismisses their complaint as malicious slander and, in some defiance, quotes St Paul against them:

'Lord, I do not regret it, nor is it enough for me — I still "spend, and will spend, for your souls!"'

More serious were the charges of moral failure and these, like Celtic satire, seem to have raised blisters on Patrick's face: 'Under anxiety, with a troubled mind, I told my most intimate friend what I had one day done in my boyhood, nay in one hour; because I was not then used to overcome. I do not know, God knows, whether I was fifteen years of age.' From all that Patrick has told us of his previous battles with the flesh, this sin may have been sexual in nature. Whatever it was it must have been suitably outrageous considering the uproar that followed, perhaps a variation of the spiteful charge by Giraldus Cambrensis that too many of the Celts seemed addicted to intercourse with cows. His confidant, in any event, was certainly a fellow cleric and a party to the thinking of the *seniores* who had planned the mission, for in happier days 'he had said to me with his own mouth, "Behold, thou art to be promoted to the rank of bishop," of which I was not worthy.' Now, many years later and in desperate straits, Patrick finds himself betrayed at home, as his friend — 'to whom I trusted even my life' — reveals the sin to his superiors. 'But when did it occur to him', Patrick writes bitterly, 'that before all, good and bad, he should publically put discredit on me, although he had before of his own accord gladly conceded that honour to me? I know in part', he continues, 'that I have not led a perfect life, as other believers. But I confess to my Lord, and I do not blush before Him, because I lie not: from the time that I knew Him in my youth, the love of God and His fear have increased in me; and until now, by the favour of the Lord, "I have kept the faith." I have said enough.'

If Patrick was ever formally recalled we know nothing of it. From the anger and humiliation that runs throughout the *Confession* it is doubtful he would have answered a summons to return. The *Confession*, he seems to point out, is a final statement.

The *Epistle to Coroticus* is more of the same and again contradicts the triumphant tone of Patrician myth. One historian speaking of Ferdomnach, the scribe who transferred Patrick's writings into the Book of Armagh *c.* 806, says he 'meant to copy' the *Epistle* but somehow never got around to it. Actually the defeatism of Patrick's letter explains more accurately the cause of its omission.

Coroticus was a pirate. Ironically he was not Irish but either British or Welsh, and if not himself a Christian he certainly lived among many who were. His outrage had been to raid a strip of Irish coast. On the day before his attack Patrick had baptised a number of converts who dressed themselves according to custom in the white robes of a neophyte. 'While the annointing was yet glistening on their foreheads they were cruelly massacred and slaughtered with the sword by those abovementioned.' The few who escaped with their lives, mostly the women, it would appear, were carried off as slaves.

Patrick's anger with these 'ravening wolves' was provoked most of all by their knowledge of the peoples' innocence in the sight of the Lord — their white robes. To him this made the awful crime something more — a sacrilege — but his efforts to gain the release of those enslaved met with the laughter of Coroticus and his men. The *Epistle* reflects his impotence, imploring those Christians living in the lands of Coroticus to shun him as diseased. The Patrick of legend, no doubt, would have smote him dead (Muirchú would have us believe that Coroticus 'was ignominiously changed into a fox, went off, and since that day and hour, like water that flows away, was never seen again'), but not so the Patrick of this letter. We hear instead a dirge for the sheep now lost, an admission of helplessness — 'The wickedness of the wicked has prevailed against us.'

I know not what I can say, or what I can speak further, concerning the departed sons of God, whom the sword has touched beyond measure severely. For it is written, 'weep with them that weep,' and again, 'if one member suffers, all the members suffer along with it.'

Therefore I grieve for you, I do grieve, my most beloved ones. But again, I rejoice within myself, I have not laboured in vain, and my pilgrimage has not been in vain; — although a crime so horrid and unspeakable has happened. Thanks be to God, baptised believers, ye have passed from this world to Paradise! I see you have begun to migrate 'where there shall be no night nor grief, nor death anymore,' but 'ye shall exult as calves let loose from their bonds, and ye shall tread down the wicked, and they shall be ashes under your feet.'

Ye, therefore, shall reign with the apostles, and prophets, and martyrs, and obtain the eternal kingdom, as He Himself testifies, saying 'They shall come from the east and the west, and shall sit down with Abraham, and Isaac, and Jacob, in the Kingdom of Heaven.'

'The thing that really endears St Patrick to anyone who has studied him are his own writings. Not what other people wrote about him, which are mostly fiction, but what he wrote himself. I believe there are very few individuals today who disbelieve the authenticity of either the *Confession* or the *Epistle*, but there are some. I had correspondence with a Franciscan who believed that the *Confession* in particular was a forgery — he wasn't an Irish Franciscan, I hasten to add, I think he was Belgian — and I must say I wasn't the least convinced by what he wrote.'

Professor Donald Binchy, smoking a small cigar and answering my questions in a frail, breaking tone of voice, does not fit my preconceived notion of a colossus. But even in his eighties, Binchy is considered just that, at least by those few remaining antiquarians who indulge themselves in what is commonly labelled Patriciology. Binchy's renowned investigation 'Patrick and His Biographers: Ancient and Modern' appeared in a 1962 issue of *Studia Hibernica*, an obscure little scholastic journal printed by St Patrick's Training College in Dublin. 'A marvellous piece of writing,' one of Binchy's admirers said to me, 'almost magisterial. It's like the Chief Justice of the highest court in the land sitting in judgment on everything ever written about Patrick, which is carloads believe me. It's so authoritative that all you can do is go along with most of what he says.' The immediate repercussions, however, were somewhat more energised. 'The response to Thomas O'Rahilly's lecture *The Two Patricks* was really bad enough', said Binchy, '— pure indignation. I wasn't in

Ireland myself that evening. It was March, during the war, 1942, and I was over in England. People here obviously felt that the proper, entrenched positions were being assailed, and the distinct reaction was one of anger. The reception given 'Patrick and His Biographers' was worse still. Some really good friends of mine were vehemently opposed to several of my conclusions. Nowadays the emotional heat has lessened a good deal, even in the orthodox camp, among the scholastics anyway. On the popular level, of course, things are much as they always have been. Look at what the Pope said during his visit about the paschal fire on the Hill of Slane — he used that for all it was worth. I doubt if anyone who's studied the subject, apart from the very few, would hold that that was historical at all. But in an article I've written, that hasn't been published yet, I've said that age, old age, has softened my acerbity a bit, and I'm perfectly prepared to listen to him say it. I don't think he's likely to make it an article of faith, or else we're all in trouble. Change does sneak in, of course, reluctantly and very slowly. Some things, for instance, have been discreetly excised. When I was a child learning the catechism I remember there was an answer to one question that read 'Ireland was converted to the true faith by St Patrick, who was sent by Pope Celestine and came to our island in the year 432.' Now I haven't kept up to date with catechisms, but I understand that 'he was sent by Pope Celestine' has been dropped. So there's always hope.'

Sitting in Binchy's office at the Institute for Advanced Studies in Dublin, which looks pretty much as it should — musty, full of papers, notebooks and galley sheets — I can't help thinking back to the old days when the controversy over how many Patricks there really were (one, two, three, even more) passed heatedly back and forth in argument and rebuttal. There must be, literally, hundreds of books, pamphlets, articles, homilies, profiles — all manner of printed literature — devoted to the Saint's life and career, which generates (at least from the vantage point of a reader far away) the impression of a world-wide, international conflict. In fact, the microcosm of disagreement is pretty much limited now to just the few, 'and we are all friends in this debate,' according to

Binchy, 'those of us still alive anyway, and we all seem to work within a few blocks of each other.'

I am most interested, naturally, in discussing the major aspects of Binchy's theories, but he is quick to point out that much of the doubt (which he refined) in the traditional picture of Patrick had been planted years ago and by many different scholars, both Catholic and Protestant. The climax was O'Rahilly's famous lecture on *The Two Patricks*, the effect of which was that 'of an atomic bomb dropped on the orthodox school,' according to Binchy. 'While it gives O'Rahilly a little too much credit to father all the ground breaking on him, he does deserve a lion's share of the honour.'

I asked Binchy to comment on some of the more famous (or infamous) points that both he and O'Rahilly developed. 'First of all I do have, myself, a rather open mind about the dating. I think I'm a person who's always prepared to accept evidence — and I mean that, *evidence* — when it hits me hard enough. I always say to my friends in this argument, 'If you can get me more definite facts, I'm prepared to accept this point or that, at least as a negative proposition,' and that's the way I feel about these disagreements on 461 as opposed to 492 as a date for the death of Patrick. As you probably know, I favour the latter. The listing of obituaries in the annals is good circumstantial evidence for the later year, in my opinion. I am not at all inclined to attach authority to any one single entry, but cumulatively they are impressive indeed because many of the Saint's reputed associates die, as they should, contemporaneously with him *c.* 491. If Patrick died in 461, as the old orthodox School maintains, one might almost think that he had preached to children, or solely to infants-in-arms.'

'What about the controversial sentence in the Book of Armagh, about Palladius "who is also known as Patrick"?

It comes, as I understand it, in a series of seemingly unrelated notes affixed to the end of Tírechán's *Memoir*. The question is, did Tírechán himself write that sentence?'

'I find it very hard to decide on that, and I think in the article I left it open as to whether it was really written by Tírechán. But it must be very old, that much I think is certain. Now I can't take that line in itself as anything like definitive proof that Palladius was Patricius/Palladius as O'Rahilly states so dogmatically. But I think it's early evidence of a tradition that Palladius was the first Patrick, and I think that's based on many other things as well. What it symbolises, the line itself, as I said in my article, is the existence in the Irish mind of 'a vague but obstinate memory of an *older* Patrick.' One other thing, most remarkable and pointed out long before me, is that the writings of the sixth century and even a great deal of the seventh century, have nothing at all to say about Patrick. If he had been the National Apostle, then it's extraordinary.

'The important thing to keep in mind are the contents of these stories in Muirchú and Tírechán. The Palladius/Patrick sentence, that's very damning, but so are the stories themselves. What I'm most convinced of is that the bulk of what's in Muirchú and Tírechán are legends or actual, purposeful alterations of the record. The whole story of Palladius, for example, has been inserted — not the story of his mission, but the story of its disastrous ending — put in simply to pave the way for Patrick to come over immediately afterwards. That's my impression as a historian, but I wouldn't like to go into the witness box and swear that it was true. Remember, the only thing you can really rely on are Patrick's own writings. I hate to keep repeating what I've written before, but the *Confession* and *Epistle to Coroticus* are the sole fifth century witnesses we have to Patrick and what he did here.'

105

The Rock of Doon, Kilmacrenan, Co. Donegal

6 *The Rock of Doon*

THE Rock of Doon, coronation mound of Clan O'Donnell in a northern reach of the Donegal Highlands — I don't believe anyone could find a bleaker spot. Even without maps and guide books I could have found this place. From afar, coming over a mountain pass and taking in the immense view, with hundreds of acres of vast and lonely bog, the Rock of Doon almost erupts from its treeless landscape, a twisted enormous projection of tribal authority and power. I drive closer, then leave my car at the side of a *boreen* or track and approach on foot, passing a filthy farmstead that abuts a holy well, itself sheltered by a scrag whose branches are festooned with rags and bits of paper. Following a worn path I walk up to the summit and find a spot in the lee of the wind to pitch my tent. In some way I feel at the prow of a ship up here, on a dreadnought really, high above the long wet fields of featureless wasteland. It seems nonsensical to think of this place as a royal preserve, but such it has been for centuries.

Tonight, well after dark and tied up in my tent, with a force 7 or 8 gale blowing overhead from the sea, is a good time to reflect on the miles (and centuries) we've travelled in the search for Patrick. It seems fair to say, without being too dogmatic, that the movements of the Saint can be identified in a general way both in time and place. No definitive conclusions can probably ever be reached, given the prodigious gap between ourselves and the Ireland of c. 450 AD and the murkiness of human memory, but the outstanding facts of his life do seem to come out with consistent clarity. We have also noted that the famed Hill of Tara, contrary to myth, was neither capital of an ancient and united Ireland nor the source of a national political power. As Binchy remarked to me in Dublin, 'Tara is very old. It may have been a prehistoric, sacred monarchy long before the Gaels came at all. But this notion of a High King of Tara in Patrick's time is all talk. The most important negative evidence that I know is that in the laws themselves, the regular canonical texts of which were all framed by the year 700 at the latest — a lot of it much earlier of course — there's no mention of the King of Tara except once, when he's called one of the local kings.' Tara's eventual overlords, a Celtic sept known to us today as the Uí Néill, were not in control there until well after Patrick's death. The Saint's association with Tara, likewise, is fiction.

It is the fiction that concerns us now as we turn ourselves to the study of myth in motion, or how it is that Patrick, far from being forgotten or lost as the generations flowed by, was instead resurrected, animated, inflated, by the exceedingly ambitious monastic federation of Armagh. Their programme of Patrician supremacy, however, would have been impossible without, on the one hand, the simultaneous rise to power of the Uí Néill, who took to calling themselves 'High Kings' of Tara long after the hill itself had been abandoned; and on the other, in typically see-saw Irish fashion, the collapse of a rival monastic federation, St Columcille's.

We are now in Columcille's domain. The Rock of Doon is his country, his world, his values — a Celtic point of view alien to that of Patrick. This is also a harder road to follow, like a wind chime. After heavy storms the strings will need untangling and redefinition. But the maze is penetrable.

Termonn *(or Sanctuary) Cross,*
Columban Monastery of Gartan,
Co. Donegal

On the seventh day of December Columcille was born, and on the ninth of June he died. And fitting to the life of Columcille in the world was the season in which he came hither, for wintry was his life in respect of cold and darkness and in respect of pain and penance and in respect of bearing adversity and hardships in the flesh. And fitting to the life into which he entered from this world was the season in which he died, to wit, the season that is purest and warmest and brightest and most shining of all the year. And it was a parable that Almighty God gave us in the life and death of his chosen servant Columcille, inasmuch as He took him from the dark and sad and gloomy winter of his life in this world to the shining glorious summer of Eternal Life.

Manus O'Donnell, *The Life of Columcille*, 1532

The morning is so clear that I decide to hike across the mountains surrounding the Rock of Doon for Lough Gartan on the other side. While several of the peaks in this area are over 1,500 feet, I can tell from the map that the trek should be an easy one, the hills for me to traverse being half that height. It is astonishing how trivial these mountains are in terms of hiking, an ironical contrast to their foreboding and unfriendly bulk. In three hours of walking I see a few cars on the track below, but not a single person.

Lough Gartan is the site of Columcille's birthplace. A modern Irish high cross and a saint's bed mark the spot, on a slowly rising pasture overlooking the water. Further on up the road is the more interesting Columcille Oratory, where the Saint established what was probably one of his earliest communities. Rough-hewn and primitive Celtic crosses mark the sanctuary boundaries of the monastery, and the neighbouring graveyard is reputedly an ancient royal burial ground of the O'Donnell kings. It is absurdly quiet here, despite the fact that I can see three tractors on the other side of the lake spreading fertiliser, amid great clouds of dirt and dust. If I didn't

know better I'd probably be inclined to see in all this serenity a metaphor for Columcille, whom the 'children that were wont to play with him,' in the words of a medieval biographer, 'called *Colum* (Dove) of the *Cill* (Church).' The character of the mountains here betray him, though. They call to mind his baptismal name, *Crimthan*, or 'Wolf', Columba, Wolf of the Church — from what little we actually know of this man, these words would appear to do him more justice.

Columcille is an elusive man to describe. He left behind no writings, and while the legends we have of his life are entertaining and seem very old, they are generally worthless as intimate guides to his personality. The Patrician juggernaut no doubt caused damage too, sweeping Columcille (along with everyone else) off to the side. Nevertheless it is still puzzling to me that in a devotional sense Columcille hasn't much of a following in this country. With the decline of Gaelic continuing, this drift will grow more pronounced in future years.

Columcille was born *c.* 524, or about thirty years after Patrick's death. His father, a Uí Néill chieftain, claimed lineage directly from Niall of the Nine Hostages and his mother was descended from the Kings of Leinster. According to Irish law Columcille was thus eligible for a crown himself, 'to have it was his right by blood'.

He was a member of Clan Conaill (later anglicised to O'Donnell), a Uí Néill sept which dominated most of County Donegal. In later years the political situation among the Northern Uí Néill would become rather complicated, with Clan Conaill competing with Clan Eogan (later the O'Neills), another dynasty centred further to the east, near Londonderry, for control of this branch of the family.

Columcille belonged to the royal *fine* of Clan Conaill and had as valid a claim to succeed his father as any brother or cousin in the family, a strange situation to those of us more accustomed to the feudal practice of primogeniture. The English, in fact, were horrified at these 'lewd customs hateful to God', 'so contrary to all law that they ought not to be deemed laws'. Not surprisingly they had the same feelings about India.

If a *tuath* was the primary political reality of Celtic

society, the *fine* was its social counterpart. Its translation is 'joint-family' and once again we find ourselves having a link with Indo-European custom. The *fine* survives today in India where it remains the basic unit of civil life despite the many years of English rule. The *fine* did not survive in Ireland. It differs from the Anglicised notion of family in its extension of perimeters to include not just the mother-father/son-daughter relationship, but also the *derbfhine* or 'certain-family': five generations (through the male line) of son to great-great-great-grandfather, in a range to include the first male cousins of every generation. In other words, starting with a son (let us say Columcille) the progression would look as follows:

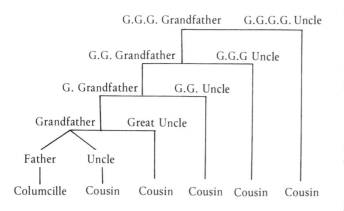

Every social, legal and political contract was based on this arrangement. In certain cases, moreover, the gates were opened to make the field even broader by extending the gap to include two or three additional generations, or sometimes by reaching out laterally for second and third cousins. In a populous family, intrigue for the succession could be extraordinarily complicated as a wide variety of kin became *rígdamnai*, or 'king material' like Columcille. Blood feuds and murder were the frequent consequence, and the custom of tanistry was evolved to cope with the problem of conflicting ambitions. As the heir apparent we saw this man at Carnfree. Spenser noted that after the king (or 'captain' as the poet insisted on calling him) had

been crowned, his two feet on the coronation stone, the tanist was inaugurated:

They say he setteth but one foot upon the stone and receiveth the like oath the captain did. And to this end the Tanist is always ready known, if it should happen the Captain suddenly to die or to be slain in battle or to be out of the country, to defend and keep it from all such doubts, and dangers; for which cause the Tanist hath also a share of the country allotted unto him, and certain cuttings and spendings upon all the inhabitants, under the lord.

The Elizabethans in particular sought to discourage tanistry, occasioning as it did 'great strife and contention', 'the effusion of blood and much mischief'. In its place they demanded the superior system (their own) whereby 'lands and inhabitants shall lynally descend from the father to the son according to the curse and Order of the lawes of England.' As the Hundred Years War and the Wars of the Roses were the direct result of problems involving primogeniture, this was a curious contention. As hindsight, in fact, it is telling to note the theory of Sir Henry Maine is his book *Early Law and Custom* that 'tanistry is the undoubted parent of primogeniture', the intent of both being to place succession 'beyond competition'. The Elizabethans saw no such parallels.

In addition to its political character the *fine* is equally fascinating from a moral and legalistic point of view. Well in the mainstream of socialist tradition, we find that ownership of property within the *fine* was held in common, and when a man died without a will or heir, his goods were distributed as the *fine* thought fair inside the family group. The bequest of property outside the *fine* was prohibited unless other members gave their permission. This became a crucial point for churchmen to consider, since without grants of income-producing property a self-supporting church or monastery was impossible. Another interesting feature was the collective responsibility every *fine* had as a whole for each of its members. If a man committed a crime and either fled or refused to pay compensation, his *fine* was held liable for damages. One really must admire these ancient customs which in lieu of central authority with its written codes of law, managed with some degree of success to create a system of bonds that were not only self-protecting and self-reliant, but eminently fair as well.

Columcille's effectiveness derived from this heritage in two respects: the first was his enormous prestige as a member of a royal *derbhfine*, the son of a king and eligible in his own right for power; and secondly, his intuitive sense of the Celtic system. Unlike Patrick, bulling right and left, confused and maybe frightened by the obdurate (as he saw them) mysteries of Irish life, Columcille ranged smoothly and confidently through the labyrinth. He was a Celt, after all, not a Briton. He was a prince, not a former slave. And he may have been the first man of any real social significance in Ireland to embrace the Cross of a White Martyrdom. In a country as status-conscious as this, such an example would not have gone unnoticed.

Christianity took over a hundred years to cement itself in Ireland. During Columcille's boyhood its progress was steady but slow, hindered in part by the misapplication of Roman methodology to an Irish system congenitally different. The foreign missionaries, Palladius and Patrick among them, had come as bishops and consecrated as bishops, but they had no source of power. They existed outside the *fine* and outside the *tuath*, and as such were literally strangers to the system. On the other hand their message seemed attractive to the Irish. Many converted to the faith though allegiance at first was often spotty under stress: Christ in times of peace and plenty, the war gods and druids in times of battle. But an accommodation was achieved in the face of this fecklessness whereby some of the more important of the pagan deities were refurbished into acceptable Christian saints pleasing to all. St Brigit, the Philomena of the Gael, is a good example.[1] Even so, the Christian machine was out of gear somewhere. The successors of Palladius and Patrick found themselves swimming against the current and somehow fatally out of step. 'Christ is my druid', said Columcille. They just shook their heads and went the other way. Druids weren't the problem or the answer, yet somehow neither was Christ.

In 548 the annals record an outbreak of the plague which 'swept away the noblest third part of the human race.' Columcille by then was in his early twenties and already a priest, having been trained since he was seven for a career in the Church. His father had made the decision, placing the boy in fosterage with a local priest instead of another noble family according to custom. Either he feared this religion or viewed it enviously (maybe both) as a potential factor in the politics of his domain, and sought to place a ready ear in its midst. Whether he expected his son to take the whole thing as seriously as he did we do not know, but Columcille proved exceedingly energetic and spiritual. As a young man he left Donegal and travelled to the most famous religious schools then operating in Ireland: Movilla in County Down and Clonard near the Boyne. He finished his studies under St Mobhi at Glasnevin, returning home *c.*545 to found his first church at *Doire*, Irish for 'oak wood', a ridge overlooking the river Foyle, present-day Derry.

> This is why I love Derry:
> For its level fields, for its brightness,
> For the hosts of its white angels,
> From one end to the other.

The plague cut a huge swath through the religious community of Ireland and had much to do with the rearrangement of religious organisation. At the head of the new tide was Columcille. For the next decade or so he courses back and forth over the north of Ireland, inflamed with the zeal of faith and spreading Christ's Word not only at the bottom of the pile but at the top as well. Columcille spoke the language of kings, he was of royal blood himself. He preached as no stranger but as an equal, and honour demanded, in part, that he be listened to. His learning and scholarship — surely his eloquence — were attributes worthy of praise and acclaim. He was a warrior without sword, an analogy the Celts could understand, and like the Desert Fathers of long ago he soon found

Monastic School of Movilla, Co. Down

The Gallarus Oratory, Dingle Peninsula, Co. Kerry

himself surrounded with followers. During these travels he founded well over a dozen churches, leaving behind in each a community of those who had heard his teachings and wished to share his life.

Hagiographical literature records the establishment of literally hundreds of churches throughout Ireland, and every saint has several score to his credit. It's an easy thing to dismiss as pious exaggeration but there are one or two points that should be noted. The first involves what we mean by the word 'church'. To us it connotes a substantial building with pews and ministers and parishioners, perhaps music, stained glass and so on. In early Ireland it meant a hut made of sticks and mud with a thatched roof, big enough for a priest and his altar, maybe a server as well. In order to 'found' a church, in fact, no more than two clerics were required, neither of whom had to be a priest. So in effect there were as many churches in Ireland as there were holy men, many of whom were hermits and solitaries. More often than not a mighty church of legend was no more than a lonely cave or an island sanctuary. At the other end of the spectrum we find the same thing: the cathedrals of Celtic Ireland, the boat-shaped oratories of Gallarus and Kilmalkedar, can hold no more than a dozen people. The emphasis lay on the eremitic principle of the individual.[2]

Columcille's foundations were larger affairs only because more people were involved, but even so the scale remained modest. His theme was that of Syria and the Desert Fathers: men should live apart, possessing no goods and living 'naked in imitation of Christ and the Evangelists'. In order to resist the temptations of accidie, however, they should find strength in the faith of their fellow hermits and should gather frequently together for the discourse of Scripture and the 'Testaments of God'. The physical result was communities very much like those of the Eastern churches where several small huts gathered round a central oratory. Hermits could live alone, each in his own *clochán*, but would join with others in the 'family' for communal prayer and discussion. Surrounding the complex would be a circular wall of stone or an earthen bank.

Once again the little signs are the strongest. Aerial photographs of the many Norman abbeys in Ireland, built anywhere from the 1200s to the 1400s, show the overlay fairly well — the Celtic buildings destroyed, their foundations either covered with a medieval church or else barely visible. Around the edges of the photograph, however, are the usual telltale signs of a cashel wall or raised earthen bank — in other words, the outline of a Celtic rath.

As Columcille's fame began to spread, petty kings and nobles sought to ingratiate themselves with this remarkable man by granting him property on which to settle his growing number of followers. Many went further and simply set aside as their gift a rath already built, enclosure and all. Some of these may well have been personal homes vacated in favour of the clergy. One or two children might be left behind as novices, yet another gift of the donor family. Negotiations to complete the transfer would ensure sufficient livestock and pasturage to support the needs of the community. In such manner Columcille would travel. When his retinue became too numerous or the countryside in particular need of Christ, he would stop and feel the political winds. If an accommodation could be made he would make it. If not he would travel on — but mostly among the Uí Néill, his own, from whom he could always expect at least a civil welcome.

The communities he left established were administered by men he chose himself. They followed the rules he stipulated and studied the texts he recommended, abiding the injunction, 'Three labours in thy day — prayer, work and reading.'

Take not food till thou art hungry.
Sleep not till thou feelest desire.
Speak not except on business.

Thy measure of prayer shall be until thy tears come;
Or thy measure of work of labour till thy tears come;
Or of thy genuflections until thy perspiration often comes, if thy tears are not free.

What gradually evolved was a feeling of solidarity, the zeal of kinship and the security of community shared with settlements many miles away and scattered to the winds.

Early Celtic Monastic Site (with later Norman abbey ruins), Canons' Island, Co. Clare

The common thread was Columcille — after his death the memory of Columcille — out of which came the notions of *paruchia* and *coarb* which sealed, if anything ever did, the fate of the bishops.

In the 600s, after Columcille's death, the position of Christianity began receiving recognition in the legal codes of the brehons. The clergy, according to their ranks, were given the rights of their civilian counterparts. Thus a bishop enjoyed the same prestige and honours as a *rí tuaithe*, or king of a *tuath*. An abbot, on the other hand, was deemed the equivalent of an overking, someone who enjoyed the fealty of several petty kings beneath him. And Columcille, it should be noted, had never been a bishop — but an abbot.

The demise of Patrick's stillborn episcopal system is a fascinating and subtle study. A bishop, of course, harking back to the Roman example, would look for a city or town in which to establish his seat. Since neither was available in Ireland he would settle for a rath, making sure it was an important rath, at least, and reasonably close to that of the *tuath*'s king. He would then determine the boundary of his diocese, which would probably correspond with that of the *tuath*, and he would struggle fiercely to retain in his hands the power of authority over any religious function or monastic body that might intrude:

If any of the presbyters builds a church, he shall not offer the sacrifice in it before he brings his bishop that he may consecrate it; for this is proper.

If a new incumbent enters the parish he shall not baptise, nor offer, nor consecrate, nor build a church until he receives permission from the bishop; but whoever seeks permission from the tribesmen (or unbelievers or laymen) shall be alien.

Any cleric who has recently entered the parish of a bishop is not permitted to baptise and offer, nor to do anything: if he does not act accordingly he shall be excommunicate.

But then, if we create a hypothetical scene, a man like Columcille comes along.

The bishop is suspicious and hostile, as well he might be. Columcille is an aristocrat and very persuasive, the sound of his voice, according to an old poem, audible 'for fifteen hundred paces (vast the distance!)'. He talks with the *rí tuaith* (whom the bishop has spent months cultivating) and persuades him to give his band a site for their community. The bishop objects, saying that only if these monks are responsive to his commands will he allow such an intrusion to his episcopal domain. Columcille agrees, the bishop remains wary, yet he has no choice but to give his approval. In six months Columcille departs, leaving just a few followers behind. The bishop is relieved. His status vis-à-vis the king is undamaged and his position remains dominant. But not for long.

The problem with episcopal controls is that a bishop has but one seat and one diocese. As Columcille[3] roamed about the countryside setting up communities, securing endowments and preaching to the people, his status was exploding in commensurate degrees. He had not one seat but many; not one diocese but dozens. And to the Irish such a string of credits was impressive. Columcille was a man of many *tuaths*, the bishop the holder of but one, and for a while these latter officials almost disappear as a power. The *paruchia* or federation of monastic communities, with their aggregate wealth and prestige, simply dominate the religious scene.

The other distinctively Celtic usage was the notion of *coarb*. Literally it translates as 'family of' or 'heir to' and it was the title usually given to successive generations of abbots. At Iona, for instance, founded by Columcille *c*. 563 in Scotland and the chief house of the Columban *paruchia*, the abbots gaining office through the years were known as the *coarbs* of Columcille. The wrinkle is that in most cases the abbot was in literal fact a member of Columcille's family. Of the nine abbots from Columcille to Adomnán, who died in 704, eight were members of Clan Conaill in County Donegal, Uí Néill one and all. Succession to the abbacy simply followed the same procedure as regnal succession, explained previously. The *derbfhine* was expanded to include a broader selection of candidates, those eligible were examined and one of these was chosen to succeed. Monasteries in the Irish system were therefore hereditary.

Iona is a mighty example, of course, the fief of Clan Conaill. The lower branches of the *paruchia*, however,

Bishop's effigy,
Ardfert Cathedral, 13th century,
Co. Kerry

reveal an accommodation (and thus a strongly preservative link) with powerful local interests not necessarily of Clan Conaill. A family that endowed a monastery with a rath and supporting property generally made certain that at least one of its members joined that particular community. Succession to the abbacy was generally confined to the *fine* of the founding father (Clan Conaill in the case of Columcille's *paruchia*) but if no suitable candidate emerged the office reverted to that of the original donor family. If anything this solidified the system of *paruchia* at the expense of episcopal organisation. When a noble felt he 'owned' something belonging to an abbey, he would consider a bishop's attempt to exert episcopal control as something worth fighting about.

A seventh-century hagiographical story, *The Life of St Samson of Dol*, illustrates this practice clearly. The *Life* is a standard devotional work written *c*. 610 and thus roughly contemporary with Columcille. It relates the holy deeds of a Celtic Briton named Samson, who like Columcille, was destined for the Church early in life. He is sent to the monastery of St Eltut, a disciple of St Germanus and a Merlin-type figure according to the chronicler — 'a most wise magician, having knowledge of the future.' Eltut sees the enormous virtue in this young boy, who at fifteen is already fasting and staying up all night in vigils.

However, Eltut had in his monastery a pupil who was also his nephew and a priest, and this priest had a brother without rank (i.e. not in orders). These men, alienated from the brothers in respect of love for Samson, and wickedly fearing lest, on account of one they knew to be better than themselves, they would be deprived of an hereditary worldly possession, could neither find any evil in him nor dwell together peaceably and lovingly.

Samson is aware of this hostility but cannot overcome it. The brothers attempt to murder the boy, who drinks a cup of wine knowing it to be poisoned, but survives nonetheless unharmed. If anything the story reflects how bitten with intrigue these ecclesiastical affairs could become. By the eighth and ninth centuries, in fact, the situation would degenerate to the point where an abbot was no longer required to be in orders. As a married man with issue, the abbacy would pass from father to son as though a private estate. The poem *Advice to a Prince* states the matter bluntly: 'Let the abbot's son enter the Church, let the cleric's son go on circuit.' By then the Church was very big business.

In Columcille's lifetime the situation was nowhere as complacent. All of Iona's early abbots were, like their founder, celibate and zealous, their energies primarily directed towards building the endowment that later generations of greedy men were to exploit. Columcille's task in particular was difficult because the idea of supporting the clergy with grants of land was alien to Celtic tradition and required explaining. The response of the *filid* and brehons, for example, was initially negative. 'No one bequeaths anything without the consent of his *fine*,' reads one old legal tract, a reflection of some uneasiness on the part of learned men to the growing momentum of clerical power and its acquisitive nature. 'For it is no commandment of God,' it continues, 'that the *fine* from which one is sprung and which is responsible for one's liabilities shall be prejudiced by not being left in possession of its rightful position.' The genius of the new system, however, with its *paruchia* and *coarbs*, was that it wasn't new at all, just a slightly fresher edition of usual procedure. And when kings and chieftains understood the similarities their position simply vanished. For a king the manoeuvre seemed eminently attractive: he didn't give up all that much to begin with since he retained a powerful say in the monastery's affairs; he made his bargain with the Christian god as prudence (and the sermons he'd been hearing) indicated he should; and his honour increased as the *paruchia* spread its ties throughout the land — he was part of its growing prestige. The brehons and *filid* found themselves outflanked by people more skilful than they, and many must have feared for the future. Christianity meant reading, writing and Latin, to say nothing of foreign gods. The old order, with its sense of survival keenly felt, began rearranging its priorities.

Columcille's success hit a major snag *c*. 561 when the Northern and Southern Uí Néill squabbled among themselves and fought the great battle of Cuil Dreimne near Sligo. We have no details about the extent of Columcille's involvement in the dispute but according to his biographer Adomnán, ninth abbot of Iona, he was excommunicated from the Church in the next year. The implication seems to be that Columcille may have incited the conflict, perhaps over a slight or political reverse suffered at the hands of his cousins in the south — as a later poet would describe him, after all: 'He was not a gentle hero, vehement was his work.' Whatever the circumstances Clan Conaill was victorious in battle but Columcille found himself censured almost immediately. Adomnán plays down the episode by saying the excommunication was carried out 'on a charge of offences that were trivial and very pardonable.' An assembly was apparently convoked against Columcille which he attended, but that is all we are told. In 563 at the age of forty-two he departed for Scotland, a pilgrim for Christ. It seems fair to assume that this exile was a penance.

7 Benmore Head

IN October of 1842 William Thackeray, gathering material for his *Irish Sketch Book*, travelled northwards from Dublin to the Antrim coast, his main objective the famous Giant's Causeway. Above Carrickfergus, a medieval town of great interest, the main road follows the shore almost as far as Benmore Head, then turns west until Londonderry. The circuit is justly renowned: the Nine Glens of Antrim carved into the mountains and falling down to the sea, great ocean cliffs and romantic castles, and of course the Giant's Causeway itself. For Thackeray the coast road presented vistas 'of the most beautiful landscapes of this most beautiful country,' and he is not far wrong. At Cushendun the main road cuts inland from Ballycastle, but the intrepid driver not afraid of s-curves and frightening grades should continue with the ocean and follow a lonely track along the shore. Soon the road begins climbing, and loses itself in mountain valleys and steep fields. Scotland is clearly visible across the open sea.

Most of the minuscule glens that lie hundreds of feet below me were, incredibly, heavily populated in Patrick's time by a Ulaid tribe known to us today as the Dál Riata. Uí Néill expansion from the old Ulaid holdings in Tyrone had pushed the Dál Riata east to these meagre holdings with predictable and catastrophic results: slim resources proved inadequate to feed their growing number. Around the year AD 500 a sizeable contingent of the clan, with a chieftain of characteristic daring named Fergus mac Erc, sailed for Scotland and fought with the indigenous Picts for a foothold there. With a bridgehead successfully established a long series of migrations took place, until the major Dál Riata strength no longer lay in Ulster but in

Scotland, an interesting development with regard to Columcille's later career.

This afternoon I am lucky to catch a meal in the otherwise boarded up seaside resort of Ballycastle, where the panorama includes Rathlin Island out in the North Channel and Benmore Head to the east. Benmore exudes a majestic, weathered character, and for no other reason I pick it out for the evening's campsite. A long and gently rising ridge of cliffs leads out from the town for a couple of miles before the promontory is reached and I drive for about half that distance before gathering up my gear to walk the remainder of the way. A few little cottages, called the 'village' of Cross but seemingly lifeless, mark an entry into the wilderness: acres and acres of bog stretching onwards to the sea cliff, itself more than 650 feet above the ocean. Trekking further in the overwhelming solitude of the place reminds me of Thackeray's discomfort with the melancholia of Irish countryside, 'sweet, wild and sad even in the sunshine', as he put it. Adding to the desolation is a tarn or bog lake that I come across, several hundred yards in circumference, and in the centre sits an ancient *crannóg*, the water-borne equivalent of a Celtic rath. It is a small artificial island, 120' × 90', constructed of boulders, timber and assorted fill. A retaining wall of unmortared stone encloses the mound, on top of which a barrier of wickerwork or wood was probably built; within the enclosure, huts. Access to and from the *crannóg* was by curragh or dug-out log.

Crannógs are certainly Celtic. A chieftain or important retainer lived here and grazed livestock on the lonely pastures that surround the lake. Many small bodies of water in Ireland show similar traces of *crannógs*,

Benmore Head, Co. Antrim

Crannóg, *Benmore Head, Co. Antrim*

Loughrea in County Galway being perhaps the best example. But nowhere more strikingly than here is an Iron Age domain so perfectly laid out: a kingdom of its own, the borders determined partially by how far a man could roam and still be safe, still have time to flee back here and gain refuge in this island sanctuary.

Coming on to the top of Benmore Head the view is, predictably, immense, but no better really than from Ballycastle or anywhere else on this coastline. Benmore itself is more dramatic in profile, so I sit instead facing inland, the tarn below with its *crannóg*, the sweep of the empty fields drifting upwards to my feet. Having come here pre-informed, however, I can't help thinking about Scotland, enticingly close over my shoulder, yet a world away for Columcille.

8 *Glencolumbkille*

I SPENT last night in a pasture on Loughros Point, a peninsula heading out to sea from the western Donegal village of Ardara, popular in season with fishermen, and tourists in search of hand-knit Irish sweaters. Loughros Beg Bay, on the southern side of the Point, presents me with a marvellous study in the ways of the sea. As I sit up I can see the village of Maghera across this small bay, and the sparkling beach that juts out towards me right into the flow of the tide, forcing the current off into a great arc around the sand. As the tide rises, portions of the beach are cut off by advancing waters. Soon individual rip-tides and eddies swirl about in countless numbers, each seeking an accustomed pool or waterside marsh. In front of Maghera the permanent strand is gradually delineated, the sea coming as high as it will, the waves seeming to break hundreds of yards before they reach the sand. The white of their foam makes the bay a garden of ribbons, alternating with the blue-green shimmer of unbroken water. Behind Maghera the Glen of Owenree curves up nine hundred feet to a vast and empty plateau. Above it stand the mountains of Slievetooey. Morning sun, almost summerlike, warms up the bay sufficiently to allow for a swim. I would never have thought this possible for March.

Later in the day I drive along the other side of Loughros Beg Bay. The map indicates a dead end at Maghera, but a single-lane cart path leads up the Glen, and I follow it. Beautiful wild flowers and brown stained mountain streams parallel the track. At the top of the pass, facing south, the great plain of bogland — almost a desert were it not for a few stacks of peat visible here and there — stretches on for about ten miles to the famed mountain mass known as Slieve League. Off this plateau, a few minutes drive away, is the Glen of Columbkille.

Three hundred churches did Columcille found in Erin and Alba; and a hundred of these were fast by the sea.
The Life of Columcille

The glen of Columbkille is one of three facing the Atlantic off the enormous projection of Slieve League and Slievetooey, the others being Port and Malin Bay. I have camped down by the small beach that even on fine days is rough with surf. In old times the men here used to fish for a living, but down by the dock and moorings only a handful of small battered boats can be counted, evidently used by lobstermen, each with a few traps scattered here and there off the rocky coast. Fishing, I'm told by one of them, was never a secure livelihood for the men of Glencolumbkille. Consistently foul weather, the mighty ocean swells, dependence on the tiny curragh, all made catches spotty and unreliable. Even today the only sizeable trawlers in the area berth at Killybegs, and many of the younger men never go to sea, preferring to work factory shifts instead at the local processing plant.

Walking along the shore I recall the appalling irony of the Great Famine — massive starvation on the one hand and a multitude of fish on the other. The problem was

The Glen of Owenwee and Croagh Ballaghdown, Loughros Beg Bay, Co. Donegal

*Incised Cross,
Glencolmbkille,
Co. Donegal*

Incised Cross,
Glencolmbkille,
Co. Donegal

catching them. Curraghs are too frail and too low in the water to allow the substantial use of nets, but the great runs of fish are all in deep water, several miles offshore, where nets are mandatory. Tricky weather and rough Atlantic waters sealed off the venture to any but the foolhardy, and so the people starved amidst the plenty. Even so one still hears the slur now and then that the peasants were too lazy to fish. But watching the surf along this coast would drive me to drink too.

I have seen this place, Glencolumbkille, in all kinds of weather, in every season of the year. The immensity of its spiritual power, to say nothing of natural splendour, has yet to fade for me. An aura of the primitive Celtic church — aloof, removed, intensely pure — is more easily perceived here, I believe, than any place in Ireland. 'It extends into the ocean,' a visitor wrote in 1835, 'and is horrible with craggy mountains and promontories which hang over the sea.' Horrible and also barbarous, as Patrick might say. Glencolumbkille is an apt illustration of two cultures in collision, Somehow a Roman temple would seem idiotic in this locale.

This evening, walking along the beach (as did Columcille 'right often' according to one ancient biography) I meet a priest, a French Benedictine, in Ireland on holiday. He is familiar with Columcille and together we cross the dunes and climb up a rocky outcrop of the northern valley wall, where the ruins of Columcille's foundation lie. There is little to see of what was, supposedly, his most favoured settlement: the clustered ruins of old cashels and an oratory, with a St Columcille's Bed and an incised cross. There are several fine examples of these in the Glen, especially worthy of note because they reflect the interim period between pagan and Christian Ireland, when pillars and ogham stones were adapted for Christian use, heathen markings overlaid with Christian crosses and similar devotional designs. The next step in progression is the famous high cross, but there are none of these here.

It is interesting being in the company of a priest, a man who, through faith believes in the wondrous deeds of saints and holy men. He brushes aside my generalised remarks about miracles and superstition, however; what we read in saints' lives is pious exaggeration, nothing more. The great marvel is the effect of holy example on human life. 'There must have been something remarkable about Columcille,' he says. 'People wouldn't have written about him with so much devotion if he hadn't been a rather attractive person. He had a special dynamism and, I think, a rash, impetuous nature ... very Irish. A touch of the fanatic as well, except that's a bad word these days. He would probably brook no opposition at all and yet, to ride so heavily over people like that, quite evidently one must have considerable leadership qualities. Which we must assume he had. We can do worse than emulate a man like that, if we have his righteous faith. For myself, I prefer the spiritual action of faith. That would be Columcille's lesson to me. Men of physical action, in the religious sphere anyway, often cause more trouble these days than it's worth.' The next morning, at first light, the priest says mass among the ruins. I watch him from higher up on the mountain side. When he's finished, we climb further on to an old watch tower for the view.

The beauty here is almost vicious, and in a strange, chemical fashion it rubs off on the clumsy and awkward remains that still stand — the oratory, the pillar stones, the cashel walls. In the process they merge, become as one: the zealot's faith, the tiny particles of his temple, all a work of nature in this wild, rough setting.

There is a gray eye, that looks back at Erin.
The Amra of Columcille

Exile for Columcille, say all the legends, was bitter hardship. Tradition has it he landed first on the island of Oronsay in Scotland near Jura and Islay, but that the view of his native land drove him further north to Mull. Most of these western islands and the coast from Kintyre to Mull had been settled by the Dál Riata, and the mainland region is still known today as Argyll, from the Gaelic *Aier*

Gordell, or 'Country of the Irish'. Being a prince of the traditional Uí Néill enemy does not seem to have been a hindrance for Columcille since that same year he was granted the island of Iona off Mull by the king of the Dál Riata, and there he settled with his companions. The island is a small one, only about three miles in length and one in width. There is barely a tree to be seen. On a hill overlooking the bay to the south is an ancient cairn, known to this day by the name Columcille gave it — *carn Cul ri Eirinn*, or 'Cairn of the Back Turned to Erin'. Two years later in 565 he set out on the mission which gained him enduring fame, the Christianisation of the Picts. In his own lifetime the Word was spread all over the Highlands and beyond to the Hebrides. His *coarbs* carried it further to the Orkneys and then south into the kingdom of Northumbria. The *paruchia* of Columcille, with links throughout the Celtic world, was settled now in Iona. It was the most renowned Celtic monastery, and perhaps in its way the most influential, ever founded.

In 575 Columcille returned to Ireland (it appears in some triumph) accompanied by forty priests, twenty bishops, thirty deacons and fifty students. The occasion for his trip was the Convention of Druim Cett.

If the popular historians of Ireland, past and present, are to be believed, the purpose of this council was to deal with the *filid*. Mythologists are fond of their claim that Columcille was himself a *fili* and thus in sympathy with the plight of his fellow poets in the hour of their need. The kings of Ireland, it seems, had had enough of satire and the huge expense of maintaining these schools of bothersome, haughty scholars. Even when paid on a regular basis they never could be trusted, for many was the time a noble king was insulted with a sarcastic paean:

> I have heard he gives no horses
> in reward for poems: he gives according
> to his nature — a cow!

The solution was to get rid of them completely, expel them from the country en masse, but Columcille (according to legend) intervened and appealed to the lords of this noble assembly to rescind their judgment, which they did. The *filid* were placed instead on a probationary status, in the expectation that they would moderate their ways. As a sidelight to the more important business of Druim Cett all of this may well have happened, although claims that Columcille was a *fili* seem far fetched. The more intriguing aspects of the Convention were somewhat more machiavellian, and offer insight into the byzantine nature of Celtic politics.

Obituaries in the Irish annals reveal that in the year of Druim Cett the fate of the bishops hung in the balance (rhetorically speaking). Prior to the Great Plague of 549 nearly every notation of death applied to a bishop. They were the churchmen of note, their office the most important. Between 550 and 600 the scales begin to tip as the annalists enter the obituaries of abbots in a roughly 50/50 split. From 601 to the 650s we find hardly any mention of bishops at all, the laurel of recognition passing completely to the abbots. Columcille's mission to the Convention, therefore, marks the very point of transition, the period when the Celtic system pulled right away from Patrick's.

The provocation may possibly have been Armagh's, the diocesan seat established by Patrick near Emain Macha. The tidal wave of *paruchias* and spider web confederations had been humiliating for the older, more established communities like Armagh. In fact for many years Armagh had existed outside everyone's orbit, her former patrons now boxed up in Downpatrick and her new masters, the Southern Uí Néill, preoccupied and indifferent. These were lean times for Armagh and her clergy began thinking in terms of survival. It was emulate the *paruchia* or fade away.

Armagh's good fortune was the split between the Uí Néill. The Southern branch of that dynasty was now alienated from the family *paruchia*. The logical strategy for Armagh was to enter the vacuum and nail its fortunes to theirs. Airgialla, after all, belonged to the Southern Uí Néill and an alliance would make sense. The problem was making Armagh attractive enough for the Southern Uí Néill to be interested in the first place. Her clergy would somehow have to dredge up an image or identity forceful enough to rival that of Columcille. The only thing they

Carn Cul rí Eirinn, *"Cairn of the Back Turned to Erin"*, *Iona, Argyll, Scotland*

had was their founding father, Patrick the Briton, whose cult was so far purely local and embarrassingly Ulaidian. But it would do for a start.

Columcille was probably unaware of these intrigues as he directed his mission to the Picts from Iona, but his primary motives were just the same. He was concerned for his *paruchia* and wanted its future guaranteed. His allies in Scotland — the patrons of Iona — were secure: Áedán mac Gabráin (known as 'the Wily'), King of the Dál Riata, and Brude mac Maelchon, King of the Picts, called *rex potentissimus* by Bede. Áedán, in fact, had been crowned by Columcille himself in 574, the first such ecclesiastical coronation in Irish history, and indicative of Columcille's ability to form the bond between Celtic and Christian tradition. Any plot on the part of Armagh or even the Southern Uí Néill could do nothing to threaten these arrangements. The danger to his *paruchia* lay in the homeland. He had been away from Ireland for over ten years now, and a new king of Ulster would awaken him to the dangers he faced there.

Báetán mac Cairell, King of Ulster, won his crown in 574. In the time-honoured fashion of a newly crowned Irish king, he rumbled forth a call for pledges and hostages from his capital in Downpatrick. As men of Ulster, the Dál Riata still remaining in County Antrim were legally required to obey these demands. The point of contention was the Dál Riata settlements in Scotland, now of considerable size and importance. Technically speaking they too were men of Ulster, and Báetán, intent on a Ulaid restoration, regarded these colonies as part of his province. In particular, he wanted their fleet.

All this proved highly alarming for the Dál Riata. If they pledged submission to Báetán, both branches of the Uí Néill would feel threatened. Ulster was still the traditional foe of song and legend, and warlike postures by Báetán could be counted upon to elicit a response. The Northern Uí Néill in particular were uneasy about the fleet and might invade what was left of Ulster if the warships were handed over, their route taking them through Antrim where the Dál Riata still left In Ireland would likely be trampled. To ignore the demands of their rightful king, on the other hand, would provoke retaliation from Down-patrick, and at the moment Báetán was far stronger than they. Áedán the Wily turned to Columcille, who took the discussion one step further.

If the Dál Riata were overwhelmed on the mainland, whether by the Uí Néill or by Báetán, what were the consequences for him? In the immediate sense probably nothing, but in the long run just about everything. Columcille's prestige, like Patrick's with the Ulaid, was now intimately wrapped up with the Dál Riata. Iona and all its Scottish churches would survive no matter what happened in Ireland, but a Dál Riata disaster in County Antrim would scatter his Irish *paruchia*, the daughter houses he and his disciples had established over the course of many years. No link however personal could maintain the unity and influence of the federation. It would fall apart, if not then, certainly on his death, the pieces picked up by other hungry *paruchia*, most notably Clonmacnoise or perhaps Armagh. Columcille's long exile from Ireland had left him without any firm allies there. He found himself dependent on the weakest link of all — the Dál Riata, themselves caught in the middle of a gigantic squeeze.

Columcille's response was the Convention of Druim Cett, most probably his idea as the guest list indicates. Báetán, King of Ulster, was not invited, nor were the Southern Uí Néill. The council was held near Limavady in Dál Riata territory, and Áedán the Wily presided although Columcille spoke for him. The most important figure there was Áed mac Ainmuirech, King of the Northern Uí Néill and a member of Clan Conaill. He was also Columcille's cousin.

The bargain they arranged was cagey and self-serving. For Columcille the objective was to throw the Dál Riata in the safest corner possible. This meant placing them with the Northern Uí Néill. For Áed, who according to an old poem 'had many questions here,' the strategy was to ensure that Scotland's fleet stayed out of Irish affairs, or at least out of Uí Néill affairs, permanently. Otherwise he might destroy what was left of the Dál Riata in Ireland, the pawn he held. Negotiations achieved both these goals. The fleet was judged part and parcel of Dál Riata holdings in Scotland. The claims of overlordship which Báetán

St Martin's Cross,
Iona, Argyll, Scotland

The Mullagh, Site of the Convention of Druim Cett, Limavady, Co. Derry

Glencolumbkille, Co. Donegal

believed extended across the sea to Argyll were deemed void. The submission rightly owed Báetán by the Dál Riata, namely troops, was recognised by Áed in such a way as to save face for the Ulster king, but in reality the message was made even plainer: the Dál Riata, as far as Áed was concerned, were now wards of the Northern Uí Néill.

Báetán mac Caerell understood the implications of these proceedings pretty clearly. His career was henceforth directed towards the east in an effort to colonise the Isle of Man with settlers from Ulster, a venture only partially successful. In 582, with an irony truly Irish, Áedán the Wily so ravaged this community with his Scottish fleet that it never recovered. Báetán lost out in just about every way.

For Columcille the Convention was a vindication of his earlier misfortune. He had re-entered the Irish political swirl with a vengeance. By allying Dál Riata to his cousins he had forged a link that assured survival for the Columban *paruchia*. There would be no scraps for other jealous communities on his death. Áed had been guaranteed during conference that the abbacy of Iona, head church of the entire federation, would forever be the heirloom of Clan Conaill. Who knows, maybe Columcille even named a tanist as special reassurance. The responsibility of supporting Columcille's 'investments' in Ireland was thus transferred from the weak to the strong, from the Dál Riata to the Northern Uí Néill. In doing so Columcille had drawn the lines of contention. There was no longer any pretence of alliance within the Uí Néill. The Southern branch would now support Armagh or some other faction, there was little doubt of that, and any slippage on the part of either side would affect the fortunes of the *paruchia* involved. But for the moment, Columcille and the north were ascendant.

Columcille died in his monastery of Iona in 597 and was buried there, although his remains have long since been scattered. The news of his death occasioned the oldest piece of Irish literature still in existence, a mournful poem composed by an unknown *fili* and called the *Amra of Columcille*:

> A tale I have for you. Ox murmurs,
> Winter pours, summer is gone:
> Wind high, cold: sun low;
> Cry is attacking, sea resounding.
>
> Very red raying has concealed form,
> Voice of geese has become usual:
> Cold has caught wings of birds;
> Ice-frost time: wretched, very wretched
>   a tale I have for you.

9 *Lough Erne*

LOUGH Erne is a large lake about eighteen miles long and five across at its widest point. Over forty islands, many of them wooded down to the waterline and resembling mushrooms, cluster mainly in the southern reach near Enniskillen. Monastic settlements were founded on several of these, the best known being Devenish or *Daimhinis*, 'the isle of oxen'.

In Celtic times, before the forests had been cut down — the lands drained, roadways built — lakes and rivers were primary routes for inland travel. Devenish served a dual role, the major gateway into the northwest and, being close to the Connaught/Ulster border, neutral ground for parleys between warring tribes — 'Devenish of the Assemblies' in the words of one admiring annalist. By motor launch the trip is a short but scenic five minutes, and I find only three other visitors on the island rummaging through the ruins. Nothing survives from the earliest Celtic monastery, whose buildings were probably wooden and thatched. Two churches of stone and a fine round tower, dating from the 1100s, still stand, along with the remains of St Mary's Priory, a fifteenth-century building that occupies higher ground. From here the view is far-reaching — Devenish and its seventy acres, various old crop lines and agricultural enclosures around the community itself, the curving reach of Lough Erne spreading north.

Devenish was founded by St Molasius 'of the Lake', one of the Twelve Apostles of Erin and a friend of Columcille with whom he studied at Clonard under St Finnian. The Twelve Apostles, in fact, were reputedly all students of Finnian, but the makeup of this exclusive fraternity turns out to be very variable on closer examination. My first list from one old story, for example, corresponded with only five names from a second, which contradicted a third that claimed seven names not mentioned in either. Membership was apparently open to just about any saint then known to have existed — the Twelve became Hundreds.

Molasius was taken with Devenish from the start, seeing here on this island the same qualities that so many other Irish monks found in their own remote and obscure hideaways, 'a prison of hard narrow stone'. The local druids, according to the standard hagiographical pattern, did all they could to arouse opposition with the usual calamitous results: the local king, one Red Conall, flies to the lake seeking a confrontation, but anger turns to fear as his horses are frozen in mid step, his boat is swamped, two prize steeds with crimson tails and manes drop dead for no reason and so on. Molasius, his point made, restores all to life again saying to the king, 'Make we now a bargain: I of my Lord's part will grant this region to thyself and to thy son after thee, and leave thou me this spot of land upon which I am.' Red Conall, his panic turning again to indignation, 'I thank thee not for that: mine own land and my father's and grandfather's before me!' Upon which the Saint curses his seed forever and blinds the poor man as a warning to his followers.

The saints of Ireland as a general rule were rather free with their anger, from Patrick on down. The usual fate of a blaspheming druid or recalcitrant king was to be smouldered into nothing or else have his innards smashed to pieces after a spin in the air ('his body, frozen with hailstone and snow mixed with sparks of fire, fell to the ground in sight of all'). Red Conall's fate was actually rather modest by comparison but then again Molasius was

Tower of St Mary's Priory, 15th century, Devenish, Co. Fermanagh

a gentle man, whereas many of his friends were not. Ruadhan of Lorrha,[1] for example, another of the Twelve Apostles, was a legend all his own. A poem of c. 695 described him as the saint who 'loved cursing' and by that the poet meant something stronger than oaths or swearing — he meant casting people into hell.

Molasius was evidently a witness to Ruadhan's most famous outburst of temper, the cursing of Tara. After founding Devenish, Molasius made a pilgrimage to Rome, a journey that was accompanied with many adventures and miraculous happenings. After gathering together several holy mementoes — 'some of Mary's hair and Martin's anklebone; somewhat of Paul's relics and of Peter's, a share of Laurence's relics and that of Clement's, and of Stephen the Martyr's relics' — he returned for home, landing near the Boyne. He was immediately summoned by Ruadhan to come as quickly as he could to Tara, for there the Twelve Apostles were fasting against the king.

While embellishments to this story are no doubt mythical, the rudiments seem to have a basis in fact. Ruadhan's quarrel with the king, for instance, is probably accurate. Legends and stories do agree that Dermot mac Cerbaill, King of Tara, in his legal pursuit of a killer did indeed violate a monastic sanctuary to which the outlaw had fled seeking refuge. The prisoner was apparently a relation to Ruadhan, who accordingly felt the sacrilege very keenly and despite the man's guilt, pledged to humble the king. Ruadhan called as many of the Twelve as he could find and together they went to Tara. There they fasted on the king, while he, 'relying on his kingly quality and on the justice of his cause, fasts on them'.

The practice of fasting against one's enemy is very ancient indeed, perhaps the first attempt by man to solve grievances without recourse to violence. Once again we hear the call of Indo-European custom. Up until 1861 it was a fairly common sight in India to see a Brahman moneylender fasting outside the house of someone in his debt. In Hindu the procedure was called *dharna* or 'detention', in Sanskrit *prayopaveçana* or 'sitting down to die by hunger'. According to Whitley Stokes, a well-travelled nineteenth-century scholar, 'the person fasted upon incurs divine displeasure if he lets the faster die. In

India, by the rigour of the etiquette, the unfortunate object of (the Brahman's) arrest ought to fast also, and thus they both remain until the institutor of the *dharna* obtains satisfaction.' Provisions in the British Penal Code of 1861 forbade this practice and it slowly died away, although every now and then one reads of its recurrence.

In Celtic Ireland the *dharna* was standard procedure, involving as it did the issues of status and prestige. To break the fast on either side would be to lose face and, in effect, acknowledge defeat.

According to the legends this greatest of all struggles outside Tara lasted over a year, both parties 'being every second night without food,' Dermot within his rath, the clergy in tents outside. 'The clerics chanted psalms of commination now, and rang their bells against the king.' Most of the saints' lives credit Brendan of Clonfert with the idea that finally broke the deadlock. He ordered the Twelve to stand outside Tara and pretend to eat for all to see. Rather than actually consume the food, however, they were to drop each mouthful down the inside of their cowls. Dermot's men reported the breakthrough — they had seen the monks eat with their own eyes — whereupon the king ordered a great feast and broke the fast himself. His bitterness when he discovered the ruse was intense. 'I am the tree,' he said, 'the foreigners that chop it down are the clergy cutting short my life, and by them also am I fallen.'

On the morrow the king rose and went to the place where the clergy were: 'ill have ye done,' he said, 'to undo my kingdom for that I maintained the righteous cause. At all events,' he went on, 'be thy diocese the one that is ruined in Ireland and Ruadhan, may thy monks desert thee!' The saint retorted: 'May thy kingdom droop speedily!' Dermot said: 'Thy see shall be empty, and swine shall root up thy churchyards.' 'Tara shall be desolate,' Ruadhan said, 'and therein shall no dwelling be forever.' Dermot said: 'May shameful blemish affect thy person,' and straightaway one of Ruadhan's eyes burst. Ruadhan said: 'Be thy body mangled by enemies, and thy limbs disintegrated so that they be not found in one place.' Dermot said: 'May there a wild boar come that he grub up the hill on which 'thou shalt be buried, and thy relics be scattered; also at nones, continually be there in thy churchyard howling of wild wolves, and the alarm-cry every evening.'

'Alas for him,' were Dermot's last words, 'that to the clergy of the Churches showeth fight; woe to him that would contend. Tara shall be clean swept.' Of all the twelve only Molasius was saddened by the fall of the king — it was 'a lamentable thing' and 'stirred his pity.'

Whether Ruadhan actually cursed the king or whether these events ever happened is, again, open to dispute. Ruadhan's character as a hostile, turbulent man is confirmed by many other stories, however, all of which would seem to indicate that his behaviour at Tara was true to form. 'Better be doomed to perish than be a feeble wretch' was his philosophy, a point of view so militant that even Giraldus Cambrensis was taken aback. 'The people of this nation,' he wrote in 1187, 'are beyond all others irascible and prompt to revenge.' The saints, in his opinion, were of especially 'vindictive temperament'.

St Columbanus was not a member of the Twelve Apostles although his squabbling with kings and warriors was certainly Heroic and maniacal. In many ways he is the best known of the early Irish saints, having left a good deal of correspondence behind, much of it with popes and fellow clerics. His interest for us is two-fold: in the first place his cantankarous personality is genuine and not obscured by myth. This alone makes his story intriguing. But secondly, the goals for which his anger was utilised represent the first extensive expression of a purely Irish orientation in religious matters. Though twenty years the junior of Columcille, Columbanus did more than even he to articulate the character of the Celtic Church, of which Iona was the figurehead. For the first time we lean on an Irish commentator. Curiously enough, the majority of his adult years were spent on the continent.

Three chosen men, on fire with belief, withdrew from the Irish nation. They sewed a boat from bull's hide in secret, they provided a week's food for themselves, they kept sail up seven days and seven nights, and they arrived in their boat in Cornwall. Leaving their boat, which had not been brought by tackle nor by ample shoulders, but rather by a nod from Him who sees all things, they went to Alfred, king of the English . . . Then they directed their course to seek Rome as Christ's teachers are wont frequently to do.

The Chronicle of Aethelweard, 891

Columbanus is the most renowned of the early Irish *peregrini* (Latin for 'wanderer' or 'pilgrim') but in his own lifetime he was considered a nuisance and a bother. Many were the clergy who wished he would quietly disappear. We know very little about his career in Ireland except that he was born in Leinster and, like Columcille, spent many years as a student and priest in the shadow of more celebrated holy men. He seems to have remained for some time in the company of a hermit before moving on to the monastery of Bangor, outside of Belfast, where he completed his studies. This interchange between the two extremes of asceticism and learning was by now a common feature in Irish religious life. Whereas the desert ideal of Antony and the Eastern Fathers had been notably anti-scholastic, the Celtic variation was exactly the reverse. Columbanus was a severe man much given to fasting and corporal punishment but he was also highly educated, at least by Celtic standards. He could read and write, knew Latin fluently, had a smattering of Greek and Hebrew and was fascinated with biblical commentaries. In much the same fashion as Columcille he did not divorce himself from the values of Celtic society which honoured men of learning.

Columbanus heard the call of God while at Bangor, directing him to a missionary life abroad. Europe, as we know, was struggling at this time. Pagan and semi-Christian kings ruled where governors and Roman generals had once held authority. The only vestige of civilised control and orderly respect for the law that remained lay with the bishops, who sought to impress on their new masters the benefits that would result from acceptance of Roman customs and religion. Contemporary chronicles relate many examples of bravery on the part of these churchmen as they confronted a warrior king here or a marauding army there, trying at all times to secure the best possible terms for the Christian communities about to be inundated. But the scales were turning against them, the dual responsibilities of religious and civil affairs were proving too much.

During all this strife the bishops felt very strongly about the *peregrini,* whether Irish or not. Monastic communities electing their own superiors and following their own, often quixotic Rules, were ignoring the paramount needs of the endangered flock and undermining episcopal controls. In the opinion of the bishops, this made the task of dealing with barbarian generals and wandering freebooters doubly difficult. Particularly galling was the vulturous habit these monks had of electing one of their own to a vacant bishopric. Many times a newly appointed bishop arriving to take the post of a deceased predecessor would find an abbot in the bishop's palace with monks in every office of control, upsetting the status quo everywhere. The response was often angry and confused. Pope Celestine, the bishop of Rome who authorised the mission of Palladius to the Irish, wrote a lengthy letter in 428 condemning these aberrations, in the course of which are several heated digressions: These '*peregrini et extranei* (wanderers and strangers) who have not grown up in the Church act contrary to the Church's usages. Coming from other customs they have brought their traditional ways with them, clad in a cloak and with a girdle round their loins. Such a practice may perhaps be followed by those who dwell in remote places and pass their lives far from fellow men. But why should they dress this way in the Churches of God, changing the usage of so many years, of such great prelates, for another habit?'

Columbanus, in imitation of Christ with twelve disciples, landed in Gaul *c.* 575, or roughly the time of the Convention of Druim Cett. His behaviour symbolised just about everything that Celestine and successive popes and bishops thought wayward in the habits of *peregrini:* pride, wilfulness, the dogmatic assertion of individual freedom. And far from being defensive about their distant and uncouth origin, these men acknowledged no order of wisdom superior to their own. In a letter that must have shocked its recipient, Pope Boniface IV, Columbanus stated their position precisely: 'We, all the Irish, dwellers at the ends of the earth, who accept nothing beyond the evangelical and apostical teaching. No one among us has been a heretic, no one a Jew, no one a schismatic; but the Catholic faith, just as it was first transmitted from you, to wit, the successors of the holy apostles, is maintained unchanged.'

Columbanus spent over twenty years in Burgundy. He founded three monasteries there. Annegray, Luxeuil and Fontaine. His relations with the local kings appear to have been cordial (except on matters of morality) until a series of violent arguments led to his exile *c.* 610. At first the Gaulish clergy left him alone, allowing his little community to fend for itself in the hideaways he chose as monasteries, Columbanus and his monks patiently scratching a living from the soil and going their own way as God decreed. 'Bishops and monks have different vocations,' he pointed out, but 'we are all fellow-members of one body.'

The dating of Easter, that most confusing and strident of disagreements, brought all this to an end. One scholar has noted that 'the Easter Question is not the most enthralling of subjects' and he might have a point, though to lose sight of the controversies that obsessed these men is to cut ourselves off from their histories. The Easter problem is certainly arcane and more than a little technical, but its essential meaning involves character. We have through this dispute one of our clearest glimpses into the Celtic mind — arrogant, wayward, distracted, yet irrepressible and free of artifice — during an age centuries ago when it was truly a life force in the civilised world. The behaviour alone makes the mechanics of Easter worth a look and gives it some life of its own.

The core of the problem was set out by Christ himself: 'It came to pass when Jesus had finished all those words that he said to his disciples, "You know that after two days the

Passover will be here; and the Son of Man will be delivered up to be crucified."' His prediction of martyrdom was indeed all too accurate, for Jesus was executed on the day of Passover, that major Jewish feast which commemorates the liberation of the Hebrews from Egyptian slavery. To the early Fathers of the Church, however, it seemed grotesque that a festival as important as Easter should coincide with an equally joyous celebration on the part of his Jewish murderers. To avoid the continuance of this scandal the Council of Nicea was convened in 325 which sought to deviate from custom and arbitrarily change the date of Easter.

Previous to the Council, Christians had celebrated Easter on the day it fell, in much the same fashion as Christmas. It was thus a 'fixed' day and computed no differently than Passover: the 14th day of the new moon in the Jewish month of Nisan. The first point to bear in mind is that the Jewish calendar was lunar in its orientation, that is, it looked to the cycles of the moon as a calculation of time.[2] The Council of Nicea decreed instead that henceforth Easter could be observed only on a Sunday to be determined and announced by the Church. Its decision each year would be balanced by astrological calculations on the one hand (involving a solar, rather than lunar, orientation, to determine the vernal equinox), and aversion to Passover on the other. Easter was thereby transformed into a 'moveable' feast more commemorative than factual, a loss felt by many in the East who immediately slipped into heresy. They were called Quartodecimians, and though perfectly orthodox in faith, 'in ritual were addicted to Jewish fables'. The Emperor Constantine wrote a letter in praise of the Council's work and summarised its motivations:

We would have nothing in common with that most hostile people, the Jews; for we have received from the Redeemer another way of honouring God (the order of the days of the week), and harmoniously adopting this method, we would withdraw ourselves from the evil fellowship of the Jews. For what they pompously assert, is really utterly absurd: that we cannot keep this feast at all without their instruction ... It is our duty to have nothing in common with the murderers of our Lord.

The new provisions might have worked had everyone been agreed on their cycles. The problem was twofold at the start: first of all the Julian calendar (solar) instituted by Caesar was not perfectly accurate. The length of each solar year is exactly 365.2422 days, not $365\frac{1}{4}$, a difference of 11 minutes and 14 seconds, not much really, but enough to add up over several decades, and by the year of the Council (325) the Julian calendar was out by four days. In itself this was not important, but the Church's decision to establish Easter on a Sunday, no matter what, altered the situation radically and resulted in a second, related problem. Easter is the pivotal feast of the Church's calendar from which every other holy day is calculated. Without being able to predict the exact Sunday in any given year upon which the Easter designate would fall, the task of formulating a perpetual annual schedule known and followed throughout Christendom became impossible. The Council backed into this realisation when it sought to overlay an orderly, standardised calendar (its line-up of feasts and holy days) on a changing solar calendar, only to discover that efforts to harmonise the two were impossible given the swamp of conflicting cycles.

To make up for the lag in the Julian calendar, and to determine the exact day (year in, year out) of the vernal equinox, a variety of astronomical schemes had been advanced which added or deleted days in the course of many years to come up with the even and precise calculation of time that ecclesiastical schedules demanded. Depending on the particular cycle one happened to favour, however, whether the 15-year cycle or the 19, whether the 8, 28, 76 or even the 532, the forecast as to Easter would vary accordingly. The chaos that ensued was predictable. In 368 the Eastern and Western Churches celebrated their respective Easters almost five weeks apart.

Efforts to harmonise these vagaries into a coherent, uniform system took several decades. Pride in mathematical and calculative skills was very real especially in Egypt, the intellectual centre of the Eastern Church for over three centuries, and professional reputations were frequently at stake. A cycle based on 19 years was finally adopted c. 467, the problem being that by that late date the Celts were accustomed to and happy with their own 84-year cycle and refused to give it up. Not only that, they quarrelled with the vernal quinox and the arbitrary Sunday.

The vernal equinox occurs when the sun 'crosses' the equator in its movement from the winter to the summer solstice. March 21 is usually the day of this happening and the harbinger of spring. The first full moon falling on or just after the vernal equinox is called the Paschal moon (from the Jewish *Pesach* for 'Passover'). In order to avoid any possibility that Easter might fall on the same day as Passover it was decreed that the feast be kept on the Sunday of the third week of the Paschal moon. According to Rome the third week (heavy type in chart) began on the 15th day, which on the hypothetical calendar below would delay Easter until the 21st, well beyond Passover:

	S	M	T	W	T	F	S
new	0	1	2	3	4	5	6
moon	7	8	9	10	11	12	13
full							
The Passover	14	**15**	**16**	**17**	**18**	**19**	**20**
moon							
Easter	21	22	23	24	25	26	27

The Celts, however, insisted that the third week started on the 14th day, Easter thereby falling, as shown below, a full week earlier and, coincidentally, on the same day as Passover:

	S	M	T	W	T	F	S
new	0	2	2	3	4	5	6
moon	7	8	9	10	11	12	13
The Passover full							
&	**14**	15	16	17	18	19	20
Easter moon	21	22	23	24	25	26	27

Easter thus shared its glory with that of the Jews, but more germane than that was the full moon.

Monastic customs for celebrating Easter were fairly uniform: the Holy Week of Christ's death marked by special fasts and penance, followed by the vigil of Holy Saturday and the midnight mass in the first hour of Easter day. The major celebration of the feast, therefore, occurred in the dead of night. Celtic objections stemmed from the fact that by delaying Easter a full week or more, the Roman system ensured a 'dark' Easter — the mass would be celebrated during the waning moon. The Celtic cycle, though more likely to conflict with Passover, guaranteed the heavens would be bright with the moon still full and shining vigorously. In their opinion anything else was a contradiction of what Easter, the Feast of Light and Ecstasy, was all about. 'We ought not to keep Passover with the Jews?' wrote Columbanus, 'What has that to do with the question?' In terms of the sixth century, very little.

For the Gaulish clergy the presence of an Irish community in their midst following customs alien to their own and the Pope's, was what the *peregrini* problem was all about, and they eventually took steps to coerce these foreigners into conformity. Columbanus refused to cooperate, apparently in no uncertain terms, the feud burst into the open and the disagreement suddenly became ugly. The question of Easter, and to a lesser degree other arguments regarding tonsure[3] and differing procedural habits, had hitherto been discussed but seldom explosive issues. In the 590s they became so as positions hardened. While the correspondence that survives does not expressly say it, most of those involved seemed to realise that the real controversy was one of authority not of hairstyles or Easter. The Gauls were determined that Abbot Columbanus would obey their commands. Likewise Columbanus was steadfast in his opinion that the bishops should leave him alone. 'Liberty was the tradition of my fathers,' he wrote the Pope in 612, 'and among us in Ireland no person avails, but rather reason.'

In 603 a council of Gaulish bishops was convened at Chalons sur Saône to deal with Columbanus, who refused to attend: 'I have not dared to come myself in person,' he told them in a letter, 'lest I should show myself too contentious. I am not the author of this strife.' He was apparently censured during these proceedings for he appealed to the Pope immediately upon the adjournment for a definitive statement on Easter. He was not, he said, a Quartodeciman.

The most revealing commentary ever written on this question was a lengthy and often sarcastic letter by Columbanus to Pope Gregory the Great, who ruled in Rome from 590 until his death in 604. In it the pride of this stubborn abbot is barely concealed, and his contempt for the Roman cycle open and blunt. There is reason to believe that Gregory, a conscientious correspondent, never answered this communication, and the opening salutation is perhaps a partial explanation: to that 'most fair ornament of the Church, a certain most august flower, as it were, of the whole of withering Europe, I, poor dove of Christ, send greetings. I am pleased to think O holy Pope', he continues,

that it will seem to thee nothing extravagant to be interrogated about Easter, according to that canticle, 'Ask thy father, and he will shew thee: thine elders and they will tell thee.' What, then, dost thou say concerning Easter on the 21st and 22nd day of the moon, which (with thy peace it is said) is proved by many calculators not to be Easter, but in truth a time of darkness?

Then follows a lengthy condemnation (with authorities cited) on the 'absurdity' of such a position, after which Columbanus entreats the Pope to break with the decisions of his predecessors and allow the freedom of tradition:

Why dost thou keep a dark Easter? I wonder, I confess, that this error has not long ago been swept aside by thee; unless I should perchance suppose, what I can hardly believe, that, as it is evident that thou hast not corrected it, it has thy approval. In another way, however, may thy Expertness be more honorably excused, if thou art content with the authority of thy predecessors, and especially of Pope Leo. Do not, I pray thee, in such a question trust to humility or to gravity, which are often deceived. Better by far is the living dog in this problem than a dead lion.

He concludes with the acknowledgement that he may have written 'more forwardly than humbly'.

Columbanus was not, of course, the only Irish abbot involved in these quarrels, just the loudest. In Britain an official expedition sent by Gregory the Great had been hard at work since 597 trying to correct some of the more outrageous (from their point of view) of the Celtic customs. Most of the clergy involved, such as Archbishop Laurence of Canterbury, were amazed by the tenacity of the Irish position:

The apostolic see, according to its custom in all parts of the world, directed us to preach to the heathen in these western regions, and it was our lot to come to this island of Britain; before we knew them we held the holiness of both the Britons and of the Irish in great esteem, thinking that they walked according to the customs of the universal church; but on becoming acquainted with the Britons, we still thought that the Irish would be better. But now we have learned from Bishop Dagan when he came to this island and from Abbot Columbanus when he came to Gaul that the Irish do not differ from the Britons in their way of life. For when Bishop Dagan came to us he refused to take food, not only with us but in the very house where we took our meals.[4]

Columbanus was finally expelled from Burgundy c.610 for arguing with a local king and spent the next five years roaming eastwards. In 612 he founded the monastery of Bobbio in a lonely valley of the Appennines in northern Italy, where he died three years later. He remains a very popular saint in Italy even today. His closest disciple, St Gall, established a community on Lake Constance, Switzerland, where he died in 630. By then the flow of *peregrini* to the Continent had become a flood. Ireland was now Christian but the Continent no longer so, and a missionary zeal fuelled by the veneration of men like Columbanus, Gall and Columcille drove the Irish into exile. Bobbio and St Gallen, along with the earlier monasteries that Columbanus had founded in France, became meccas for Irish monks, and by 700 literally dozens of additional Irish settlements had sprung up in France, Germany, Belgium, Austria, Switzerland and Italy. All were dedicated to the personal Rule of their founder, whoever he might have been, and all retained their affection for independent traditions from home. Wan-

Bobbio, Emilia-Romagna, Italy

dering monks from Iona, Bangor, Clonmacnoise, Glendalough, Arran and Lindisfarne travelled regularly on a circuit from one Continental monastery to another. The strong native ties of kinship and *paruchia* intensified the pride, fanaticism and belief in their mission as something unique. As civilisation continued its collapse, the study of Greek and Latin, the copying of books and manuscript collections, the dedication to learning on the one hand and piety on the other, survived unchecked among the Irish. These gifted yet strangely perverse men were to keep the fabric of cultural life intact for other scholars, centuries later, to learn from anew. A great deal of the classical past disappeared, needless to say, as libraries and towns were put to the torch during these distracted times, but what did remain was saved where and when it could be. If the Irish had not maintained the connection intact, the later intellectual history of Europe may well have been different.

For most of these men Columbanus was a spokesman who re-emphasised their sense of Irishness and unity. Where Easter was concerned they were all, at first, as one.

Continuing North along the eastern side of the lake I pass the Protestant churchyard of Killadeas. The site was originally Catholic, of course, and in the burial grounds several ancient pillar stones with Celtic decorations still remain. One in particular is intriguing though its purpose remains a mystery. It is a stone about three feet high with a large and bulbous face carved on its forward 'prow' rather like a figurehead. A Celtic design of interlacing filigree continues to the ground, perhaps a representation of the body but it's difficult to say. On the side of the stone is another carving, that of a cleric carying a bell and crozier. An inscription in Irish (illegible) curves up his back. Local people call it 'the bishop's stone'.

The remarkable thing about this sculpture is that it exists in the first place. Aside from the smaller carvings of scriptural scenes on the later high crosses, there is very little representational stone carving in the country, and a significant portion of what there is seems clustered in or around this lake. This is puzzling since in Celtic Gaul there are hundreds of examples of this sort of portraiture, grotesque and semi-pagan. The fate of the White Island statues may partially explain their scarcity.

White Island, like Devenish, is served by a ferry, but the shoreline is deserted and I cannot see any boats for hire. After prowling about for half an hour or so I hear, then see, an ancient contraption puttering by with a little Seagull outboard, so I hail it over and ask for a ride. Two men, one of whom is clearly the captain, shift about and make room. Luckily I'm wearing a pair of heavy rubber boots, the 'Wellingtons' worn by nearly all the farmers here, since there seems to be a good two feet of water sloshing about inside the boat. With three of us, it droops to its waterline. Our conversation is at first rather dry, mostly comparing the merits of various motors, about which I know nothing. The one interesting point that I do pick out is that while both men are native to this lake, neither has ever been to the island.

The ruins of the church on White Island are nothing special, but when Board of Works men were here in 1928 to repair the structure they found several statues embedded in the wall and buried in the adjoining grave-yard, apparently on purpose. In 1958 another was discovered bringing the cache to eight figures in all and (it is possible) several more may lie buried nearby. Six of the eight deserve a close look, being from right to left: 1) a rather strange figure with legs crossed and cheeks bulging, as though filled with food; 2) another male, seated, holding a book or reliquary; 3) definitely a cleric, likely an abbot or bishop since he, like the figure at neighbouring Killadeas, holds a bell and crozier; discovered in 1958 head down, buried in the wall of the church; 4)

145

The Bishop's Stone,
Killadeas, Co. Fermanagh

Curios,
White Island,
Co. Fermanagh

possibly a cleric with his left hand pointed to his mouth for no apparent reason; 5) in contrast this figure, seated, is probably a layman since he sports a curly head of hair; he is holding what appear to be two sheep, sacrificial? 6) a prince or warrior, also seated, holding shield and sword. The seventh figure is a rough-out, apparently discarded when a flaw in the stone was discovered, and the last is a single head.

All of these statues are a mystery. They are primitive and somewhat incongruous, and may have been corbels set in the wall to support cross beams or roof posts. But why they were purposely hidden when the church was rebuilt or enlarged during medieval times is an interesting question. Some have said that perhaps their style was offensive to Norman conquerors who, like John de Courcy, preferred more orthodox decorations in the English manner. That is possible but White Island is remote even today and Norman pressure here was never as strong as in the eastern and southern portions of Ireland. They might instead have reflected something a bit too pagan or cultic for later more sophisticated Christian minds, although this is just a guess. The fascinating corroboration of this sort of theory, however, is possibly the Lusty Man.

The captain is not very interested in all of this. A beautiful day like this should be spent on Lough Erne absorbing its beauty and besides, he says, if we leave his boat unattended too long it will sink. We hurry on back and bail for a few minutes, then take leave of the island.

We go another way to the shore, a bit longer, giving us more time to chat. My guide is personable, in his forties, with a moustache like a pencil line across his lip. In the course of our ride he offers some unsolicited remarks on the current political situation. He was formerly a B-Special and proud of it. When the B's were disbanded he and his fellows joined the Ulster Defence Force, a legal organisation that at first allowed them to keep almost everything they had as B's. He spends about eight hours a week with the UDF, has a uniform and several guns. Most of his duty is little different from that of any militiaman, guarding power installations, police stations, schools and the like. As B's they used to do a great deal of nighttime

roadblocks and interrogations, but that would be risky business nowadays. He has been fired upon several times, mostly at border stations when the IRA would shoot Russian-built rockets at them from the Republic. In response they would open up with everything they had — one time he fired over 600 rounds. The British regulars, according to him, would never join the indiscriminate fusilades, in fact they deplored the wastage though refusing to interfere. 'They just sat there and called us stupid bloody micks,' he says.

Boa Island, just three miles from White Island, is the largest in Lough Erne. A long low salamander of a hill, it is connected at either end of the shore with brand new bridges. To my surprise there is no sign pointing out the whereabouts of the Lusty Man, and two farmers that I ask just shake their heads. They know, of course, but why they won't help out with directions is their business. Making a rough approximation from the scanty description in my guidebook ('about 1 mile from the bridge') I quit the road and head for water.

I am looking for a graveyard once again. My hopes that it may stand out from the scrub and overgrown pastures of the area are quickly dispelled, however, and I end up slogging around in bog pits, thorn bushes and drainage ditches for well over an hour before a rusty iron gate, smothered in undergrowth, gives the clue. Struggling through a veritable wall of entangling burrs I finally blunder into the cemetery, completely buried, most of its headstones thick with ivy. With some difficulty I pick out the Lusty Man.

In fact, there are two of these figures in the Caldragh graveyard. The Lusty Man originally stood in a cemetery on Lustymore Island, an islet just a few hundred yards from here but somebody dug up the statue and brought him here for some reason unexplained. Of the two he is the less impressive due to size and vandalism in some long

Lusty Man II,
Boa Island,
Co. Fermanagh

*High Cross
Inishmacsaint,
Co. Fermanagh*

forgotten age. His brother is taller and in perfect condition, and for want of any other name I dub him Lusty Man II.

The Lusty Men are two-headed figures with carvings back to back on each side. Lusty Man I was defaced so that today only one portrait is complete. Lusty Man II, on the other hand, retains both so there are, in effect, three portraits here. The representation in each is of a huge face cut in the shape of a diamond, the lower chin and crossed arms covering a barrel-like body dressed in a tunic with waistband. In Lusty Man II a cleft was hollowed out between the two heads to form a bowl, perhaps for offerings, which implies some sort of pagan ritual. It is difficult to see in these bizarre statues anything Christian, but the streak of grotesque is certainly a common thread uniting them to White Island and Killadeas — both supposedly Christian. The fact that in all of Ireland only here, along the shores of Lough Erne, do we find such figures in these numbers, leads to the inevitable conclusion that some sort of distinctly local cult was practised in this region that somehow infected the character of its later Christianisation. This would not be surprising: as a first step in converting any area, missionaries would often simply reorient pagan beliefs into nominally acceptable channels that could be adjusted to a more correct theological position later on. The cult of Brigit is a good example, and also attempts by Columcille and others to reshape pagan festivals of spring and harvest into Christian feasts.[5] Here at Lough Erne the heathen ritual perhaps survived for too long and in too militant a fashion, producing Christian statues of dubious artistic purity and hence the inevitable embarrassment and cover-up, at least in terms of White Island.

As the progenitors of these later abnormalities, the Lusty Men are obvious candidates. For as long as superstition reigned supreme among the peasantry, and it certainly did well into the nineteenth century, clandestine assemblies in this boggy, weed-ridden graveyard and that on Lustymore Island were probably common. The linkage is intriguing between the rituals practised here and those performed on White Island, only a few miles away.

Leaving Boa Island I drive south along the western shore of the Lake, near to completing the full circuit now. I have planned for a last stop at Inishmacsaint, the 'isle of the plain of sorrel'. For once I have no difficulty in finding a boat to hire, and row off into a late afternoon breeze.

Inishmacsaint is another scruffy morass of a little island, visited mainly for its high cross, an early example tentatively dated AD c. 700. The ruins of the church it guards are scanty and not impressive. The cross, however, is huge, over twelve feet high according to my measure. It consists of three pieces: a base, a shaft and the cruciform pattern of the cross itself. There is no decoration anywhere on it, nor the familiar Celtic ring around the cross. It is a transitional piece standing midway between pillar stones with crosses carved on them (incised, as at Glencolumbkille) and the more famous ringed crosses with pyramidal base (Moone, for example). Inishmacsaint represents the interim artistic struggle: whoever built it had something novel in mind and came up with this, a 'rude structure' according to one early traveller, only an 'early effort'. That may be true but in many ways the overall effect, while primitive, is more pleasing.

Lovely season of May! Most noble then is the colour of trees;
blackbirds sing a full lay, when the shaft of day is slender.
Irish, seventh century

10 *Armagh*

HAVING thought and read so much about Armagh it is a relief to be here finally, though the experience is bittersweet in a way. My own ancient companion, a battered copy of L Russell Muirhead's *Blue Guide to Ireland*, refers to this city's 'atmosphere of ancient dignity,' with its 'quiet streets' and 'dignified Georgian houses'. Yesterday's local newspaper called Armagh 'a wilderness', and that pragmatic note, unfortunately, is the more appropriate observation. Outside of Strabane and portions of Belfast and Londonderry, no other place in the North has suffered such material damage. I was amazed to find entire streets and blocks in this venerable (though small) town totally boarded up and deserted. Within sight of Patrick's Cathedral hill, acres of a ghost city spread before me. And the violence continues, despite the vast and heavily fortified British Army camp only a mile or two away, with its constant patrols of armoured vehicles and mobile check points. Just last week a hotel on Lower English Street, the Charlemont, was shattered by a car bomb, estimated by police to have weighed 600 pounds. A soldier I talked with said the explosion was probably heard by his parents in faraway London. Muirhead notes that Armagh has been burned and pillaged so many times in its past that little if anything old remains, most of the finer buildings dating from the Georgian period. If the current seige continues, nothing even new will be left. My strongest impression of Armagh is that of a place being evacuated.

This is, naturally, a disaster since few cities in Ireland are more naturally pleasant than Armagh, with its curious and Celtic arrangement of streets and boundaries. Dominating everything are the two cathedrals of Protestant and Catholic archbishops, both of whom are Primates of Ireland. The Protestant Cathedral, thanks to the Reformation, occupies the more ancient site of the two, where in the fifth century one of Patrick's modest little churches once stood, given to him by the Ulaid kings of Emain Macha, just two miles off to the west. The limits of Patrick's hilltop rath and the extensive ecclesiastical community that eventually developed around it are most graphically illustrated by aerial photography, which shows how the present plan of streets and roadways, shops and homes, simply follows a more ancient arrangement. On the other side of the city sits the twin-spired Roman Catholic Cathedral, a rather ugly structure built solely to overshadow and dominate that of the opposition's, a lower and squatter building of basically eighteenth-century appearance. It is a shame, aesthetically speaking, that the enormous surge in Catholic church building that began in Ireland, near the midway point of the nineteenth century should have coincided with the mania for gothic. The results of this enthusiasm lie all over Ireland (to say nothing of Boston and Chicago) yet here at Armagh we see it at its worst, the Italian variation. Inside this leaden structure is a virtual cornucopia of marble and brass glitter, almost blinding in its weight. I am all for spectacles but this is disproportionate — a Mediterranean flavour entirely false to a setting so wet and deeply green. It is impossible to digest.

The Anglican Cathedral is a more dignified structure and reminds one of England, as no doubt it was intended to. Union Jacks hang overhead and memorials to the Royal Irish Fusiliers, headquartered in Armagh, are everywhere. The custodian takes me up to the tower

Protestant Cathedral, Armagh.

The outline of the central rath now occupied by the cathedral on top of the hill can easily be traced. Spread around on the slope and also circular in plan was the larger 'city' rath of monks, students and artisans.

where I have a fine view of the wooded countryside and hills surrounding us.

While Armagh, given the present circumstances, is an easy place to bypass, its role in Irish history is the reverse, which is the only reason I've come here. Armagh, to use the term collectively, represents some of the coolest political thinking since Columcille's performance at Druim Cett in 575. At that point, as the reader may recall, the pre-eminent position of Columcille's *paruchia* was established beyond question throughout the north of the island, with Iona as its primary house. Columcille's death in 597 aged seventy-six in no way altered the situation.

These early years of the seventh century were times of reckoning for Armagh. The failure of episcopal controls and the lessened status of bishops were direct setbacks for the older, non-monastic churches of which Armagh was one of the more important. Communities of a 'third world' status — new, independent or non-aligned — gravitated slowly to the wings of *paruchia* federations where the lion's share of royal favour and patronage were usually in evidence. Places like Armagh survived on what little was left. If it hadn't been for Easter things might never have changed.

The *paruchia* of Columcille was fanatically opposed to concessions on the Easter question. We saw in the behaviour of Columbanus a typical example of Celtic inflexibility, and Bede's pervasive eye (in his *Ecclesiastical History of the British People*) chronicles their continuing disobediance throughout the 600s. But changes to the south of their influence in both England and Ireland eventually began to press and hit home until even Iona was pushed aside, into nothingness, by the distant finger of Rome. By 700 the struggle was just about over.

At first the threat was remote and seemingly unrelated. Anglo-Saxon barbarians, following the time-honoured tradition of moving west under pressure, had gradually established themselves in England during the 500s as Roman authority there crumbled. Pockets of Christianity survived in the west (Cornwall and Wales) and to the north in Scotland there was Iona, but everywhere else the religion went underground to surface again, quietly, only when the heathens settled down to what they had won.

Celtic missionary activity, bottled up in the extremities of the island, kept to itself.[1]

In 597 Pope Gregory I sent an official mission to England of forty monks, headed by the future St Augustine of Canterbury, in the hopes of reconverting the former colony to Christ. The expedition was deemed by those who were sent as exceedingly dangerous, if not impossible, and missionary zeal seemed to ebb away as the monks, 'seized by a panic of foreboding' in Bede's words, sat down one night in France and refused to go on. Augustine retraced his steps to Rome as representative of the group, and pleaded with Gregory to relieve them of 'this journey so perilous, so toilsome, so uncertain,' but the Pope refused. Augustine finally landed in Kent and the mission began.

The curious aspect of this activity is that Augustine had little or no contact with the Celtic monks of Iona during the ten years of his labour in Britain. They were buried in the mountain fastness of the Highlands, of course, and their cousins in Wales and Cornwall, though closer, were also not easily available, but the complete lack of communication between them all is still surprising. Augustine worked on, oblivious to his co-religionists, and established rules and customs as the Pope had decreed which, naturally enough, were utterly at variance with local Celtic habits.

Even so, initial contacts between the Roman and Celtic parties were inevitably made, mostly after Augustine's death, and they appear to have been amicable enough, at least in the west. It seems that many of the Irish monks living in Cornwall and Wales had no problem conforming to official instructions for the dating of Easter, as we have some evidence that by 630 the entire southern half of Ireland, dominated by Cashel, observed the feast after the Roman fashion. The reader will recall the important and traditional ties between these two areas which no doubt explain the relative ease of their decision to accept a papal authority from Rome. But the men of the north were a different breed. As the distribution of ogham stones indicates, their kinfolk and affections lay not in Wales but in Argyll, and according to contemporary accounts they were a far less easy-going group of people.

The establishment of links between Iona and the Roman mission is rather more fully known that that of Cornwall and Wales. In 623 Edwin, the pagan king of Northumbria (northernmost of the Anglo-Saxon kingdoms) took as his queen Aethelburh of Kent, a Christian. Her confessor, a member of the Roman party, converted great numbers of pagans (but not the king) and settled York as his see. Edwin was killed in battle some years later by a rival warrior named Cadwallon, and his son Oswald fled further north. Tradition has it he found refuge at Iona and was converted there by the monks. In 634 Oswald regained his throne (over Cadwallon's body) and out of respect for the new religion he invited missionaries into his kingdom to proselytise the populace. The call, significantly enough, went not to Canterbury, the spiritual home of the Roman faction and of his own mother, but to Iona, the monastery that had taken him in. A direct result was the foundation of Lindisfarne, one of the truly romantic spots in the British Isles, by the Abbot Aidan in 635. Almost right away, in typically Irish fashion, the spider web of daughter houses began to spread, Melrose and Lichfield being notable examples. With Oswald's death, however, a confrontation ensued: the king's brother, sympathetic with Iona, took the crown but soon discovered his family' preference for Canterbury. The result was the famous Council of Whitby.

Bede has given us a rather fanciful description of the bickering that took place at Whitby, some of which (certainly the dialogue) is fictitious. But the central Solomon-like question by the king, Oswiu by name, about who held the keys to heaven, St Peter or Columcille, is probably accurate and Bede's rhetorical inventions seem consistent with the known positions of the two parties. On the basis of these points the scene he creates is more or less historical.

Oswiu's rationale for calling the conference was logical enough: the feud over Easter had become disruptive, his own son had turned against him on account of it, and these meddlesome monks did nothing but quarrel over the issue incessantly. Whitby was meant to settle this controversy one way or the other forever as far as Oswiu and Northumbria were concerned. The two combatants were Colmán, third abbot of Lindisfarne and spokesman for the Columban *paruchia* and Wilfrid, later canonised, a priest and adherent of Canterbury. Wilfrid began by charging that 'the Easter we keep is the same as we have seen universally celebrated throughout the whole world, wherever the Church of Christ is scattered, amid various nations and languages. The only exceptions are these men and their accomplices in obstinacy.' To which Colmán replied that anything good enough for Columcille and his successors — whom 'I have no doubt were saints' — was good enough for him. Lengthy arguments went back and forth until Wilfrid arrived at his central point, that 'even if this Columba of yours — yes, and ours too if he belonged to Christ — was a holy man of mighty works, is he to be preferred to the most blessed chief of the apostles, to whom the Lord said, 'Thou art Peter and upon this rock I will build my Church and the gates of hell shall not prevail against it, and I will give unto thee the keys to the kingdom of heaven"'?'

The king [then] said, 'Is it true, Colmán, that the Lord said these words to Peter?' Colmán answered, 'It is true, O King.' Then the king went on, 'Have you anything to show that an equal authority was given to your Columba?' Colmán answered, 'Nothing.' Again the king said, 'Do you both agree, without any dispute, that these words were addressed primarily to Peter and that the Lord gave him the keys to the Kingdom of Heaven?' They both answered, 'Yes.' Thereupon the king concluded, 'Then, I tell you, since he is the doorkeeper I will not contradict him, nor will I condone any who do. Otherwise, when I come to the gates of Heaven, he who holds the key may not be willing to open them. As long as I live I shall abide by this decision.'

Oswiu's judgment proved the first in a series of reverses that finalised Iona's slide from pre-eminence. Colmán, given the choice of conforming or exile, chose the latter course and with all the Irish monks of Lindisfarne (plus thirty or so of its British brothers) travelled north to Iona and then home to Ireland.[2] The expansion south into England of the Columban *paruchia* stalled instantly as the Roman party gained control of both their existing communities and the sources of revenue, royal patronage, hitherto undisputedly Iona's.

The Abbey Church, Iona, Argyll, Scotland

*St Peter with his Keys,
tomb carving, 16th century,
Jerpoint Abbey, Co. Kilkenny*

In Ireland tensions also mounted. The south conformed without much dispute, their ties with Gaul and Britain easing the transition. But in the north, virtual fief of Iona for decades, there was no giving in among the die-hards even as abuse and pressure grew. The pride of Columbanus in the Irish as 'dwellers at the end of the earth' gave way to the taunt of a Romaniser 'and I might say, a pimple on the chin of the earth.' Papal influence was surrounding Iona even in its hideaways, yet the final crack, ironically, came from within.

Adomnán, ninth abbot of Iona and famous for his biography of Columcille, a member of Clan Conaill of the Northern Uí Néill and literally the *coarb* of the great saint himself, was the instrument of Iona's eventual submission. Bede informs us that Adomnán was a 'good and wise man' but implies (as a strong adherent to the Roman party would) that the Irish monk was rustic and backward. On a trip to visit Aldfrith, King of Northumbria, Adomnán found himself surrounded with canonical enemies 'better instructed than he,' who harangued him with the evil of his ways and those of his followers in Iora. Adomnán proved malleable, for 'he altered his opinion so greatly that he readily preferred the customs which he saw and heard in English churches to those of himself,' and he returned to Iona convinced that at long last conformity was necessary, a decision his monks refused to recognise. Somewhat discouraged he crossed over to Ireland and apparently went on circuit from one house of the *paruchia* to another, trying to convince his monks to change their ways. He was more successful this time for in 697 he presided over the Synod of Birr which, among other things, formalised the acknowledgment that henceforth the universal writ of the Church as decreed by Rome would apply to Ireland. The final blow came in 717, after Adomnán's death, when the king of the Picts forcibly expelled recalcitrant monks from Iona itself, leaving only those in peace who were prepared to celebrate Easter in the proper fashion. For all practical purposes the Columban *paruchia* disappears as an influence.

The events of these hectic years, the 630s on up to the purge of Iona in 717, serve as a backdrop to Armagh's series of manoeuvres. Alone of the northern churches Armagh quickly and forcibly attached itself to the fortunes of the Roman party, a logical alliance given the early associations of this community with Patrick and episcopal (i.e. Roman) values. This resurgence of both Armagh and Rome in Irish affairs was best served by the extraordinary utilisation of Patrick the Briton.

We have seen how Patrick fled Armagh when Niall of the Nine Hostages destroyed the Ulaid in battle, and that he ended up in Downpatrick. These were Armagh's bleakest years and it didn't help that when Patrick died his body was not returned to Armagh for burial. Tradition is consistent in recording that troops were sent to recover the corpse, for what good was an ancestor figure if you didn't have knucklebones, hair, ankles, heart, toenails or personal effects which pilgrims could travel from afar to venerate (and in the process make the church which owned such relics rich)? Unfortunately these military forays (there seem to have been several) were bloodily repulsed by the Ulaid and Armagh never did get his body, a problem later apologists energetically explained away as best they could.[3]

Even so Armagh pushed ahead, claiming Patrick as its own true father and setting out to refurbish his image as a genuine champion of Rome. This primarily explains why Patrick was sent to matriculate in Gaul and become a pupil of Germanus, a fervent episcopalian if there ever was one, and accounts for the many legends of his reputed travels in Italy as well. To have left poor Patrick as a simple, uneducated monk straight from Britain would have been altogether too dry. Muirchú's *Life of Patrick*, written *c.* 680, is therefore simply a compilation of the official line invented and spread about in the interests of Armagh, and Tírechán's contemporary *Memoir* represents the political extension of this same Patrician material.

Tírechán's *Memoir of c.* 675 is not really a biography of Patrick as much as a set of claims for a non-monastic *paruchia* to compete with those of Columcille, Ciarán, Comgall and the others. As a forerunner of a new wave (Patrick and Rome) Armagh required a political framework that could absorb and express the power it hoped was coming towards it. Episcopal organisation was out of the question as two centuries of futility had proven, so Armagh in effect joined the system and established a federation all its own. Tírechán made claim to free, non-aligned churches through the person of Patrick, now a national apostle, whose travels about the entire island were fabricated to legitimise an All-Ireland *paruchia*. For if Patrick never preached in Connaught or Leinster or Munster, how could the many independent communities in those parts of the country possibly justify their allegiance to a Patrician federation? The traditions of many a local saint were submerged in just this fashion, as churches began claiming Patrick as their founder. This sudden pervasiveness of the Patrician cult, especially when translated into the financial picture of endowments and patronage, was apparently viewed with alarm by the older monastic *paruchia* as Tírechán himself implies. 'My heart is troubled within me through love of Patrick,' he writes, 'for I see with what hatred the renegades and robbers and soldiers of Ireland regard Patrick's *paruchia*, in that they have taken away from him what is his and they are in fear, since, if the heir of Patrick were to demand his *paruchia*, he could recover as such almost the whole island.' With the disintegration of Iona over the Easter question in the latter half of the seventh century, Armagh was poised, eagerly, to take its place. Our first real sign of this comes *c.* 680 when Bishop Áed of Slébte,[4] Muirchú's patron, travelled to Armagh and pledged 'his kin and his church to Patrick till Doom'. It was only the beginning.

By AD 700 with one foot crossed over the body of Iona and the other ready to follow, Armagh's fortunes took another more drastic step forward. The Uí Néill kings of Tara were beginning to make a rather startling assertion (inasmuch as it was absurd) that they should henceforth be recognised as High Kings of all Ireland. On the face of it the notion was incredible: everyone knew that disunity reigned supreme among the Uí Néill with warfare almost every other year between the Northern and Southern septs. How could they possibly expect anyone to take a centralising idea such as this seriously? But deep in the Gaelic heart there was a twitch of excitement, the recognition that here was something unique, the notion of a singular titular king ruling over the country as a whole. And the kingship of Tara was if anything titular and symbolic. To the Celts, loving the extravagance of it all, this particular bit of bluff on the part of the Uí Néill was genuine entertainment. Everyone sat back to see how things would go, except Armagh.

The idea of an authoritative high king, someone who could rule over the land in fact as well as in theory, was an exciting idea to the ecclesiastical family of Armagh, and their ambition began to feed off that of the Uí Néill. For hand in hand with a high king — logically — went the idea of a dominant all powerful church to which all others owed tribute and obedience. What other candidate than Armagh? And so the wheels began to turn, with Armagh's fidelity to the Uí Néill, a tradition dating as far back as the 500s, bearing fruit at long last. In the process a single remaining piece of the Tara puzzle, and with it centuries of confusion over Patrick, fitted snugly into place.

Tara looked no different in AD 700 than it does today, a lonely, empty set of fields. The title King of Tara, however, flourished among the Uí Néill, the ceremonial appellation won by the man who could claim the obedience of both family branches. And now a culmination: the High King of Tara to whom every king was to owe fealty. To prove their loyalty, and in the process advance their own cause, the clergy of Armagh set out to justify the claim. In a way they handled the public relations for this spectacular new product by giving it a history. Into the stew they threw everything they had — Patrick, Easter, Tara, a high kingship, everything — and came out with a legend that has endured more strongly in Irish folklore than any other. We see it most clearly in Muirchú: Patrick the agent of Rome and its universal, correct rule, lands in Saul at the start of his mission. Seeking to begin at the top he looks around to see who it is he should convert first. We have

Early Christian Cross, possibly 5th century, Sleaty, Co. Leix

noted previously that he travelled to Emain Macha in Ulster and settled less than two miles away on the hill of Armagh to work on the Ulaid kings, the most prestigious in Ireland. But in seventh-century terms power no longer lay with the Ulaid and certainly not at Emain Macha, but with the Uí Néill who ruled from Tara — or, to be as specific as possible, who ruled from the idea of Tara. Thus, again in seventh-century terms with the Uí Néill claiming a high kingship of Tara, it became necessary to institutionalise the office as an ancient historical fact. Niall of the Nine Hostages, ancestor of the Uí Néill but never more than a warlord, becomes a fourth-century High King of Tara ruling over all of Ireland, and so too his progeny, who did indeed rule from Tara Hill but only as indeterminate regional kings. Muirchú and his companions (and later the unwitting annalists) threw a non-existent crown back through the centuries simply to justify a political innovation of the seventh century. Patrick is hauled south to the Hill of Tara to confront Laoghaire, the 'High King,' on, of all days, an Easter Sunday — a nice bit of Roman emphasis on Muirchú's part since Patrick stood for the correct Easter and who, from among the mighties of the *paruchia*, stood for that noble and, more importantly, correct principle in the year 700? The *coarbs* of Patrick, naturally, the bishops of Armagh. And who were the high kings of all Ireland that Patrick converted? The Uí Néill, ruling from Tara. The maze straightens out as we follow the logic of this sequence, for if the Uí Néill ruled this island in Patrick's time they had every right to claim it in AD 700. And if Armagh (in the person of Patrick) and the Uí Néill were allies then, surely their friendship could progress even further towards mutual, self-serving goals in AD 700. Or so the argument went, and by 1843 when Daniel O'Connell and all the rest were roaming up and down on Tara these distinctions and realisations had all but blurred away leaving confusion in their place. For that is the way of myth, religious, historical or otherwise: the price is paid by later generations when the memory of debate falls back in time. In just four or five decades, possibly less, Muirchú's tale was probably accepted as the truth of God. Many people today still think it is.[5]

Armagh's claims for ecclesiastical primacy specifically evolved from their association with the Uí Néill, without whom a document like the *Liber Angeli* would have been impossible. The *Liber Angeli* or 'Book of the Angel' is the ultimate expression of Armagh's ambition. It is relatively short and was included in the Book of Armagh c.806 by Ferdomnach, the scribe evidently responsible for the edited version of Patrick's writings. The more important sections seem to have been originally composed at a far earlier date than 806, however, possibly around 730 at a time when Armagh was rapidly emerging as the single most powerful church in Ireland. It represents the formalisation of Tírechán's first claim in the format of a conversation between Patrick and an angel of the Lord:

Once, therefore, S. Patrick went forth from the city Armagh to baptise, teach, and heal the multitudes of both sexes of the human race beside the spring which is close to the eastern part of the aforesaid city. And there, before dawn, he waited for many who were gathering from all parts to the knowledge of the faith. Suddenly, then, sleep prostrated him, because, for Christ's sake, he had beforehand been wearied from his night vigils. And behold, straightaway an angel came to him from heaven, and raised him gently from sleep. And S. Patrick said: 'Here I am. Have I done anything wrong of late in the sight of the Most High? If it has happened, I seek pardon from God.'

The angel reassures Patrick that nothing is amiss, only that the Lord wishes to grant his faithful servant certain rights and privileges, not the least of which are 'all the tribes of the Irish by way of *paruchia* to you and this city of yours which is called *Ardd Machae* in the Irish tongue'. In the light of this rather broad concession Patrick goes on to fill in the details: of how a special tax — 'rightly to be rendered' — is now due Armagh from every independent church in the country;[6] of how Armagh's *paruchia* is entitled to encourage and accept gifts of land and treasure from secular rulers 'through the will of their own freedom'; how the archbishop of Armagh and his retinue are entitled to gratuitous and appropriate lodging in every monastery and church of the island during the course of their travels; of how it is unlawful for any bishop or abbot to oppose the authority of the *coarb* of Patrick, for 'God has given to him (Patrick) the whole island,' and 'by privilege and by the heavenly authority of the most high bishop, its founder (Armagh) precedes all the churches and all the monasteries of the Irish'; and finally how the direct link with Rome is formally established, as all disputes incapable of resolution are ordered sent to the bishop of Armagh for arbitration, and he, if he so desires, will send the matter on to his fellow primate the pope himself for a corroborating opinion. Furthermore it is stated that any violation of these provisions will be witnessed, and remembered, by Patrick himself. His mystique seals the grant because [and this is new] 'he will judge all the Irish in the great day of terrible judgment in the presence of Christ.'

Many historians feel the *Liber Angeli* is a fragment of the *Lex Patricii* or 'Law of Patrick' which the annalists record was imposed on many of the *tuaths* of Ireland in the early decades of the eighth century. It appears that an ecclesiastical 'progress' was made throughout the north and midlands by the clergy of Armagh to enforce collection of the tax mentioned in *Liber Angeli*. To make the tribute somewhat more palatable the relics of Armagh were paraded around too, as a reference in the Annals of Ulster suggests for the year 733, 'Transfer of the relics of Peter and Paul and Patrick to enforce the law.' Nearly all the larger *paruchia* were soon engaged in similar fund-raising activities until there sprouted up more 'laws' in Ireland than there were saints, to say nothing of the relic trade — an 'evil' exploitation according to one poet, when 'any wretched pitiful thing will be used as a relic'. The eighth century, as many authorities have pointed out, became the riptide of commercialism within the Irish church, the beginnings of lay abbots and massive ecclesiastical wealth. Temporal claims for lands and endowments even led to religious wars as armies of monks engaged in open battle, killing and hacking each other like regular soldiers. At the forefront of the rush was Armagh, so powerful by the year 800 (and rich) that even the Uí Néill seemed a bit in awe. By that time the ideals of the the early fathers — Patrick, Columcille, Columbanus, Molasius — had all been compromised, and the phenomenon of the Céli Dé drifted through in response.

I had hoped that the Archbishop of Armagh and Primate of all Ireland, Tomás Cardinal Ó Fiaich (anglicised Thomas O'Fee) would be available to see me during my stay in the city. Ó Fiaich has written several articles on St Patrick over the years, generally adhering to the orthodox point of view with its maintenance of the traditional highlights of Patrician legend, most especially those regarding Slemish Mountain in Antrim as the locale of Patrick's captivity; the almost instant death of Palladius and the equally swift arrival of his replacement, Patrick; and the whole Paschal fire episode at the Hill of Slane, prior to Patrick's cataclysmic confrontation with King Laoghaire at Tara. All of these events have been deemed more or less unhistorical by the majority of academicians engaged in Patriciology, and I felt it would be interesting to hear arguments from the other side.

Most especially, I wanted Ó Fiaich's comments. He is not a casual scholar by any means. Prior to his elevation as a cardinal he had been in charge of St Patrick's College in Maynooth, the famous seminary for Irish priests first established in 1521 by the 8th Earl of Kildare. More intriguingly, he is reputed to have been a prime historical quarry from which John Paul II gleaned most (if not all) of the background material used in the twenty-two addresses and homilies of his recent papal visit in 1979. These I had read in paperback form in Dublin, and not surprisingly the emphasis on Patrick had been extremely pronounced, particularly in the Pope's speech at Drogheda, near the Hill of

Slane. I had been amazed when going over that sermon by the Pope's choice (or was it Ó Fiaich's choice?) of two excerpts from Patrick's *Confession*. Both had been omitted from the Book of Armagh. The irony of John Paul re-emphasising Patrician myth on the one hand ('In the words of the Easter liturgy, celebrated for the first time in Ireland on the Hill of Slane . . . ' etc.) yet in the same breath using language of the Saint's that had been censored by the monks of Armagh, was not lost on me. I wondered about the Cardinal's response.

Several phone calls from Dublin to the Cardinal's secretary in Armagh convinced me, however, that an interview would not be easy to arrange. 'St Patrick is it? Well you know the Cardinal is a very busy man, a very busy man indeed, and since he left Maynooth two years ago he's been far behind in his reading, far behind. Call me tomorrow, could you do that?' And so on. Friends in Dublin recommended more forceful steps: appear on his doorstep. Within sight of the Cardinal's residence, I phone again. 'You're in Armagh? Oh dear. Let's have a look at the Cardinal's schedule. . . . Could you call me back, I have no idea where the Cardinal is at the moment?' Ten minutes later: 'Ah well now, you see the Cardinal had confirmations tonight in Portadown, and confirmations tomorrow night and the night after. Then he's travelling south.'

'Could he squeeze me in for just thirty minutes or so?' I reply.

'Well actually, the truth of it, you see the Cardinal is disinclined to see you or talk to you. Or anyone else for that matter. And he has these confirmations to do this evening.'

Questions involving Patrick are not, of course, journalistic by nature, and while I am not a journalist, the distinction (over the telephone anyway) is probably unclear. Nor is Cardinal Ó Fiaich an elected official responsible to me or the public. The rebuff is more comical than momentous. In expectation of failure, I had in my notebooks the name of an alternative. I arrange to see Joseph Duffy, Roman Catholic Bishop of Clogher, the next day at his cathedral seat in nearby Monaghan. Then I drive out to Emain Macha, capital of the Ulaid until its

destruction by Niall of the Nine Hostages *c.* 480, and just two miles away.

Like Dun Aillinne in Leinster and Tara in County Meath, it occupies the summit of a hill surrounded by a great trench. The royal rath of Ulster sits within, and the twin spires of the Roman Catholic Cathedral are just visible over the intervening ridge. Typically there is little to see here, but the associations are enormous, preserved in song and poem through hundreds of years: Deirdre, Cú Chulainn, the Knights of the Red Branch, Niall of the Nine Hostages, St Patrick himself. But as the day wears on I find my eyes not seeing this place. Perhaps it's the noisy, chalk-encrusted factory at the foot of the hill. Maybe it's just fatigue. After just thirty minutes I leave to search out a camp site. Enough for one day.

The Bishop of Clogher, like the cardinal, is both a Maynooth man and a published writer on the life of St Patrick. His colloquial translation of the *Confession*, while awkward in spots, has proven very popular as an inexpensive, accessible paperback, and has run through at least two editions. My expectations of finding a hopeless reactionary are unfounded, however. Joseph Duffy, young to be a bishop, is the polished defender of a more respectable, semi-orthodox view of the Patrician legends — he is not behind the times. 'Would it disappoint you', I asked him first, 'if it was established that St Patrick never did half the things or visited half the places we're told he did?'

'No, not at all. I think St Patrick is a much bigger character than one to be almost spied upon as he made his way around the country. It's rather his impact on the island as a whole that is the reality, and the physical minutae don't really count. In terms of historical research and the ability of documents to fill in his movements, it is

Emain Macha, *Roman Catholic Cathedral in distance, Co. Armagh*

fairly obvious that it's impossible to state with any sort of accuracy where St Patrick actually was and where he wasn't, apart from one or two places, one of which would be Armagh, the primatial seat. Even though there isn't any documentary proof to say that he was in Armagh, the whole circumstantial evidence is such that it is virtually certain. And then the other place, of course, is the famous *Silva Focluti*, or 'Wood of Foclut', which is mentioned in the *Confession* as the place where he heard the voices, and that has been I think, reasonably identified as a place in western Mayo, fairly near the Reek.'

'Should I assume from what you've said that the question of Slemish Mountain in County Antrim as the spot of these visions does not interest you too much as a controversy?'

'That's right. Slemish is interesting in other ways, but not that one.'

'What about Patrick's supposed sojourn in Gaul, with Germanus at Auxerre and so forth?'

'Well I think one has to agree with Professor Binchy in most of what he says about Patrick being a rustic and all that. He obviously was closer to Britain than he was to the Continent. But I think even Binchy wouldn't go so far as to say that he wasn't *ever* on the Continent. And again, I think the Continental influence is possibly more important than his actual physical presence on the Continent at any given time. When I read the *Confession* it makes more sense to me personally to assume that he was on the Continent for at least some time. It helps in understanding the controversy which arose over his mission back in England, the way he was taken to task by his fellow bishops, and so on, in terms of the larger controversy surrounding the mission of Germanus of Auxerre to Britain in the fifth century. I am much impressed, by the way, with a curious fact that has been brought out by at least one very substantial scholar, Christine Mohrmann, a linguist. She found elements of the Latin of Gaul, colloquial Latin, in Patrick's speech. And the only possible explanation is that Patrick was in fact brought up in that area. As to whether he went to school or not in France, that's an open question, we just do not know.'

'I'm interested in your thoughts on the mysterious Palladius. Or more to the point, the reliability of Muirchú and Tírechán.'

'It's a question of what you mean by reliable. As factual biographical accounts of the saint, I don't think you could say they were reliable by modern standards. But then again, it's only fair to say that their work wasn't intended to be that kind of biography. A comparative example would be the Bible, which admits of several different literary genres and where you've got to interpret what's there in the understanding that it's written for a particular purpose. It would seem to me that Muirchú and Tírechán, and particularly Tírechán, wrote to bolster up a political theory that the Uí Néill were inheritors of the primitive Patrician church. You can say, correctly, that this work is propaganda. Now that may have been the purpose of it, but I feel that doesn't take from these two the value of their writings. Look at Tírechán. It would seem that what Tírechán did was go round the churches of the time which had the tradition of Patrick alive in them, and he did a tour. Instead of just saying "I took a tour of churches reputedly founded by Patrick," he called it a Patrician circuit. In other words, he made of Patrick a literary device, he made him in fact go round these churches. Well you see, there's a very real connection between the two things. While on the one hand it may seem to be just a tissue of falsehoods, on the other it's the most obvious way to look for Patrick's remnants — where in fact the Patrician tradition was strongest. And this is where Tírechán came in. He did the circuit and he listed those places that had a real closeness to Patrick. He employed artistic license in writing his piece, but I don't find that objectionable, nor do I find his writings useless. The majority of places described are consistent with where we think Patrick practised his ministry, in line from Armagh over to the northwest.'

'We do have, though, the rather crudely altered version of the *Confession* in the Book of Armagh. And while the word "conspiracy" has been in the news frequently over the past years, and conjures up all sorts of evil things, is it applicable to Armagh? Did these monks really sit about and conspire to do things like alter records, in a kind of criminal fashion, or did it seem to them a decent and appropriate course of action?'

'I would say it seemed a perfectly natural, innocent thing to do.'

'In the tradition of writing a saint's life?'

'Absolutely so. There wasn't a trace of malice in what they were doing. In fact, it was a labour of reverence and love.'

'So you don't believe they were thinking, "Here we are with the Columban *paruchia*, we have to do something about them"?'

'Well, maybe something like that insinuates itself into it. It's very hard sometimes to separate the baser motive from the purer motive, isn't it? They were well-intentioned people who were devoted to their subject, and who felt deeply about it, and if they didn't give a detached, objective account as the sort we would want, well who's to blame them? We must remember that all this took place hundreds of years ago. We sit here and debate the reliability of Muirchú and Tírechán and all the others. For some people, baffled by the seeming contridictions, the overlapping and confusion over dates and facts and so on — these people say it's spoiled the Saint, made a sort of corpse out of him for inspection, carving up his anatomy. I don't feel that way, personally. As a subject of study, St Patrick is fascinating and this, I think, is where Binchy has succeeded so well. He has gone through the sources, thrown out many of the wilder things that have been said, a lot of the slagging that went on, and just zoned in on what is really important, the only two really basic documents on which to establish any credible life of the Saint — the *Confession* and *Epistle to Coroticus*. He demonstrates clearly how poorly moored sources like Muirchú and Tírechán are to your recognisable events and incidents of the fifth century. They're interesting in their own right, but not as witnesses. Now the Old School of Thought on St Patrick, quite honestly, would have to be considered passé today, with their heavy reliance on poor, far removed sources. They've been superseded by a new generation of scholars who would lean, oh undoubtedly, towards O'Rahilly and Binchy, principally Binchy.'

'Would a Roman Catholic priest, do you think, have any difficulty abandoning the traditional line on St Patrick, and agreeing with the theories of Binchy?'

'Absolutely not. I'd dismiss the idea immediately that Binchy's approach is in any way counter to an acceptable portraiture of Patrick in Catholic terms.'

I remark on my impression of the Pope's speech at Drogheda, with its affirmation especially of the Slane saga. 'Was there any suggestion made to the Pope, that you know of, that he use the Hill of Slane in his address?'

'Oh yes, very much so. I think you're begging a big question when you ask, in effect who wrote the Pope's speeches. I think the answer to that is he wrote them himself, in collaboration with a number of people from this country, notably the Cardinal, who would have filled him in on Irish history and Irish life. I think that the working out of his speeches and thought processes were entirely his own. There's no question of that. And the Slane thing, you're right, it just made a good story and we're not tied to the historicity of it in the strict sense.'

'I know, but should it be used, do you think? I mean, it isn't true, it never happened.'

'Well, it's not true in the sense that it's a verifiable fact. It's a legend. And I think it's accepted nowadays that legends have a truth of their own, in that they rather conveniently encapsulate a way of looking at a thing, certainly a way of reflecting on something, and insofar as they put it in story form, and tell it graphically and dramatically, that has a very powerful effect on people.'

'As a metaphor.'

'Right. And they have their own truth.'

'So you saw the use of it as a teaching tool?'

'Absolutely.'

11 *Tallaght*

Come to me, loving Mary, that I may keen with you your very dear one. Alas that your son should go to the cross, he who was a great diadem, a beautiful hero.

A poem by Blathmac, a Céli Dé, *c.*760

THE cult of the Virgin Mary did more than even the teachings of Christ to promote the ideal of clerical celibacy, but the veneration of her 'example' was apparently a posthumous development. Jesus, interestingly enough, never once insisted that a priest remain celibate and there still exists considerable debate over the actual virginity of his mother. References in the New Testament would seem to establish the fact, for example, that Joseph only refrained from intercourse with his wife until *after* the birth of their first son (which the angel of the Lord instructed him had been 'begotten in her by the Holy Spirit'), whereupon the couple went on to enjoy normal conjugal relations, the fruit of which were several children. St Matthew's description of the virgin birth confirms the former point ('And he did not know her til she brought forth her first born son') and scattered references to the brothers and sisters of Jesus tend to corroborate the latter.[1]

The growth of Mary into a perpetual rather than temporary virgin came later during the second, third and fourth centuries with the appearance of the so-called 'apocryphal gospels' whose fabulous content elaborated her role (sparsely etched in the earlier, more authentic gospels of the apostles) into a full-blown, centre-stage production. Despite the efforts of the Church to control

fables (the Decrees of Pope Gelasius, AD 492-496) the cult spread contagiously.

Among the more inspired contributors to Mary's legend were early monks, the Desert Fathers that we've heard from before, who chose to live apart and in celibacy. Mary became their special patron and efforts were made to explain away the inconsistencies brought up by St Matthew and the others. Joseph, for instance, was gradually transformed into an elderly widower whose marriage with Mary was one in name only; the brothers and sisters mentioned in the gospels became his children by an earlier wife as opposed to Mary's, and thereby half-brothers and half-sisters to Jesus. This preoccupation with straightening the record grew somewhat demented with the passage of time: monks began theorising that Mary's hymen, unbroken by intercourse, remained sealed even after Christ's birth, the delivery painless and without bleeding. One Irish opinion had it that 'Christ was born from the Crown of the Virgin's head,' bypassing her vagina altogether. The logical culmination to this entire sequence was the doctrine of Immaculate Conception, which after centuries of unofficial acceptance was formalised into dogma by the Pope in 1854.

The development of monasticism in Europe on a large scale did much to entrench these traditions. The Virgin was the highest ideal of all to emulate, and saints such as Jerome and Ambrose even went so far as to say that true holiness could never be fully achieved within the state of lawful matrimony. Columbanus was little different. Abstinence from sexual relations between man and wife was a fine penitential exercise: it gave a person more time to pray.

The secularisation of the Irish church, personified by the proliferating involvement in business affairs by Armagh, Clonmacnoise, Durrow, Kildare and the rest, saw the erosion of these values among the monks. Warfare between the clergy and the grotesque appetite for lands and riches was bad enough, but married abbots, married monks and the passage of church property from a clerical father to a clerical son made the whole situation immeasurably worse. To the Céli Dé, 'the laity and the people of the great old churches yonder are of little worth,' and their admonition 'Take not the world, O cleric' began spreading through monastic circles.

The Céli Dé, or 'Companions of God' (also known as Culdees) were reformers. Their most famous saint was Máelruain who founded the Céli Dé monastery of Tallaght outside of Dublin and died there in 797. The movement is interesting primarily for the perspective it forces us to take in our examination of the Celtic church. For we have travelled since Downpatrick a span of over four centuries, yet even that almost unimaginable gulf flies quickly through the pages. The Céli Dé serve as a reminder of the passage of time. The Age of the Saints had passed away in Ireland, its highwater mark being the plague of 666, and with it to a large degree went that amazing religious fervour that had lasted one hundred and fifty years. In typically cyclical fashion the years of sainthood had given way to years of power and wealth, corrupting factors inconsistent with the precepts of the earlier evangelical fanaticism. And now the inevitable reformation, that stage in the affairs of any organised religion or movement where the desire is to go back, to return to the ancients.

The Céli Dé were not organised, regimented bodies of men. Only a few specifically Céli Dé monasteries were ever actually founded. Instead it represents a state of mind

or attitude and many were the Céli Dé who lived within the walls of unreformed communities, set apart from the rest only by the ways in which their service to God was individually interpreted. For the most part they were passive, seeking to reform by example only those who wished to be reformed. Some withdrew completely to revive the eremital zeal of Athanasius and Skellig Michael. In whatever circumstance it was constancy of purpose that mattered. Máelruain, whose Rule most completely summarises the Céli Dé ideal, instructed his pupils 'to abide always in the place where thou were wont to be. Meddle not with worldly disputes. Go not with any man to a law court, nor to an assembly, to plead on account of any man, but continue in prayer and in pondering thy reading, and in teaching, if there be any that desire to receive instruction from thee.'

we lift up a ready heart
we cast down our faces.

Máelruain's teachings, which are somewhat fragmentary, inferentially reflect the political scandals so offensive to the Céli Dé. The practices of 'the lax folk', as the power magnates in clerical circles were derisively called, came in for substantial condemnation as did many of the habits so popular with the everyday monk such as pilgrimages to faraway lands ('desertion') and asceticism for its own sake ('excessive'). The most revealing of the revivals, however, had to do with sex.

The Céli Dé in effect attempted to resurrect the puritanism of Columbanus in hopes that the virtue of Mary, mother of God, would again become the prevalent custom of Irish monastic life. To Máelruain the problem was one of appetite. A person who ate too much or too frequently increased the amount of blood running through his veins, and too much blood meant 'desires excited'. Monks who were given to such temptations 'need strict abstinence to subdue them. Afterwards, when the blood fails, then lust and desire fail.' He tells the story of Copar, the sister of St Molasius, upon whom 'desire lay heavy, for it is a third part as strong again in women as in men.'[2] Molasius prescribed 'a measured pittance' of food for the girl who returned in a year saying the situation was no better. 'Then he thrust a needle thrice into her palm, and three streams of blood flowed from her hand. Then he said, "No wonder if it is hard for the body, wherein are all these strong currents, to contain itself." Then he diminished her meals a second time.' This procedure went on for three years until at last no blood spurted forth when her hand was jabbed. 'In future,' he concluded at that point, 'keep on this pittance until thy death.' Aside from blood pressure the monk was admonished to be on his guard for the devil in disguise, who can and did strike everywhere with sexual trickery. 'Now the privy houses and the urine houses, they are the abodes of demons. Let these houses be blessed by anyone going thither, and let him bless himself when he enters them, and it is not lawful to say any prayers in them except "Deus in adjutorium" to "festina."'[3]

A far greater proportion of Céli Dé writings involved the aftermath of sin. They seem to have been somewhat pessimistic over the odds against them of really changing the ways of their brothers, and took the morbid pleasure of discussing punishments as a result. Most of these involved the scheduling of specific penances for specific sins, the minor varieties of which entailed a simple three day fast or a night vigil in a cold church or wilderness cell. More grievous sin required proportionally greater effort, anything in the range of a week's strict penance or forty days on bread and water, to fifty nights of vigil or a year's worth of penance; the 'black fast' came next and then a provision for seven years on bread and water. There were even forms of penance unrelated to sin, undertaken to achieve some exalted motive such as the rescue of a soul from hell. The most popular penitential exercise was the vigil, a category all its own with many variations: the famous cross-vigil, for instance, also called the 'corselet of Devotion,' was highly regarded. It involved standing in church[4] with the arms outstretched 'until weary — "beseech pardon of God," "May I receive mercy," "I believe in the Trinity," that is what one sings without ceasing.' In this same position genuflections, often in the hundreds, would be performed and later perhaps several dozen 'properly administered lashes', all the while 'praying withot respite, as though one were at the very gates of hell'.

The Céli Dé were a significant force in Irish life c. 800, but political turmoil later on in that century prevented any lasting effect on the Church. Another more telling reason that the reformers never really caught on was that the Céli Dé were just too passive and independent. A St Benedict or a St Gregory with more organising talents or a coherent, simple Rule, might have made something out of the zeal that people like Máelruain engendered in their followers. Instead we have a wild jumble of penitentials and prohibitions, a disordered and almost private fanaticism that appealed no doubt to the unruly Irish mind but proved incapable of permanent root. And perhaps, though some might disagree, there just wasn't any widespread support among their fellow brethren for the ascetic reform. In 824 the nearby community of Kildare utterly ravaged the monastery of Tallaght, taking off booty and leaving many dead behind. That kind of hostility goes a long way towards illustrating their ultimate failure. 'The wise man's work is in his mouth,' wrote one of the Culdees, 'the ignorant man's work is in his hand,' a prophetic remark given the flames that ravaged Tallaght and all it stood for.[5]

12 *Clonmacnoise*

O Shannon of Conn of the Hundred Fights, it is hard to follow thy leaps:
I have not seen one like thee on this side of Ireland's sea.

O stately river of smooth fish, on whose bank is many a habitation of saints.
Irish, fifteenth-century

THE Meadow of the Sons of Nós, better known to us today as Clonmacnoise, is level boggy land. A ridge of sorts, only fifty feet or so above its surroundings, overlooks the Shannon as it winds and meanders south from Athlone to Lough Derg and on past Limerick to the sea. Here we find the Seven Churches of Clonmacnoise founded by Ciarán, son of the carpenter, in 547. The monastery would survive for a thousand years until 1552 when the English from Athlone would come with mules and wagons. 'There was not left', say the Four Masters, 'a bell, small or large, an image or an altar, or a book or a gem, or even glass in the window, from the wall of the church out, which was not carried off. Lamentable was this deed, the plundering of the city of Ciarán, the holy patron.' Between foundation and dissolution Clonmacnoise was witness to repeated acts of violence: 'It was burned down thirteen times between 722 and 1205, sacked eight times by Viking raiders who sailed up the Shannon, attacked twenty-seven times by native Irishmen in various feuds and disputes between 832 and 1163, and six times by Anglo-Normans between 1178 and 1205.' Ciarán, it is said, dying from the plague in 548, foresaw these misfortunes to come and warned his followers to disperse:

When he knew that the day of his death was at hand, he prophesied bewailing the later evils which would be after him in this place. Then the brothers said to him: 'What then shall we do in the time of these evils? Shall we stay here by your remains? Or shall we proceed to other places?' To them St Ciarán said: 'Hasten to other quiet places, and leave my remains just like the dry bones of the stag on the mountain, for it is better that you should be with my spirit in heaven, then to be alongside my bones on earth with scandal.'

This advice was never followed. In the age of great *paruchiae* few were stronger or more famous than Clonmacnoise. In the fields by the river a city of huts and timber buildings housed hundreds of students, craftsmen and visiting monks, many from Britain and even the Continent. Up the Shannon in Lough Ree, north of Athlone, hundreds more lived an eremital existence on island sanctuaries and wooded retreats, secure in the protection of Clonmacnoise. Monarchs and nobles from the three great provinces which bordered the site — Munster, Connaught and Leinster — enriched the monastery with patronage and fine stone buildings, and soon the churchyard was cluttered with royal graves:

May Christ of the arts hold in His keeping the son of my king, Cathal of the Red-Hand!
May God save the person who comes: that is a wish for every cemetery!

Clonmacnoise is arranged in the usual Celtic manner. There is not one church here but seven, the custom being to build an extra chapel when the others became over-crowded, rather than one huge edifice. St Ciarán's is the smallest, probably built on the site of his original wooden oratory and possibly the spot of his initial grave. Excavations there uncovered two very fine croziers, now in Dublin's National Museum. Scattered about are the ruins of later churches, each somewhat larger than its pre-decessor, capped by the Cathedral (a rather portentous categorisation) that in no way resembles the mighty gothic buildings so familiar to us from travel posters and art books. The Cathedral, nonetheless, is a specifically Irish pleasure — scaled to life, modest, and best of all, often deserted. As a result the few architectural embellish-ments that remain (there are two fine doorways and some examples of interior stonework still in place) stand out with a clarity I find remarkable. In some ways, perhaps, the less there is to see the better.

What has managed to survive, both here in the Meadow of the Sons of Nós and at all the other monastic sites in Ireland, are gravestones. Clonmacnoise accumulated a sub-stantial portion of its wealth from burying the nobility of Ireland, supporting in the process a variety of craftsmen and workers. Over five hundred examples of their skill, with Celtic crosses and lovely, tortured Gaelic inscrip-tions, lie scattered about in the cemetery. Some of the better slabs have been set in a wall, and the wealth of variations and styles is impressive. There is no better place in the country to examine the graphic designs of Celtic stone work than here at Clonmacnoise. In addition there are three high crosses and several eighteenth- and nine-teenth-century memorials of considerable interest; also a ruined castle just a few hundred feet away and the Nun's Church, a five-minute walk through the fields. But the real thing to notice here is the river. From a hillock about a half mile from the monastery the entire flat tabletop of central Ireland spreads as far as the eye can see. And curling slowly through its heart, the Shannon.

Men will quake with terror
Before the seventy sea-oars
Are given deserved respite
From the labours of the ocean.
Norwegian arms are driving
This iron-studded dragon
Down the storm-tossed river
Like an eagle with wings flapping.
The Orb of the World

Norwegians initially appeared off Irish waters at the turn of the ninth century. Like their fellow Scandinavians, the Danes and Swedes, they were a rapaciously daring people with enormous vigour. Their mask could vary as occasion demanded — merchant, colonist or warrior — but the objective was always the same: to find a foothold and to keep it.

The Norwegians were the first of the Viking peoples to leave their Baltic homeland for the simple reason that they were the first to run out of space. Essentially a farming and fishing people they found their population too large to sustain given the mountainous, wintry character of the country; what fertile valley fields they possessed had long since been settled. Expansion east was impossible for most of the same reasons, the Swedes too feeling pressure all their own and looking to Finland and the Slavic lands for release. In Jutland and the Southern Baltic islands the Danes were settled, and comfortably so, not yet at peak capacity. But only war of a scale unimaginable could forge a Norse community there, and prospects were apparently thought better out in the North Atlantic amid foreign ter-ritories. Around 790 the first of the great migrations began.

The Orkney Islands, seventy in number and grouped off the northeastern coast of Scotland, were the key to these preliminary Norwegian expeditions. The idea was to find land, uninhabited if possible, and fertile. Resistance, if slight or disorganised, was considered an acceptable risk in the process of colonisation, but at first the raiding and pillage that is synonymous with the word Viking was low key or non-existent. The barren Shetlands, an island group seventy miles further north than the Orkneys, were also populated, and farming setttlements peacefully

171

Grave slab,
Clonmacnoise,
Co. Offaly

Grave slab,
Clonmacnoise,
Co. Offaly

established on the Outer Hebrides, due west of the Scottish mainland. Trouble began when scouting parties began coursing further south on either side of Scotland and discovered communities of men living in complete isolation amid gold and silver. The temptation was too strong, and the fall of the monasteries commenced.

The first recorded instance of a Viking raid in the British Isles is dated 793 — the sack of Lindisfarne, the Holy Island, a monastery of Columcille's *paruchia* off the eastern coast of northern Britain. Alcuin of York, tutor to Charlemagne, the first of the Holy Roman Emperors, wrote home to the King of Northumbria that

Lo, it is nearly 350 years that we and our fathers have inhabited this most lovely land, and never before has such a terror appeared in Britain as we have now suffered from a pagan race, nor was it thought that such an inroad from the sea could be made. Behold, the church of St Cuthbert spattered with the blood of the priests of God, despoiled of all its ornaments, a place more venerable than all in Britain, is given prey to pagan peoples.

One year later in 794 the Norwegians returned 'like stinging hornets' to sack Jarrow, another coastal monastery further south than Lindisfarne. In 802 they raided Iona, and Inishmurray off the Sligo coast in 807. That same year they returned to Iona and this time burned it to the ground. Over sixty monks were slaughtered.

At first the Norwegian attacks were sporadic and non-committal. Only island sanctuaries and the more remote of monastic communities were plundered and mostly during summer. With the coming of winter gales the Vikings returned home to their wind-swept ocean havens and became once more peaceful herders and farmers. Only the utilitarian genius of their finest creation, the longship, developed the raids into something more devastating.

The Viking from birth was a man of the sea. Denmark is made up of over five hundred islands and Norway, with its villages in fiords and isolated mountain valleys, was dependent on water-borne transport for communication and trade. Shipbuilding and navigational science were high art among the Scandinavians to an extent unknown anywhere else in the world. To leave behind the sight of land was no great feat for a Viking, to sail where man had never gone, no fearful journey.

The key to all this was the longship, one of the sturdiest and most seaworthy of craft ever built, and the key to it was the keel. The keel is a centre beam running along the bottom of a boat, prow to stern. From it support beams radiate to form the frame of a ship, over which outer planks are affixed in overlapping fashion. The keel was a Viking discovery and it revolutionised Scandinavian society:

It is not known when or how they evolved the keel, but the significance of this detail of construction is clear. With it they could make their ships broad and flat. Keels gave them seaworthiness and stability, and at the same time made them easier to propel. This stability in turn permitted the use of mast and sail on the open sea, thereby increasing range and speed. The construction below the waterline was strong, and at the same time so elastic that it could yield and still resist the powerful pressure of the waves.

The Gokstad Ship,[1] discovered in 1880 in a Norwegian burial mound and thought to date from *c*.850, is representative of the ocean-going longship: seventy-six feet in length, seventeen feet wide and six and a half feet from keel to gunwale. With a ship's crew of seventy men, estimating their weight at about 175 pounds each (making a total of 12,250 lbs); weapons and ship's gear at 3,655 lbs; food and water 5,500 lbs; miscellaneous cargo at 2,200 lbs; and actual ship's weight at 18,750 lbs, we come to a total of over 42,000 lbs, or twenty-one tons. Fully loaded, however, the Gokstad ship's draught (how much of it lay below the waterline) is a remarkable thirty-six inches. That measurement alone spelled devastation for Clonmacnoise.

In the 820s the Norwegians became bolder and began to raid mainland monasteries largely in search of plunder. Their technique was generally the same: a sudden arrival off sandy shores, their longships rowed full force onto the beach, a spewing forth of warriors, the fast pillage of everything portable and the torch to huts and roofing, the indiscriminate murder of monks or their capture as slaves, a quick retreat back to their boats and out to sea again — all before native levies could gather from outlying raths to organise an attack. Skelligs in 823, Iona again in 825 and Bangor, Downpatrick and Movilla that same year, Clonmore and Armagh in 828 and so on every year with increasing frequency. In 840 the Vikings ranged inland.

The warfare was more or less continual from that date on. The Norse were no longer returning home each winter to the Orkneys but settled along the Irish coast, founding towns and villages (the first in Ireland) such as Dublin at the mouth of the Liffey, Waterford on the Suir, Limerick on the Shannon, Cork on the Lee and Wexford at the Slaney. Expeditions were carried forth from these bases to a host of targets ranging from Ireland itself to southern Britain and even Gaul. Norse raids up the Loire and Seine rivalled Danish attacks along the Frisian coast and the Rhine. Nowhere seemed safe from Viking terror:

> The grey eagle's talons
> You reddened with blood, great king;
> On all your expeditions
> The hungry wolves were feasted.
> *The Orb of the World*

The series of Ordnance Survey maps (½ inch to the mile) published by the government in Dublin is the best introduction I can think of to an impact study of Viking strategy. They chart the mouth of the Shannon Estuary as far as Limerick City, for example, following the river from there upstream to Lough Derg, then passing Clonmacnoise to Athlone and Lough Ree. Tracing your finger further north the Shannon's source can be found, Lough Allen in County Leitrim, over two hundred miles in all. An exercise such as this draws two conclusions, one quite obvious — the prodigious reach of the Shannon. It plunges straight into the country's interior, then due north for most of its course, an almost ideal highway.

And secondly, the ½ inch maps are excellent in their identification of monastic and ecclesiastical ruins still remaining. There are literally dozens and dozens of such sites on either side of the Shannon and the lakes it feeds, and these represent but a fraction of the total number that existed in the 840s. Islands in particular were overrun with churches and while the actual wealth that may have been stored in any but the greatest of these communities (such as Clonmacnoise and Clonfert) was probably insignificant, the disruption of religious life by a Viking presence must have been immense. In 844 the Vikings in their shallow-draught longships came up the Shannon from their settlement in Limerick, led by a Norse chieftain called Turgesius. Clonmacnoise was burned to the ground and Ota, wife of Turgesius, 'gave heathen oracles' on the high altar. The fleet continued to Lough Ree and there, to the horror of all, encamped as a permanent feature. Ranging at will the Vikings plundered everything in sight. When local levies arrived to contest them, more often than not the Vikings retreated to their boats and simply rowed out to the middle of the lake to hoot and laugh. In Ulster the same thing: shallow-draught boats were sailed and hauled up the Bann to Lough Neagh, there to roam at pleasure. In Carlingford Lough, open to the sea, yet a third fleet was stationed. Bangor, renowned for over two centuries as the monastery of Columbanus, was so reduced that it never really recovered, and many were the smaller houses that simply disappeared.

As far as the Norse were concerned the complicating factor at this point was not Irish resistance but competition from the Danes. Since 835 Danish raiders had been content to confine their activities to the channel coasts of the Continent and eastern Britain, but in 849 a Danish fleet of over one hundred ships turned up off Ireland. This internecine feud went back and forth for about four years, the Danes winning Dublin in 851 and the huge battle of Carlingford Lough the next year. That struggle had lasted a full three days on both land and sea, the fight at first going well for the Norse. Irish annals record that in despair the Danes went so far as to pledge fealty to St Patrick (in the form of an offering, gold and silver) should they emerge victorious. With the Saint's

Clonmacnoise, Co. Offaly

assistance they did in fact end up triumphant and, as if out of the blue, Irish messengers appeared to collect payment. These riders were horrified to find the Danes calmly eating dinner on top of mangled corpses lying scattered on the battlefield, the heat of their campfires causing the bellies of these deceased foes to 'burst, revealing the welter of meat and pork eaten the night before. The messengers reproached them but they answered that their enemies would have wished to do the same to them'. In accordance with their pledge they turned over a large chest of treasure, 'for the Danes had at least a kind of piety,' according to the annalists, 'they were for piety's sake capable of ceasing for awhile their eating and drinking.' In 853 the Norse regrouped and bloodily regained Dublin, and discouraged by the tenacity of the contest, many Danes withdrew to England.

These scuffles between Dane and Norse reveal the basic instability of the Viking position. Despite the recapture of Dublin by the Norse and the resumption of unlimited warfare it was really only a matter of time before their effectiveness was countered. The Norwegians were essentially too few in numbers. Hit-and-run raids, the propaganda of their cruelty, the savage terror of sleek dragon ships, were diluted once the Norse settled among the Irish and became preoccupied with trade. They intermarried with Celtic families of noble blood to secure their positions, became allies and enemies along the usual Irish lines and generally began to lose themselves in Gaelic society. Their own lack of unity had much to do with this evolution. None of the Norse towns was allied with any of the others nor did the ties of nationalistic kinship mean a thing. In the Orkneys, for example, raids during summer months were oriented as much towards the homeland as towards the Irish or Britons. In 875 the first king of a united Norway, Harold Haarfagr, actually led an expedition himself to the Orkneys to deal with their anarchistic ways and defeated the local jarl decisively. He granted the earldom to a follower named Rögnvald, who in turn passed it on to his brother Sigurd. Rögnvald is interesting in an Irish context only because of his son, Rolf the 'Ganger' or Walker, better known to us today simply as Rollo.

Rollo was apparently something of a problem child. His deadly temper (and the depredations that followed) were enough to brand him an outlaw in Norway itself, and he fled to the Hebrides with a band of renegades. From there he led a life of banditry, mostly in the form of expeditions into Ireland, until the political climate there forced him to travel elsewhere along with other predatory warriors too wild to settle down. Tradition has it that he gathered round him a sizeable number of Danish pirates and c. 910 entered France by way of the Loire. Early successes brought him more and more men until by the time he reached Chartres, just south of Paris, Rollo found himself at the head of an army. On 20 July 911 he was checked there by the Emperor Charles III (called 'the Simple') but not so badly that a bargain wasn't struck between them. Charles, like all the Frankish kings, sought to emulate the Roman custom of hiring savages to fight his battles for him, preferably at the extremities of his domain, thereby sparing interior counties the devastation of constant warfare. In Charles's case, since terror always came by way of the sea and inland waterways, the smart idea would be to settle these mercenary, bloodthirsty people at the mouths of important rivers and let them absorb the shock of future attacks. In return for a small grant of land around Rouen, at the foot of the Seine, and a subsidy of gold and silver, Rollo pledged fealty to the emperor and pledged death to any Viking so bold as to enter France by means of that river. He also became a Christian, ostensibly as further proof of his loyalty.

Rollo's new lands, to bring this adventure full circle, formed the nucleus of the later kingdom of Normandy, and the Normans, after their conquest of England in 1066, would try their hand in Ireland just a hundred years later. As descendants of a Viking pirate, William the Conqueror and Richard FitzGilbert de Clare, the Earl of Pembroke, but better known by the nickname Strongbow, would return in force to the scene of Rollo's first adventures. Curiously enough they would do so without any particular realisation of their Viking heritage; to the Normans, many of whom were illiterate, their background was simply irrelevant. The Conquerer and Strongbow represent an end result, the evolutionary product of earlier generations of Vikings who simply jettisoned (no doubt unconsciously) the ethnic individuality of their Scandinavian culture. Within just a few decades of Rollo's death the dukes of Normandy had been thoroughly Gallicised.

We find this same characteristically Viking assimilation in Ireland, to the point where linguists can find barely a trace of any Scandinavian influence on Irish place names, and aside from a few loanwords (mostly connected with the sea or shipping terminology), Viking settlers seem to have had an utterly neutral effect on the Gaelic vocabulary, a startling analysis, given their two centuries of presence in this country. The impression we are left with is that once their raids were checked (Turgesius, for instance, was finally caught by a powerful chieftain and drowned in Lough Owel) the Norse in Ireland turned mostly to mercantile affairs. The easing of population pressures from Norway may also serve to explain their lessening impact on Irish society. The Faroe Islands had been discovered *c*. 800 and Iceland in 870.[2] Further expansion, with each additional social squeeze, was due west — Greenland in 985 and Labrador after that. Ireland remained important, as Clontarf was to indicate in 1014, but the Norse generally fade away with time. Unlike the Danes who did indeed conquer and then hold great portions of England, and even placed a king, Cnute the Great, on its throne, the Norwegians never achieved anything more than a transient authority. As for that great rogue Rolf the Ganger, he seems to have died in his bed, a whoremonger and killer to the end. Out of respect for his clerical advisers he paid a great sum of money to neighbouring monasteries to have commemorative masses sung for the repose of his soul, but at the same time he ordered the execution of a hundred Christian slaves to appease the Viking gods of war.

Although Irish life survived the Vikings many changes came about as the result of their intrusions. The Church, for instance, underwent a reverse purgation of sorts as the Céli Dé reform halted dead. Despite the Culdee opinion that Viking terror represented God's personal dissatisfaction with Irish monastic abuses, the response of the regular clergy proved worldly and realistic: they wanted protection not prayers. Many communities simply put themselves completely under the authority of local chieftains and their *fine*, or sought to scramble as best they could for the services of powerful warlords from far away. The result was a predictable surge in the secularisation of Church affairs rather than a cleansing of the spirit. For the abbots involved there seemed little choice if they wanted to preserve the wealth of their communities. The Celtic law of compensation was a generally effective restraint if the offender was a Gael, but what good were the brehon codes with heathen Vikings, 'those valiant, wrathful, purely pagan peoples'?

Furthermore there was now the problem of Celtic renegades, men who saw no Viking struck down by lightning when they burned a church or killed a monk. 'In this year,' wrote the annalists for 854, 'many forsook their Christian baptism and joined the Norwegians, and they plundered Armagh, and carried away all its riches.' Perhaps the worst of these offenders was Feidhmid mac Crimthainn, King of Munster, who took advantage of Viking chaos to plunder (among other monasteries) Kildare in 836 and Clonmacnoise in both 832 and 846. He is reputed to have killed the vice-abbot of the latter community on the front lawn, along with that unfortunate man's wife, servant and dog.[3]

Paradoxically, many of the more powerful *paruchia* became even stronger in the course of these evil times. Clonmacnoise derived enormous profit from the destruction of lesser communities in its locale. Survivors of a Viking raid were generally eager to place their holdings under the protection and management of a mightier house, no matter how many times it too had been pillaged. But some of the *paruchia* were not as fortunate. Iona, so long the figurehead of the Celtic church, was almost completely deserted by the monks of Columcille in the year

178

The Abbot and 15 monks were murdered by Vikings here, AD 986 Iona, Argyll, Scotland

Traigh Ban na Manach
'White Strand of the Monks'

Irish Illuminated Manuscript
"Codex 51", *c.* AD 750:
St John the Evangelist and Initial page of St John's Gospel
Stiftsbibliothek, St Gallen, Switzerland

814, most preferring the inland sanctuary of the Columban monastery at Kells in Ireland. They took with them a reliquary containing the bones of Columcille and their illuminated copy of the gospels only just begun, since known as the Book of Kells. In 996 this place too was destroyed in an expedition led by Sigurd the Stout, Jarl of Orkney, who himself would fall in 1014 at Clontarf. Luckily the Book was saved.

The Book of Kells, according to Muirhead, is 'the most beautiful book in the world'. It sits in splendour, a page turned each day, in the Library of Trinity College in Dublin and may well be worth the hyperboles showered upon it. The work is not, however, an isolated example of genius. Illuminated Irish manuscripts of the eighth and ninth centuries lie scattered throughout the libraries of Europe, wherever *peregrini* fleeing terror at home found refuge and settled (and wherever their work survived the later confusion of the French Revolution and its cousins). I mention this only to emphasise the pervasiveness of Irish talent. The monks of Kells had no private vision, no artistic monopoly. They stood in the very centre of a widespread cultural ability.

Illuminated manuscripts are a most fragile treasure, of course, and Viking raids probably saw the majority of these destroyed. It is interesting to inquire, given the fact that not a single Irish monastery seems to have been spared a visit from the Vikings, how any survived at all. That purely Celtic strategem — the round tower — provides the answer, a functional piece of architecture so simple, so utilitarian, and yet so inspired, that it provides the finest working definition of art that we are ever likely to see.

In the nineteenth century there were many antiquarians, mostly Protestant Anglophiles, who refused to credit the Celtic mind with ingenuity enough to design and fashion these incredible structures. Not surprisingly this interest in the question was largely political, to reinforce their prejudice of moral superiority over the standards of a captive and Catholic populace. Civilisation existed before the Celts and after the Celts, but nowhere in between. Racial theories as odd as these helped infect the wild and ingenious tales that have periodically arisen to explain the round tower: that they were built by Phoenicians or Canaanites from the Holy Land, that they served as fire temples or places of communication with the stars, of how African 'sea champions' constructed these 'pillars' as altars to their gods. I even had an Irish lord tell me over dinner some years ago that they were essential to the pagan fertility worship of the penis. At first I thought he was joking, but my wife told me later he was serious. William Stokes had the right idea when he wrote in 1868 that 'a ready method of testing the sanity or insanity of an Irish antiquary is to ask him his opinion as to the round towers,' and the observation still holds true today.

George Petrie was the man who finally settled this controversy. Searching through original source material he found ample reference to these towers as monastic belfries, and ascertained that the stimulus for their construction lay squarely with the Norwegian intrusion. They served multiple functions in those times of great insecurity: as a watchtower, capable of seeing from afar the approach of any raiders; as a signal tower (bell or torch) to warn the monastic community and surrounding countryside as a whole that danger was near; as refuge, a place strong enough where the monks could hide until local forces assembled to drive the enemy away (who never lingered any longer than necessary); as a warehouse where the treasure of chalices and reliquaries, to say nothing of the Books of the Gospels with their jewelled, ornate covers could be brought to safety; and finally as a simple belfry, tolling the various canonical hours of the day. Here at Clonmacnoise there are two round towers, the larger of which must have stood well over a hundred feet high. As it is, the top half has long since collapsed but the diameter of the base (about fifteen feet) gives some indication of its great size. The doorway, as is usual in nearly all the round towers, is about six feet above the ground. A wooden ladder reached up to the entrance which the monks pulled after them when the last of the community had piled in. The door would then be barred, the monks pressed together on the three of four levels of the tower (these would be wooden floors, connected again by a movable ladder) waiting for help to arrive. In a way the first Viking

MacCarthy's Tower,
Clonmacnoise, Co. Offaly

The Round Tower of Ratoo, Ballyduff, Co. Kerry

who saw this ploy in actual use must have admired its simplicity. If he had a few days to spend at leisure it would be an easy thing to make a scaffold high enough to reach the entrance way, then batter through the door to the treasure inside. But successful raids were generally quick raids, and so he'd take what he could but rage over that which he couldn't, locked up as it was with the several dozen hens whose prayers and chanting would seem to mock him from above.

Clonmacnoise was a rich enough place that it could afford a second tower (though smaller, only forty-eight feet high) and it remains a perfect example of the genre with its conical roof still intact.[4] As many architectural writers have observed, these towers represent a logical extension of the beehive principle: sturdy base and then slightly tapering walls until the apex is reached. The decisive factor for a structure so tall, of course, was the use of mortar.

In a way it seems to me that round towers and the delicate yet bizarre illuminated gospels of the scribes have much in common, aside from the fact that one came to depend on the other for its existence. They seem to share an originality of spirit, a resourcefulness very tightly rooted in an imagination profound and yet eccentric. Oscar Wilde, who gave this subject some thought, once wrote that 'everything that is made from without and by dead rules, and does not spring from within through some spirit informing it' was 'dreary' and 'much to be regretted.' He had in mind, among other things, Raphael's frescoes, Palladian architecture, Alexander Pope, St Paul's Cathedral in London and formal French tragedy, to which he contrasted the vitality of the romantic movement which he felt himself to be a part of. And it is interesting to note his opinion that in great art 'there is somehow, and under some form, Christ, or the soul of Christ.' 'There is something so unique' about him, he added later, and staring at the Book of Kells in Trinity Library or the round towers here at Clonmacnoise somehow brings these strands together. The creation of lasting beauty (for want of a better word) in the midst of alarm, terror, violent death — this is an achievement to the lasting credit of the Celtic mind and Clonmacnoise, though little seems to be here, is a full though battle-weary expression of this wayward genius.

13 *Monasterboice*

IT is raining today, wet and soggy underfoot. The whine of trucks and heavy traffic from the Dublin-Belfast road just a mile away somehow blends in perfectly with this weedy, overgrown, depressing cemetery. The moisture gives Muiredach's Cross a sheen, but it's a dull and grimy sort of glitter. This most famous of all the high crosses in Ireland in a way leaves me cold.

The Vikings, as we've seen, bent the pattern of Irish life but failed to break it open. The changes which did occur on their account were more evolutionary in nature than radical, a speeding up of social alterations in progress already. The secularisation of the Church is a good example, most graphically illustrated by the clerical adoption of Gaelic as the ecclesiastical medium as opposed to Latin. The monks were no longer writing for themselves in a private, priestly language. In need of secular support they turned their pens to saga lore and Celtic legends, writing in Irish for the amusement of a lay audience and in the process preserving much of an oral tradition that might otherwise have disappeared. We owe the *Táin Bó Cualigne* to just such a set of circumstances and in the *Tripartite Life* of Patrick we see the inevitable result of this involvement in popular entertainment: written for the people, in Gaelic, these stories relate Patrick's emergence as a Christian Cú Chulainn, a gigantic Hero with extraordinary powers.

Displacement of a great many monks from their accustomed homes was another direct consequence of Viking terror, but Irish individuality survived wherever they travelled. Substantial numbers emigrated to the Continent as a second wave of *peregrini* in emulation of Columbanus (but in defiance of the Céli Dé), many of these enriching the Carolingian Renaissance begun in the reign of Charlemagne. The masters of the palace school established by that great king were invariably Celts, throughout the 800s, the best known being John Scotus Erigena, called by one writer (in uncharacteristically awesome terms) 'one of the rare isolated geniuses in the history of culture'. Erigena, a formidable master of Greek (rare for those distracted years) simply appeared on the doorstep some time around 840 and so impressed Charles the Bald that he was admitted to the court as a resident scholar. Just as quietly he slipped away in 877. The work to which he mainly owes his fame dealt with the problem of predestination — *The Division of Nature*, still relevant and still read.[1]

Artistically speaking the Vikings again had a prodding but not entirely original effect on the ways of the Irish. The round tower, devised in self-defence, followed pretty closely the more venerable example of beehive construction, but some might say this evolution is more architectural in nature than artistic — which is why I've come to Monasterboice. This ancient monastery, said to have been founded *c.*530 by a saint called Buithe, is typically Celtic: a minuscule enclosure, two very small churches, a ruined round tower and hundreds of graves. Of more interest are the high crosses.

We have followed the progression of these crosses from as far back as the neolithic pillar stone, but no stage in their development came as quickly or as dramatically as in the 800s when Viking raids provided a stimulus for change. What the Irish needed was something precious that in fact wasn't worth a thing. Also, in the light of the Norwegian penchant for burning what they couldn't steal, it had to be fireproof. And just in case a Viking chieftain decided out of spite to plunder the artifact in question anyway, it had to be heavy enough to discourage the thought. The high cross was a logical solution.

Irish craftsmen turned to stone as their medium in the ninth century. No more jewelled gospels or metalwork, no more chalices or precious vestments, at least for the time being. Stone sculpture and mastery of the chisel, these were the means of earning a wage from clerical employers. Muiredach's Cross, built *c.*900, is probably the best known of all their work. It stands about seventeen feet high and was carved from a single block of stone. Two important features distinguish it from the earliest high crosses, an example of which we saw at Inishmacsaint on Lough Erne: the enigmatic ring (a halo?) that encircles the top half of the crucifix itself, and the addition of carving along the base, shaft and arms of the cross. The latter development in particular is interesting (given the ring is a mystery and will likely remain so forever) in its Viking orientation. The sculptures are like pages from a book, each panel telling a story from scripture — the sacrifice of Isaac, the murder of Abel, Daniel in the Den. The most important lesson is naturally that of the crucifixion itself which occupies the very centre of the cross. What we have here, it seems, is a Book of Kells in stone, something permanent and safe, an instructional medium of great beauty and obvious sanctity, but valueless in terms of gold or silver. Let the Vikings come, there wasn't much they could do to a monument like this except push it over and that was a sacrilege the monks could remedy. It wouldn't take much to right it again.

Muiredach's Cross is remarkable for its nearly perfect condition, a kindly fate that many other high crosses haven't had the luck of sharing. In the north, for instance, a large number have been mutilated beyond recognition over the years by sectarian. vandals, and in the south a great proportion were broken up in the course of Irish rebellions by English troops, most particularly Cromwell's. But Muiredach's Cross looks as though it was carved yesterday and somehow that makes it rather dull. It radiates, for this traveller anyway, a decidedly lumpish aura which may be due to its monolithic construction. The sculptor of Muiredach's Cross worked from one great rock, which naturally must have determined the shape and outline of his work. It seems to me this factor imprisoned his spirit, for the form is so heavy and squat that it throws away the grace we come to expect in the finest of Celtic art. Muiredach's Cross is antiseptic and somewhat industrial, as gray as the mist.

Ireland being what it is, a land of plenty, just a few feet away stands the West Cross, as it is called, a contemporary of Muiredach's dated *c.*900. As at Inishmacsaint it was made from three separate pieces of stone and the end result is a sleek, inspired piece of work over twenty-one feet high. There are some two score of panels — enough for several Sunday sermons — wedged in wherever space allows, again dominated by the central theme of Christ's death on the cross. More satisfying, however, is that this particular specimen more appropriately looks its age (many of its biblical carvings are barely decipherable), an assertion of antiquity that is indispensable to the Irish landscape, an arousal of what Rose Macaulay called that 'strange human reaction to decay'.

The full decline of Viking influence on Irish affairs has traditionally been dated to the Battle of Clontarf in 1014 when Brian Bóruma, reputedly the first authentic High King of Ireland, defeated the Norwegians outside of Dublin with a united Irish army. But as is usual with Irish history there is more invention here than fact.

Brian Bóruma is certainly a famous figure but nationalistic historians tend to confuse the extent of his powers (to say nothing of his hopes and visions) with their own ideas of what a high kingship really was. We must begin to accept the fact that then, as now, there was no such thing as a united Ireland.

The high kingship of Ireland, since we last saw it being fictionalised by the monks of Armagh, had become reality

The West Cross,
Monasterboice, Co. Louth

by the year 1000, at least as an idea. In practice its existence was a bit more shadowy: Uí Néill kings who were strong enough to make their fellows bend a knee were recognised as high kings. The appellation was symbolic and honorary and did little to affect the comings and goings of everyday ambition within the several dozen minor *tuaths* of Ireland. It made, in other words, little difference practically speaking who the high king was. Life went on as usual.

Around the year 963 a characteristically convoluted struggle for power unfolded in Munster, the end result of which saw the kingship of Cashel wrested away from its traditional guardians, the Clan Eóganacht. The new kings were of another dynasty altogether, the Dál Cais, whose territorial origin they'd barely recognise today, the environs of Shannon Airport. The second king of their line was Brian mac Cennétig, who spent most of his early life warring with the Norse of Limerick, whom he finally destroyed (and that appears to be the correct word) some time in 977. He then seems to have turned his attentions to Leinster with an eye, like the Uí Néill before him, to forcing it to recognise the suzerainty of Munster. Leinster appears to have given in by 984 and offered pledges, which made Brian supreme in the south, from whence his name 'Bóruma,' or Brian 'of the Tribute'.

The supposed high king at this point — the strongest of the Uí Néill — was Maelsechnaill mac Domnaill, a warlord of the Southern Uí Néill. In 980 he had defeated in open battle the Viking chief of Dublin, Olav Cuaran, and then sacked the town after a short seige, thereafter claiming its tribute on an annual basis. Nineteen years later Brian was encamped at the very same gates for the very same reasons, and Sigtrygg of the Silken Beard surrendered just as his father had before him. To cement their alliance Sigtrygg gave his mother to Brian in marriage, and himself took as wife Brian's daughter from a previous union. With the Norse of Dublin behind him Brian then turned on Máelsechnaill and forced him to cede the title over. In 1005 on a royal circuit of Ireland Brian paid an official visit to Armagh, sanctuary of the Uí Néill, and recognised its ecclesiastical primacy and that of Patrick in his offering of twenty ounces of pure gold, placed formally on the high altar. In return, on a sheet in the Book of Armagh, his title was ritualistically recorded — 'imperatoris scotorum', Emperor of the Irish.

This single entry in the Book of Armagh has done a great deal to complicate our picture of both Brian and the kingship, to say nothing of his role at the Battle of Clontarf. In point of fact Brian was no different a high king than Máelsechnaill, the only distinction being that Brian, an outsider, had wrenched the honour from its hereditary custodians, the Uí Néill. He was not a ruler of the entire country (nor had Máelsechnaill been); he made no impact at all on the Northern Uí Néill, who remained aloof from both Máelsechnaill and the Vikings; he had no direct control over the internal affairs of Leinster itself; and he made no attempt to consolidate his power by eliminating the many smaller kings and their petty *tuaths*, as any forward-looking Richelieu might have deemed essential. The biggest fable of all, moreover, is that Brian's success at Clontarf was a national effort (All-Ireland) against a national enemy (the Vikings), when in truth the battle represents just a larger than usual internecine feud.

Into the picture now strides a rather forceful personality, that 'most beautiful woman', Brian's new wife Gormlath. At the time of their marriage Brian was getting on, over seventy years of age according to some accounts. Gormlath too was no longer a young woman, but we have no exact idea how old she was. We do know, however, that she had passed from hand to hand enough times to make her dangerous.

Gormlath was an Irish princess, the daughter of a Leinster chieftain. The Icelandic saga *Njál of the Burning* relates she was indeed a beauty but used her assets to ill advantage, exhibiting 'the best qualities in all matters that were not in her own power, but in all those that were, showed herself of an evil disposition.' While she was still a young girl, her family won the kingship of Leinster, her brother Máelmórda being the first of their line to wear the crown. In a political move she was married to the Viking chief of Dublin, Olav Cuaran, an important alliance given that city's strategic position between Leinster and the traditional Uí Néill foe. She bore Cuaran a son, Sigtrygg of the Silken Beard.

In 980, as mentioned previously, Máelsechnaill the Uí Néill high king defeated Cuaran and forced the Vikings to break their pact with Leinster. Cuaran reputedly saw in this downfall a punishment for his many sins, renounced Gormlath as his wife, converted to Christianity and set sail for Iona where he lived as a humble brother until his death. Máelsechnaill in turn married Gormlath, only to divorce her just a few years later. She returned to Dublin where her son Sigtrygg now ruled, just in time for Brian Boru's expedition of 999, the result of which was her third marriage, this time to the aged king. When Brian withdrew to his lands in the west, Gormlath went along as well.

These political marriages, as one Norwegian historian has remarked, 'were desperately entangled' and that holds true of every aspect of the Clontarf affair. At some point between 1000 and 1012, for instance, Gormlath was cast aside yet again — Brian divorced her. Brooding in Dublin she began needling her brother Máelmórda, the king of Leinster, over his payment of tribute to Brian. On a visit to the 'emperor' in 1012 the indignity of it all finally reached a peak and insults were exchanged. Máelmórda returned to Leinster and renounced his allegiances. Sigtrygg Silkbeard, King of Dublin, had little choice but to side with Leinster. If he hadn't his own mother might have slit his throat.

Nationalistic historians, convinced that Ireland was benevolently united and Brian a king in the modern sense of the word, have termed Maelmorda's behaviour as 'treason', which is not an accurate assessment. He was feuding, true, but there was nothing unusual about that, and Brian's reaction was certainly low key: it took him a year to bother and come himself to deal with Máelmórda, and his first seige of Dublin (where the King of Leinster and Sigtrygg had united forces) proved a lacklustre affair. He withdrew in the winter of 1013.

Sigtrygg, who is an interesting figure throughout all of this, was apparently unenthusiastic about fighting with Brian. If it hadn't been for his vindictive mother he probably would have avoided the quarrel completely. His best chance of survival, he concluded, lay in attracting other chieftains to come in and carry on the fight themselves, easing the pressure of having to be in the forefront, and hedging his bets in case Brian won. Máelsechnaill, the former high king and former husband of Gormlath, was unlikely to join them against Brian however — the Uí Néill hated Leinster more than Munster — so in true Viking fashion he set out to sea and headed north.

Icelandic sagas record the arrival of a 'king of Ireland, who was named Sigtrygg, the son of Olaf Kvararan' at the court of Sigurd the Stout, Jarl of Orkney. After a week or so of heavy drinking he persuaded the Jarl to try his hand in Ireland. Svein Forkbeard, the Danish warrior, after all, was setting up a kingdom in England and just a few years later his son Cnut the Great would rule there as monarch. Here was Sigurd's chance to do the same thing, and as inducement Sigtrygg promised the Jarl his own kingdom of Dublin as well as the hand of Gormlath in marriage (she must have had striking looks). Sigtrygg sailed home with promises that the Jarl of Orkney would be in Dublin by spring. He made one additional stop on his return, to visit Brodar, the Norse King of Man. Once again there was heavy drinking, once again a discussion of the incredible Svein Forkbeard, once again the offer of Dublin's throne, once again Gormlath pledged in marriage, and once again a promise made to be in Dublin harbour come spring. Sigtrygg must have gone away happy. In his opinion his only problem now was to keep Sigurd from talking with Brodar, otherwise if the two compared their conversations with Sigtrygg serious complications could develop. Other than that there wasn't much more he could manipulate that hadn't been done already.

On Good Friday 1014 all of these intrigues were resolved outside the gates of Dublin town, on ground occupied today by the suburb of Clontarf. The opposing armies give some indication of the purely regional and private aspects of the fight. On Brian's side were levies from his own Dál Cais and their immediate allies, as well as Norwegian soldiers under the command of Olaf Ospak, the brother of Brodar, King of Man, who evidently saw some chance of profit here for himself. Not included in the 'Royal' army were the Northern Uí Néill or men of Connaught, who ignored the struggle completely. Opposing them were Máelmórda with a Leinster contingent (only men of northern Leinster, however; the

Clontarf, Co. Dublin

kings of southern Leinster had no wish to offend Brian and refused to come); Sigurd the Stout from the Orkneys and Brodar from the Isle of Man. Cagily enough, both sides had question marks: Máelsechnaill, the former high king and supposedly allied with Brian, jockeyed back and forth with his army on the edge of the battlefield but never committed his forces; and on the other end of the field, viewing the fight from his own city walls, stood Sigtrygg of the Silken Beard with many of his Vikings. These two figures apparently saw the coming battle for what it was, a fight for private prestige and profit, otherwise known as feud, and were sufficiently uncommitted to be willing to sit it out until one side gained the day.* If that side happened to be their nominal allies, then perhaps they'd fight.

And it will be one of the wonders of the day of judgment to relate the descriptions of this tremendous onset. And there arose a wild, impetuous, precipitate, furious, dark, frightful, voracious, merciless, combative, contentious vulture, screaming and fluttering over their heads. And there arose also the satyrs, and the idiots, and the maniacs of the valleys, and the witches, and the goblins, and the ancient birds, and the destroying demons of the air and of the firmament; and they were screaming and comparing the valour and combat of both parties.

Irish, eleventh century

Brian himself, a man of eighty-six now, watched the battle from a nearby hill, the army under the command of his eldest son Murchadh, who was over sixty himself. We have no idea how many men were actually involved but there is little doubt from the hyperbolic descriptions in both Irish and Icelandic sagas that it was the biggest battle ever seen in Ireland. The struggle was brutal, imprecise and lengthy, lasting the entire day. The saga writers

*However, tradition has it that Sigtrygg's wife (Brian's daughter) yelled encouragement to the Irish from the walls, upon which her husband hit her several times in the face, knocking most of her teeth out.

invented a great many personal duels between some of the more notable warriors ("Where is Domhnall," he said three times. Domhnall answered and said, "Here thou reptile."') but it seems more likely that the battle was one huge hacking line surging back and forth, a maze of soldiers stabbing and spearing, grappling and killing. Sigurd the Stout eventually fell, and one of Brian's grandsons, Turlough by name; so too, finally, did Murchadh but only after heroic battling, for then did Murchadh

put the foreigner down under him, by force of wrestling, and then he caught the foreigner's own sword and thrust it into the ribs of the foreigner's breast, until it reached the ground through him three times. The foreigner then drew his knife and with it gave Murchadh such a cut that the whole of his entrails were cut out, and they fell to the ground before him. Then did shiverings and faintings descend on Murchadh.

And last the Vikings and men of Leinster broke and fled. Some traditions insist that Sigtrygg, seeing the cause as hopeless, barred the gates of Dublin to Viking survivors who then fell victim to the pursuing Irish; others maintain that many were drowned by the rising tides as they tried to reach their longships riding at anchor in the bay. By whatever means these legends do agree that the casualties were fearful. Only the death of Brian in the aftermath of battle was seen as a more amazing loss.

Brodar, King of Man is the villian here. He had been a scourge of the Irish in the beginning of the fight but a Norwegian chief fighting for Brian, Wolf the Quarrelsome, finally 'struck him down three times and sent him flying'. As he wandered about on the fringe of the battlefield he came upon the king, unprotected, and slew him. Brandishing the old man's head he is reputed to have yelled 'Let it pass from mouth to mouth that Brodar felled Brian!' Ubiquitous legend salvages some dignity from this disaster by crediting Brian with a fearful stab before Brodar took his head, a fatal wound from which the Viking died. But Icelandic sources suggest a more gruesome fate for Brodar, his capture by Brian's body-guard, who 'slit open his belly, led him round and round an oak tree, and in this way unwound all the intestines of his

Christ Church Cathedral, Founded by Sigtrygg of the Silken Beard c. 1035, Dublin

body, and Brodar did not die before they were all pulled out of him.'

Brian's body and that of his son and heir were taken in holy procession to Armagh for burial, a great coup for that church. Máelsechnaill, whose behaviour on the battlefield has been questioned, resumed the high kingship once again and held it until 1022. Later saga writers were generous enough not to accuse the old/new high king of any wrongdoing at Clontarf, and suggested instead that he was simply waiting for orders to move up. Interestingly enough, his role as a close but uninvolved spectator was used to its greatest advantage in a literary context: his report proves the most evocative in the entire repertoire of saga concerning Clontarf which was, not surprisingly, immense. 'I never saw a battle like it,' he is reputed to have said,

nor have I heard of its equal; and even if an angel of God attempted its description, I doubt if he could give it. But there was one circumstance that attracted my notice there, when the forces first came into contact and each began to pierce the other. There was a field and a ditch, between us and them, and the sharp wind of the spring coming over them towards us; and it was not longer than the time that a cow could be milked, or two cows, that we continued there, when not one person of the two hosts could recognise another, though it might be his son or his brother that was nearest him unless he should know his voice, and that he previously knew the spot in which he was; we were so covered, as well our heads as our faces and our clothes, with the drops of gory blood carried by the force of the sharp cold wind which passed over them to us. And even if we attempted to perform any deed of valour we were unable to do it, because our spears which were over our heads had become clogged and bound with long locks of hair which the wind forced upon us when cut away by well-aimed swords and gleaming axes; so that it was half occupation to us to endeavour to disentangle and cast them off. And it is one of the questions of Erin whether the valour of those who sustained that crushing assault was greater than ours who bore the sight of it without running distracted before the winds or fainting.

As for Sigtrygg of the Silken Beard, his last minute change of heart when he saw the Vikings and Máelmórda break apparently freed him from any lasting penalty for his role in bringing on the battle. The next year Máelsechnaill attempted to re-establish the tribute that Brian had usurped from the Uí Néill as far as Dublin was concerned, but we have no real information if he was successful. Sigtrygg did convert to please the Irish and built the nucleus of Christ Church Cathedral, still standing, in the centre of Norse Dublin. None of this prevented him from looting Christian monasteries in the immediate vicinity, but in that respect he behaved no differently than any other Celtic king. Some twenty years after Clontarf he finally fell victim to intrigue, the Norse king of Waterford forcing him to flee. Tradition relates that he followed his father's footsteps and ended his days in penance at Iona. What happened to his mother is not known.

Monasterboice slips off behind me as the mist turns to steady rain and the little road runs away southwest past mighty trees, glistening leaves. The last we hear of this ancient place is the death of its abbot in 1122, after which it simply fades away, overshadowed by events too momentous and too fatal. The purge of Celtic Ireland begins, the Vikings give way to a more consistent, united energy. Mellifont Abbey lies just a few miles away, but the warp of centuries lies between.

No church or holy city, no great dun or great rath, green wood or plain that shall not pass away and become unrecognisable.

Irish, c. 1100

14 *Mellifont*

MELLIFONT Abbey is a favourite spot for travellers today mostly on account of its wooded, pleasant atmosphere. It sits at the end of a valley, the river Mattock flowing by to the west, a ridge of hills and forest standing south and east, boxing the place in and giving it a very secure feeling. There are no high crosses here or round towers, no beehive *clocháns* or Celtic oratories. Instead a massive gatehouse, a Continental groundplan, the outline of a cloister, a classic lavebo — in all, European flavours. The 'reformation' of Ireland officially began in this obscure sanctuary. These ruins, scanty yet oddly formal, symbolise the end of a purely Celtic society. The native, insular development of an architectural style, for example, popularly called Irish Romanesque, never survived the incursion of foreign ideas and religious communities of strangers favouring more orthodox design. The famous doorway of Clonfert Cathedral — eccentric, individual, perverse — soon died away in fashion, to be replaced by Cistercian uniformity.

The political situation in Ireland after Brian's death in 1014 was that of an explosive vacuum. Ambition had truly come alive among the Irish now that Viking threats had largely disappeared. Brian's powerful personality and the legends of his kingship (which developed the novel idea of a united country) drove many warlords into deadly campaigns for far-reaching authority. The problem was that no single individual possessed enough strength to impose his will over the others, yet the strength each aspirant did enjoy was more than sufficient to keep the country in turmoil. The phenomenon of high kings 'with opposition' came into being. That phrase alone does much to explain the competition that reigned, as regional kings roved about sparking border wars with rivals, probing for the weak points that would give them advantage. In the middle of all this the Church played a prominent and conspiratorial role. *Paruchiae* took sides, many times because they had no choice, and political initiatives undertaken because of the Vikings simply continued as the times became increasingly violent. Armagh gradually emerged as the most flagrant example. Beginning in 966 and running through eight individuals until 1105, the bishops of that church were without exception married laymen with issue who passed on their position in regular tribal fashion. 'Wickedness in the crook of the pastoral staff,' as one monk lamented: 'The kings who barter the Church of God, they will be deaf in the day of Judgment, and their raths will be very empty.' St Bernard of Clairvaux was even more emphatic. The bishops of Armagh were a 'damned race,' 'an evil and adulterous generation'.

Bernard is one of the truly interesting men of the Middle Ages, a soldier of Christ with a bewildering number of masks. He was an ascetic and mystic, a man of letters and music, yet also a patron of the Knights Templar and advocate of the Second Crusade in 1146. At times he comes across as bloodthirsty and fanatical (his hounding of Abelard is a good example) and yet a piety and selfless devotion more often than not emerge to redeem his image. 'Love seeks no cause nor end but itself,' he could write. 'Its

Romanesque doorway, Church of Clonkeen, Co. Limerick

Romanesque doorway,
Clonfert Cathedral,
Co. Galway

fruit is its activity. I love because I love, I love that I may love. Love is a mighty thing, if so it return to its own principle and origin, if it flows back to its source and ever draws anew whence it may flow again. Love is the only one of all the sense movements and affections of the soul by which the creature can answer to its Creator and repay like with like.'

Bernard represents the watershed of twelfth-century Continental reform. Resurgence of the Benedictine Rule as strictly observed by the Cluniac federation of monasteries, and the spirit of Pope Gregory VII (famous for his stunning triumph at Canossa over the Holy Roman Emperor Henry IV, which later proved illusory) had presaged a broader effort to cleanse the Church of its many failings, the most serious being that of lay interference in church matters outside lay competence, and this was rampant in France, Germany and Italy as well as in Ireland. Bernard, a complicated and energetic man, somehow forced himself to the very centre of this reforming movement and gradually took control of it. His own abbey of Clairvaux, established in 1114 with just a few brethren, on his death would claim a fellowship of over seven hundred monks and countless daughter houses. His immediate pupils became bishops and cardinals by the dozen and one, Eugenius III, even became pope. Without a doubt he was the single most influential churchman of his day and the federation he did so much to create — the Cistercians — the most dynamic. His interest in Ireland, curiously enough, was to come about almost casually.

The Cluniac reforms of the 1000s had had some effect on Ireland, largely by way of Britain after its conquest in 1066 by William of Normandy. The Normans, who were masters of ecclesiastical intrigue, followed similar strategy in whatever territory they won, be it Sicily, the Holy Land, Britain or later even Ireland itself: they always supplanted the local clerical hierarchy with appointments of their own. In 1070 a Norman archbishop of Canterbury was duly installed and for the next forty years he and his successors (the most notable of whom was St Anselm) had their eye on Ireland, in particular the emerging centres of mercantile power, the Norwegian city-states.

Sigtrygg of the Silken Beard had led the way after Clontarf, converting to Christianity and ordering all his followers to do the same. Sigtrygg himself even went on a pilgrimage to Rome, coming back with suitable relics for his cathedral in Dublin. In general practice the bishops who presided over these 'urban' sees remained officially nonaligned, but many were apparently trained and educated in England, and Canterbury soon began claiming these bishoprics for its own, a direct challenge to the primacy of Armagh. In the course of this tussle, revelations of Celtic abnormalities again came into view ('a sort of paganism brought in under the name of Christianity') and again proved appalling news to those of the more civilised opposition. Even many of the Irish conceded that something had to be done, and the principles of Continental religious observance began to be discussed in earnest for the first time in years.

At the head of the list was that nagging question of clerical celibacy. The Céli Dé had denounced the abuses as far back as the 700s, to no particular advantage, and the unrest of the times had entrenched the practice of matrimony as standard monastic procedure. Some reformers within the Church apparently came around to the idea that no headway at all was possible unless the problem was attacked at its very root. Clerical sin, they decided, was merely the extension of secular sin; reform the standards of society at large and the end result would be perhaps the hoped for clerical reform.

Sexual misconduct, in terms of lawful Christian behaviour, was certainly a widespread feature of Irish life in the eleventh century. Divorce was commonly practised as a matter of policy and the keeping of concubines had long since been formally sanctioned in the brehon codes. Gormlath's travels from one marriage to another were not considered unusual by anyone but the foreign priests, and the initial response to their attempts at reformation proved sarcastic. St Anselm, writing with a Norman attitude from far away Canterbury — and trying persistently to insinuate his way into Irish affairs — lectured the king of Munster sternly on his ignorance of basic Christian morality: 'It is said that husbands exchange their wives freely and publicly with

The Rock of Cashel, Co. Tipperary

the wives of others, as a man might exchange one horse for another or any other thing for something given in exchange. If your excellency cannot yourself read the texts of Holy Scripture which forbid this wicked practice, order your bishops and religious clerks to expound them to you, so that having learned their teaching you may know with what zeal you ought to be watchful and eager to correct this abuse.' To which the brehons, with a sense of irony they surely must have enjoyed, replied with references to the Old Testament: 'There is a dispute in Irish law,' one of them wrote, 'as to which is more proper, many sexual unions or a single one; for the chosen people of God lived in plurality of unions so that it is no more impossible to commend it than to censure it ' These early exchanges proved discomfiting to the clerical party, but persistence was a virtue Romanisers had in plenty.

In keeping with previous patterns, valid for centuries past, the south of the country proved the first to bend. In 1101 on the Rock of Cashel in Munster a synod was held that methodically condemned the most serious of ecclesiastical flaws. Symbolic of the growing momentum for reform was the gift to the Church of the Rock itself, free of any obligations or dues, by the King of Munster, Muirchertach Ua Briain, a truly startling bequest.[1] The prohibitions agreed upon reflect enthusiasm in the atmosphere. Various matrimonial practices provided for by the brehons were vigorously condemned and their by-products as well: married abbots and bishops, the buying and selling of religious posts by laymen or others, plurality of bishops in a single monastery, the taking of a wife by a priest and so forth. Ten years later at the synod of Rath-breasail (also in the south, County Tipperary) a formal episcopal system was devised to separate even further cleric from layman by shattering the power of landed *paruchiae*. The island was mathematically divided in two, Cashel to be the archbishopric of one half, and Armagh of the other. Twenty-four dioceses were established (twelve under Armagh and twelve under Cashel) with a single bishop to rule completely in each, responsive only to the commands of his archbishop. Abbots were henceforth instructed to obey the wishes of bishops appointed in the dioceses where their holdings existed. The net effect, if successful, would be the drastic shrinkage of abbatical controls since the very strength of *paruchiae* derived from their widespread geographical distribution. Patrick's original scheme for episcopal organisation had at last come full circle: inception, eclipse, now finally resurrection. The current problem was implementation.

The north, as usual, refused to cooperate. By this time Armagh had beaten off the rather fanciful attempts by Canterbury to challenge its position as primate of Ireland. But in a strange reversal of roles the community of Armagh found itself in the same position as that of its arch rival Iona in 700, four centuries before. Bishop Cellach of Armagh, appointed in 1105, was like Abbot Adomnán of Iona before him a member of the 'reform party'; but his community was not, nor were the 'adulterous' family that had controlled the affairs of Armagh for over a century. Cellach had come to the post only by virtue of his being one of the family, and the fact that he happened to be a priest was considered merely a coincidence ('For they suffered none to be bishops but those who were of their own tribe, and although at times clerics failed of that blood, yet bishops never.'); by preaching and practising reform he was turning against his own kin, and tempers began to flare.[2]

In 1121 Cellach left Armagh to try his zealous hand in Dublin, another bishopric in need of improvement. He left the direction of Armagh in the hands of a kindred spirit, the future St Malachy of Down.

Malachy was an Irish Bernard of Clairvaux, born in 1095 in Armagh itself. At the age of eleven he was fostered to the Church where he soon developed a decidedly sombre outlook on life which would serve him well as the years passed by.[3] Bernard, who wrote a *vita* of Malachy in 1148, said he was 'a boy in years without a boy's playfulness. He behaved as an old man.' In his teens, as a penitential exercise, Malachy spent his time roaming through Armagh gathering up the bodies of the poor, whose burial often consisted of being rolled into ditches by the side of the road. He established a potter's field and dug graves for days at a time. His sister, 'abhoring the indignity [as it seemed to her] of his office said: "What are you doing, madman? Let the dead bury their dead." And

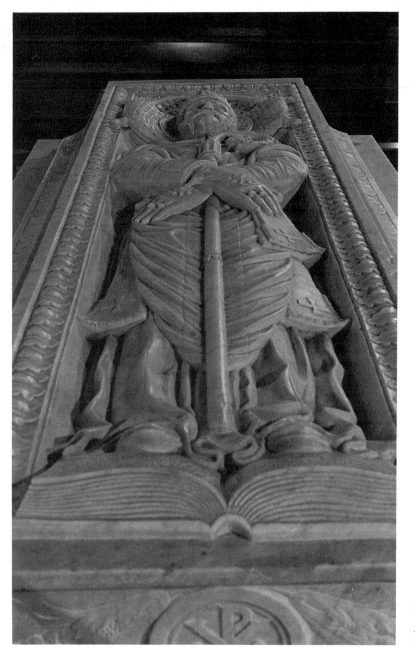

The Tomb of Columbanus,
Bobbio, Emilia-Romagna,
Italy

she attacked him daily with this reproach. But he answered the foolish woman according to her folly.' In 1120 he was ordained to the priesthood.

His handling of Armagh in Cellach's absence was sturdy enough that in five years he was consecrated a bishop in his own right, and in that capacity he attempted the reformation of the decaying monastery of Bangor. According to Bernard his work went well at first as 'barbarity ceased' and the monks were persuaded 'to admit reproof, to receive discipline'. Ranging further afield Malachy sought to cure the evil ways of his secular flock, particularly with respect to their matrimonial habits, and there he ran foul of local warlords. 'For out of the north all evil breaks forth,' and Bangor was burned to the ground. Malachy fled for his life to more congenial portions of the country, somewhere in the south, there to await a new mission which finally arrived in 1129 with the staff of Cellach.

Irish bishops enjoyed this form of deathbed calling card. Columbanus, dying in Italy, had sent his pastoral staff all the way to St Gall in Switzerland as a sign of forgiveness in a dispute that had destroyed their friendship years before. Cellach, it appears had a more political motive in mind. As the symbol of office he meant the transfer of his crozier to designate Malachy as a chosen successor. His idea was to break the secular stranglehold over Armagh that the Synods of Cashel and Rathbreasail had specifically condemned, that 'execrable succession,' that 'distorted right worthy of any sort of death'. But 'one of that evil seed,' a married layman by the name of Murtough, was legally elected to the vacant office of Patrick's *coarb* according to the usual procedure of hereditary transfer, and Malachy stayed where he was. In 1139, however, he travelled north with Cellach's staff and camped outside the walls of Armagh — a *coarb* of Patrick — 'with opposition'.

'For five years,' in Bernard's words, 'relying on the secular power, Murtough fastened himself upon the church, not as a bishop but as a tyrant.' On his deathbed, moreover, he designated one of his relatives (Niall) to succeed him in order to frustrate the campaign of Malachy: 'He was going forth to be damned' according to

Bernard's prejudgment, 'but in the person of Niall he would go on adding to the works of damnation.' The tides were running too fast for this wretched fellow, however, and in just a short time amid conspiracies and murder plots Niall was forced to flee the town, stealing the Book of Armagh and the Staff of Patrick to symbolise his frustration. Malachy entered in triumph and ruled until 1139 when Niall finally died and the relics were returned.

Through all of this (and the foregoing is but a sketch of the intrigues involved) Malachy proved himself a man of severe and forceful temperament. Like Máelruain of the Céli Dé his life was dedicated to the single goal of reform. Unlike Bernard he appears to have had few other interests, and with characteristic perseverance we find him resigning the archbishopric of Armagh once the struggle with Niall drew to an end, returning once more to Bangor to finish what he had begun so many years before. In 1139 he made his first pilgrimage to Rome in order to secure papal authority for his work in Ireland. On the way he stopped at Clairvaux.

The friendship that developed between Malachy and Bernard was a natural one from the start. Malachy couldn't help but be impressed with the constancy of Cistercian life: there were no individual idiosyncrasies, no independent choice and no variety in custom. Conformity to simple, austere rules governed the behaviour of every monk no matter what his rank or place of domicile. It seemed a perfect way to channel the natural but often unruly piety of the Irish into an acceptable format, rid forever of Celtic eccentricities. Over their Bibles and walking through the fields, Malachy and Bernard shared their vision, Bernard no doubt the more domineering and outgoing of the two, Malachy withdrawn and humourless. Yet in a way it seems that Bernard was more impressed, even overawed, by this simple friend than was Malachy with the urbane and nobly born abbot. Malachy was like a virgin in the eyes of Bernard, he was a throwback to the rustic apostles who surrounded the Lord himself. When the Irishman continued his travels south to Rome he left four of his companions behind to observe firsthand the Cistercian Rule with an eye to establishing the order in Ireland itself. In 1141 Bernard wrote to Malachy, now

Gatehouse,
Mellifont Abbey, Co. Louth

back in his homeland with the new title of papal legate, that 'the time is at hand when, by the operation of the grace of God, we shall bring forth for you new men out of the old. Blessed be the name of the Lord forever, of whose only gift it cometh that I have sons in common with you, whom your preaching planted and our exhortation watered, but God gave the increase.' the next year they arrived, 'a few grains of seed' — the four Irishmen and a handful of French Cistercians — to settle the site arranged for them by Malachy at Mellifont: the first settlers, the pioneers.

At first the tiny community prospered poorly, for most of the French wandered home to Clairvaux in 1144, disenchanted with the ways of their Irish superior, a monk named Christian, one of the original four. 'Concerning our brothers who have returned from that place,' wrote Bernard, 'it had pleased us well if they had remained. But perhaps the brothers of your country, whose characters are less disciplined and who have lent a less ready ear to advice in those observances, which were new to them, have been in some measure the reason for their return.' Christian, it seems, also retraced his steps to Clairvaux (no doubt at the wish of Malachy) to receive further training, and Bernard reported later that 'we have instructed Christian, our very dear son and yours, more fully, as far as we could, in the things which belong to the Order and henceforth, as we hope, he will be more careful concerning its obligations. Do not be surprised that we have not sent any other brothers with him; for we did not find competent brothers who were willing to assent to our wishes, and it was not our plan to compel the unwilling.'

Despite the slow and discouraging start the new community eventually settled in. Even a country as conservative as Ireland could not resist forever the inevitability of change, the essential points of which had been discussed and argued for more than three hundred years. Within a quarter of a century fifteen Cistercian daughter houses were established from Mellifont, many of which remain today as the loveliest ruins in the country: Jerpoint, Dunbrody, Boyle, Bective, Holy Cross (now restored) and so on. Augustinian communities, French and reformed, were also successful transplants. What all of these Continental orders had in common was a contempt for independent, local tradition. Conformity then, unlike today, seemed a virtue.

It all seems a little strange, walking about in the rain through this deserted place, to think that here a whole phase and era of life began its slide over the edge. But then again it's been a lengthy prelude, a thousand years of undiluted Celtic life. The Cistercians, of course, were not the truly decisive instruments of wholesale change. They represent clouds, dark and quarrelsome yes, but clouds just the same. The real storm came later, on their heels in the form of Norman warlords — Strongbow, de Courcy, Raymond le Gros, the de Burghs — and from 1169 on, the scene is seldom calm or undisrupted by foreign nations. The Christ who lived on Gaelic terms, the Irish piety of Skellig Michael, Glencolumbkille, and the hundreds of other sanctuaries that bloomed wherever life seemed bleakest here, would attempt with great vigour to absorb these tidal shocks. The Ireland of today, still true to the faith, reflects this immense effort. But the Celtic Age, the purest Celtic Age, could never survive intact. It would, over the centuries, squirm, fall back, revive, crumble. Mellifont predicts this clearly. It is Irish, but not Celtic.

Malachy bade farewell to Mellifont in 1148. Eugenius III, the Cistercian pope, had just been consecrated and Malachy departed on a second pilgrimage to Rome in the hopes that Eugenius would confer upon him even greater powers to spur on the work of reformation in Ireland. This time he never reached the Holy City. On 1 November 1148 he died in the arms of his friend at the Abbey of Clairvaux. Bernard was so moved that he had the Irish bishop buried at the foot of the high altar, taking Malachy's habit for his own and wearing it to the day of his death five years later. 'Do not take it ill that he is buried among us,' he wrote to the brothers at Mellifont, 'for God so ordered, according to the multitude of his mercies, that you should possess him in life, and that it might be allowed to us to possess him, if only in death.' When Clairvaux was pillaged in the French Revolution the remains of both Bernard and Malachy, buried side by side, were scattered.[4]

And the rain falls harder, making it difficult to hear the approach of Norman arms. Walking away from this place no Irish verse comes to mind, just some words of the Japanese poet Soin,

> Long rain of May,
> The whole world is
> A single sheet of paper
> Under the clouds.

Notes

INTRODUCTION, *Skellig Michael*
Pages 1-20
1. A village in southern Italy.
2. The official history of the Irish lights records that during the gale of 27 December, 1955, a wave knocked out the lantern here on the Great Skellig — 175 feet above sea level. The ocean 'not only put out the light but swept the lightkeeper down the stairs.'

CHAPTER 1, *Newgrange*
Pages 21-49
1. And confusion: radiocarbon techniques have themselves been undergoing re-calibration, though in general terms the conclusions reached by Renfrew and others remain confirmed, even as the dates fluctuate.
2. Specimens of burnt soil allowed archaeologists to carbon date the construction *c.* 2500 BC, now re-calibrated to *c.* 3200 BC. Interesting biological matter embedded in the matting turfs reveal the presence of both wheat pollens (showing some degree of agricultural sophistication) and plant material associated with pastures and fields, proof of extensive land clearances.
3. The composition of the Grand Menhir, a quartzite granite foreign to the immediate neighbourhood but since identified in quarries fifty miles away, leads to astonishing conclusions: Megalithic construction crews had the ability to remove this monster from a stone bedding or pit, then dressed the rock to a needle shape and succeeded in transporting it a goodly distance to the present site, finally erecting the marker with the precision its function seems to have required.

CHAPTER 3, *Tara*
Pages 55-71
1. Excavation proved the mound datable *c.* 2000 BC. Initially a megalithic passage grave contemporary with those of Slieve na Calliagh, its outer layers revealed further use during the Bronze Age. Over forty cremations from this period were discovered. No evidence of Celtic burials was found.
2. For example, even if a lesser king pledged obedience to a higher king, the latter was technically not allowed to interfere in the internal affairs of the former.
3. Later yet another splintering of caste would occur, and law would become a separate study of its own pursued by a branch of the *filid* called brehons.
4. Breton, a branch of the Celtic language once widely spoken in Brittany, was reintroduced to the Continent *c.* AD 500 by Celtic settlers from Britain.

CHAPTER 4, *Cruachain*
Pages 74-82
1. The affection that Yeats and Lady Gregory and other literati had for these sagas during the so-called Gaelic Revival at the turn of the century was not universally shared by some non-Irish observers. J. R. R. Tolkien, for example, wrote that he felt 'for them a certain distaste: largely for their fundamental unreason. They have bright colour, but are like a broken stained glass window reassembled without design. They are in fact "mad".'
2. Now preserved at Clonalis House in the village of Castlerea.

CHAPTER 5, *Downpatrick*
Pages 83-106
1. Saul in Irish is *Sabhall*, or 'place of the barn'.
2. Curraghs.
3. Meaning he had been inattentive to religious duties, even though both his father and grandfather had taken vows in the Church.
4. Between Rathlackan and Killala. Patrick mentions 'the wood of Foclut, which is close by the western sea' as the scene of his enslavement. It is the only reference he makes to an actual place in Ireland.

5. The annals today run into many editions — the Annals of the Four Masters, the Annals of Clonmacnoise, the Annals of Lough Cé, of Ulster, of Tigernach, etc. Two things should be borne in mind regarding their veracity. First, nearly all of these were begun well after the facts they relate, sometimes by as much as two and three centuries. On that count alone they are suspect. Secondly, all the editions we have today have been altered to agree with predetermined details of an official Patrician legend, and thus embody the consistencies of myth more than of fact. As far as the annalists are concerned Palladius died in 432 and Patrick in 461. As these are probably inventions, the temptation to gloss over the inconsistencies of the later obits is sometimes irresistible. This has generally been established as a dangerous procedure, and historians who base their theories solely on the annalists have not been judged fully credible. The only genuine fifth-century writings that we have are Patrick's.

6. Literally, the 'saliva' of my writing.

7. Most experts today reject the notion of this bank as a modern boundary line or continuous frontier wall. It is regarded as a series of obstacles or barriers placed judiciously across then well-travelled lanes or corridors, and primarily designed to prevent the easy passage of stolen cattle.

CHAPTER 6, *The Rock of Doon*
Pages 107-119

1. Kildare, the centre of Brigit's cult, in Irish translates as the 'church of oak wood', a reference to a huge tree that stood on the hill now occupied by a thirteenth-century cathedral. In pre-Christian times this sacred oak was the site of an extremely holy pagan sanctuary, dedicated apparently to the Celtic goddess, Brighid, a patroness of poets and artisans whose two sisters of the same name protected healers and blacksmiths, the latter frequently associated with magic charms and soothsaying. It is doubtful that a Christian saint by the name of Brigit ever existed, or if she did whether the details of her life and personality could have survived that of the better known pagan goddess and her sisters. 'One can scarcely avoid the conclusion,' writes Proinsias MacCana in *Celtic Mythology*, 'that her widespread cult substantially continues that of her pagan predecessor.' The dearth of any detail concerning a historic Brigit was more than made up for by an energetic clergy. In many of her *vitae*, for example, extraordinary stories of her birth (vague and fantistic) served to obscure the fact that no one really knew anything about it to begin with: 'Brigit was born neither within nor without a house, was bathed in milk, her breath revives the dead, a house in which she is staying flames up to heaven, cow-dung blazes before her.'

2. The Gallarus Oratory, located on the Dingle peninsula in County Kerry, is thought to date from *c.* AD 750. By Celtic standards it is huge: 22 feet long, 18 feet wide and over 16 feet tall. Like the small oratories of Skellig Michael and the *clocháns* both there and on the mainland, it stands without mortar or buttress of any kind. On a rainy day it is absolutely dry inside.

No more than a handful of monks could be comfortably accommodated during service, but then again, comfort seems to have been in little demand during the eighth century. Like most Celtic chapels, regardless of size or importance, it was built on an east-west axis. There is only one window, seemingly of very small proportions when viewed from the outside, but in fact deeply splayed like a fan for maximum interior luminescence. This was generally placed in the east wall where the altar stood, to catch the morning sun. These windows were apparently uncovered; certainly there was never any glass though a shutter or skin may have been used in stormy weather. The entrance way has two stone hinges still left where a door was probably fitted, but no such device can be seen around the window.

3. And many like him: Brendan of Clonfert, Comgall of Bangor, Féchín of Fore and so on.

CHAPTER 9, *Lough Erne*
Pages 136-151

1. A monastery in Tipperary.

2. One cycle of the moon equals 29½ days and a year of twelve cycles is a total of 354 days. This conflicts with the solar calendar which determines the passage of time more accurately by studying the ecliptic travels of the sun — i.e. the apparent path of the sun (to us on earth) through the universe as measured by the 'changing' stars in the zodiac. Observation of the stars a half hour before sunrise and a half hour after sunset (heliacal settings) confirm the progress through the skies of distinctive constellations once a year, and ancient man eventually learned to link (for example) a particular star with a particular season. Solar reckoning is relatively precise in terms of both defining what a year really is and for agricultural prognostications. It totals 365¼ days for each year, decidedly out of step with lunar calculations (a 12-month year is 11¼ days too short, a 13-month year is 18¼ days too long). Julius Caesar's calendar of 46 BC — a major reform — was solar. The crucial calculation in terms of a solar calendar is to determine the four seasons — the spring and summer equinox, the summer and winter solstice.

3. The Roman tonsure was the halo of hair — they shaved the top of their heads. The Celts were accustomed to shaving their heads in the front only, from ear to ear.

4. This incorrigibility laste well into the seventh and eighth centuries, its most flamboyant expression being the refusal of the Celtic clergy to break bread with their fellow brethren. Aldhelm, bishop of Sherborne, in fact, noted in 705 that the Irish were in the habit of throwing any food even touched by the 'Roman' party into the pigsty. The use of the dinner table as a field of battle was apparently an attempt to copy the strategy of St Monica, the mother of Augustine, who refused 'to live with me (or) eat at the same table in the house; because she shunned and detested the blasphemies of my error' — his adherence to Manichaeism.

5. As Herbert Muller wrote in his book *The Uses of the Past*, 'No religion that succeeds can be wholly new. Although it must appear to improve upon the past, it cannot break with the past; it must satisfy hopes and desires conditioned by the past; and as it takes root, it draws still more on the past.'

CHAPTER 10, *Armagh*
Pages 152-166

1. According to Anne Fremantle the Celts 'so hated the Saxons that they refused to try and convert them, lest they succeed, and the Saxons be saved'.

2. Colmán retired to a suitably bleak spot, the lovely island of Inisbofin off the western coast of Connemara in County Galway. But friction produced another split in his community 'because the Irish', in Bede's words, 'in summer time when the harvest had to be gathered in, left the monastery and wandered about, scattering into various places with which they were familiar, then when winter came they returned and expected to have a share in the things which the British had provided.' The quarrelling became so bitter that Colman finally obtained a separate grant of land on Connemara proper, near the village of Mayo (known for centuries as *Mayo na Sachsan* or 'Mayo of the Saxons') where he settled the Britons, who in turn established a university of great fame.

3. The most creative solution was that devised by Muirchú who said that an angel of the Lord appeared to Patrick and contradicted his decision to return to Armagh ('which he loved beyond all other places') to die. Upon his death in Saul God ordained that no blood be shed between armies seeking his body and raised the water of Strangford Lough to separate the warriors of Armagh and the Ulaid. A few centuries later, when in fact no one really knew where Patrick lay buried, an elaborate comparison was evolved with Moses, about whose grave there is equal uncertainty, as the Bible admits in the Book of Deuteronomy.

4. Sleaty, County Leix in Leinster.

5. On their own initiative the Southern Uí Néill made up some equally convenient legends known to us today as the *Bóruma Laigen*, or 'The Cattle-Tribute of Leinster.' Like *Táin Bó Cuailgne* these stories represent an enormous catalogue of raids, battles, forays, duels, trickery and bloodshed, but this time the struggle is between the Southern Uí Néill and the men of Leinster. The story line is that for centuries the kings of Leinster have recognised the high kings of Tara as their rightful overlords through the payment of annual tribute. Over the years the size of this tax grew and grew until Leinster began resisting the efforts of the Uí Néill to extract it. The result was more or less constant warfare which the cycle exhaustively chronicles. The *Bóruma's* theme of legal tribute and suzerainty is fictionalised, however, and was created simply to disguise and then legitimise the aggression of the UíNéill against Leinster, in their pursuit of authentic status as high kings. In this respect it differs little from the propaganda devised by Armagh.

6. The one exception being portions of Leinster. The cult of St Brigit was enormous throughout the environs of Kildare, and Armagh recognised this fact of life in the following gift: 'Between S. Patrick and Brigit, the pillars of the Irish, such friendship of charity dwelt that they had one heart and one mind. Christ performed many miracles between him and her. The holy man therefore said to the Christian virgin: O my Brigit, your *paruchia* in your province will be reckoned unto you for your monarchy; but in the eastern and western part it will be in my domination.'

CHAPTER 11, *Tallaght*
Pages 167-169

1. Revised editions of the Bible tend to gloss over the Greek αδελφοί with a very loose translation of 'cousin' or 'brethren' when in fact the literal meaning is 'brother'. These are four in number (James, Joseph, Simon and Jude) and at least eleven passages in the New Testament refer specifically to the Saviour's family. Matthew 13 is typical: 'And it came to pass when Jesus had finished these parables, that he set out from that place. And when he had come to his own country, he began to teach them in their synagogues, so that they were astonished, and said, 'How did this man come by this wisdom and these miracles? Is he not the carpenter's son? Is not his mother called Mary, and his brothers James and Joseph and Simon and Jude? And his sisters, are they not all with us? Then where did he get all this?'' And they took offence at him.'

2. This streak of anti-feminism is very common in the Rules and penitentials of both the earlier saints such as Columbanus

and those of the Céli Dé. The most frequent prohibitions generally revolved around 'the monthly disease'. Nuns, for instance, were not allowed to receive communion or approach the altar at such times ('they are unclean'), and even intercourse between a married woman and her husband was forbidden, the penance being abstention and fasting for twenty nights.

3. The 69th Psalm: 'O God, hasten to me! You are my help and my deliverer; O Lord, hold not back!' etc. A favourite Irish appeal for divine assistance.

4. Or in extreme cases up to one's neck in a freezing stream. An old Irish poem attributed to a monk of the Céli Dé records that both Adam and Eve performed cross-vigils after their expulsion from the Garden of Eden. Adam waded into the Jordan for a stay of forty-seven days and nights, praying for that river and all its frogs and fishes and birds 'to fast with him on God' for forgiveness. Eve performed a cross vigil in the Tigris for thirty days, her hair streaming behind her, gazing silently up to heaven. Bede records the hardships of a Brother Dryhthelm who performed the vigil even in winter, with freezing water 'up to his loins and sometimes up to his neck. Those who saw him would say, "Brother Dryhthelm, however can you bear such icy cold?" He answered them simply, for he was a man of simple wit and few words, "I have known it colder." And when they said, "It is marvellous that you are willing to endure such a hard and austere life," he replied, "I have seen it harder." And so until the day he was called away, in his unwearied longing for heavenly bliss, he subdued his aged body with daily fasts and led many to salvation by his words and life.'

5. Lay enthusiasm for the reform was also lukewarm and a partial explanation must certainly lie with the severity of Culdee views. A Céli Dé penance for manslaughter proclaimed that sinners guilty of that offence had to spend a night alone in an open, fresh grave with only a decomposed body for company. And as the Céli Dé opinion was that 'it is not usual for a layman or a laywoman not to have some part in manslaughter,' the prospects looked grim for a large number of people should Culdee sentiment prove contagious.

CHAPTER 12, *Clonmacnoise*
Pages 170-184

1. Fully restored and mounted in the Viking Ship Museum at Bygdøy in Oslo, Norway.

2. In both these faraway lands the Vikings found Irish hermits. The *Book of the Icelanders* relates, 'There were Christian men here then whom the Norsemen called 'papar'. But later they went away because they were not prepared to live here in company with heathen men. They left behind Irish books, bells and croziers, from which it could be seen they were Irishmen.'

3. There is evidence that some Irish chieftains prior to the era of Viking incursions did not hesitate, when raiding hostile territories, to ravage the churches of their enemies as whim or the opportunity presented itself. Since the early Celtic church was, through its system of *coarb* and *paruchia*, so involved and identified with the fortunes of donor families, it is probably not surprising to see them targeted in the various feuds of competing clans. After carefully analysing the various monastic chronicles, one historian has noted thirty entries which record the *combustio* of a church prior to 792. When compared with the destruction noted after the Viking arrival — over nine hundred between 792 and 1546 — these are generally modest figures, showing that then, as now, society had its problems with outlaws and predators.

4. Only at Devenish, where excavations beside the present tower revealed the foundation of a second, do we find another Irish monastery with two.

CHAPTER 13, *Monasterboice*
Pages 185-193

1. This work was so complex that few of Erigena's contemporaries apparently understood it or proved capable of deciphering its intent. Pope Honorius III, over three centuries later in 1225, caught the independent drift of Erigena's thought and condemned his writings as 'swarming with worms of heretical perversity', a judgment reaffirmed by Gregory XIII in 1585.

CHAPTER 14, *Mellifont*
Pages 194-204

1. It has been suggested that Muirchertach, a member of Brian Boru's Dál Cais, had politics in mind as well in making this gesture. By disposing of Cashel, long the symbol of Eóganachta supremacy in Munster, Muirchertach may have sought to demythologise the site as a political symbol. In his innermost heart he might well have wished to go further, to raze the site and, like the Romans at Carthage, sow the fields with salt.

2. Clonmacnoise was another angry opponent. In the new diocesan system this famous (though now corrupt) community had been ignored completely and just a few months after Rathbreasail it held a synod of its own to correct the situation. Duleek was dropped as a diocesan seat (without

consultation) and Clonmacnoise appointed (by its own abbot) as successor. The reformers acquiesced, probably because they had no choice. From Duleek we have no evidence of a response.

3. The early age was not unusual. Bede was seven when he entered a monastery, an offering to the Church on the part of his parents.

4. Like Cluny, Cîteaux, and many other famous monasteries in France, little remains at Clairvaux to indicate its former pre-eminence. Only the enclosure wall remains for visitors to see, and its good repair does not reflect any particular preservationist zeal among the French, but rather its current utilitarian function. The Abbey grounds and ruins now shelter a penitentiary.

References

ABBREVIATIONS

Barrow. George Lennox Barrow, *The Round Towers of Ireland, a study and gazetter*, Dublin 1979.
A Preliminary Study. D. A. Chart, E. Estyn Evans, H. C. Lawlor, eds., *A Preliminary Survey of the Ancient Monuments of Northern Ireland*, Belfast 1940.
Dunraven I. Edwin, Third Earl of Dunraven, *Notes on Irish Architecture*, ed. Margaret Stokes, Vol. I, London 1975.
Dunraven II. Ibid., Vol. II, London 1877.
County Down. Her Majesty's Stationery Office, *An Archaeological Survey of County Down*, Belfast 1966.
In State Care. Her Majesty's Stationery Office, *Ancient Monuments of Northern Ireland: In State Care*, Belfast, 1969.

J.R.S.A.I. *Journal of the Royal Society of Antiquaries of Ireland.*
Leask I. Harold G. Leask, *Irish Churches and Monastic Buildings: The First Phases and the Romanesque*, Vol. I, Dundalk 1955.
Leask II. Ibid., *Gothic Architecture to A.D. 1400*, Vol. II, Dundalk 1958.
Petrie I. George Petrie, *Christian Inscriptions in the Irish Language*, ed. Margaret Stokes, Vol. I, Dublin 1872.
Petrie II. Ibid., Vol. II, Dublin 1878.
P.R.I.A. *Proceedings of the Royal Irish Academy.*
T.R.I.A. *Transactions of the Royal Irish Academy.*
U.J.A. *The Ulster Journal of Archaeology.*

Numbers enclosed in square brackets at the end
of each entry refer to page folios in the text.

'One of the difficulties...': Eleanor Hull, *A text book of Irish Literature*, Part I, Dublin 1908, p. ii. [viii]

INTRODUCTION-SKELLIG MICHAEL
'men of the bags': see Geoffrey Keating, *The History of Ireland*, trans. David Comyn, London 1902, pp. 189-97. [5]
'Let a fast place...': The *Rule* of Columcille, trans. Curry, in *Ecclesiastical Documents Relating to Great Britain and Ireland*, eds. A. W. Haddan and W. Stubbs, Vol. II, Part 1, Oxford 1873, p. 119. [10]
'strange and incredible custom...': Diodorus Siculus, trans. J. J. Tierney, in 'The Celtic Ethnography of Posidonius', *P.R.I.A.*, Vol. 60, 1959-1960, p. 251. [10]
'We should call a man mad...': Aristotle, *The Nicomachean Ethics*, III, vii, 7, trans. H. Rackham, Cambridge 1962, p. 159. [11]
'As though they were people who can speak [the gods'] language': Diodorus Siculus, op. cit., p. 251. [11]
'Fall upon us...': see Luke 23:30. [11]

'When I am weak, then am I powerful...': Athanasius, *The Life of St. Antony*, trans. Robert Meyer, Westminster 1950, p. 25. Antony begins by quoting from the Bible. See 2 Cor. 12:10. [11]
"It is well to think over what the Apostle says...': ibid., p. 36. See 1 Cor. 15:31. [12]
'Meat and wine...': ibid., p. 25. [12]
'accusing himself of having taken revenge...': Palladius, *The Lausiac History*, trans W. K. Lowther Clarke, London 1918, p. 78. [12]
The 'Aerial Martyr': Evagrius, *A History of the Church in Six Books, from A.D. 431 to A.D. 594*, trans. Henry G. Bohn, London 1854, p. 273 [12]
'great wonder of the world...': Theodoret, 'Historia religiosa', trans. Philip Scaff, in *History of the Christian Church: Nicene and Post-Nicene Christianity*, Vol. III, New York 1884, p. 194. [12]
'built a column...': Gregory, Bishop of Tours, *History of the Franks*, trans. E. Brehaut, New York 1969, p. 195. [12-13]

'He is being punished...': Palladius, op. cit., p. 83. [13]

'Headlong, many fathoms into the sea', and following descriptions: Charles Smith, *The Ancient and Present State of the County of Kerry*, Dublin 1774, pp. 115-16. [13]

'Some were no more than low sluggards...': Scaff, op. cit., pp. 166, 167. [15]

'illumine' his fear: Sean O'Casey, *Autobiography, (Book 4): Inishfallen, Fare Thee Well*, London 1972, p. 149. [15]

'Accidie': John Cassian, 'The Institutes of Coenobia,' trans. Edgar C. S. Gibson, in *A Select Library of Nicene and Post-Nicene Fathers of the Christian Church*, eds. Philip Scaff and Henry Wallace, Second Series, Vol. IX, New York 1894, p. 266. [15-16]

'I went to him and said...': Palladius, op cit., p. 86. [16]

'a most stupid fellow...': St Jerome, trans. James Kenney, in *The Sources for the Early History of Ireland: Ecclesiastical*, New York 1966, p. 162. For complete letter see *Nicene and Post-Nicene Fathers*, op. cit., Second Series, Vol. VI, p. 499. [16]

Sin is 'not born in man...': Scaff, *History of the Christian Church*, op. cit., p. 86. [16]

'if the chastity of the heathen were no chastity...': Julian of Eclanum, trans. Scaff, ibid., p. 809. [16]

'rich, deep life of faith': Scaff, ibid., p. 790. [16]

'This is an old maxim of the Fathers...': John Cassian, op. cit., p. 279. [16]

'Greeks go abroad...': Athanasius, op. cit., p. 37; see also Luke 17:21. [18]

'I saw Satan like lightening...': ibid., p. 54; see also Luke 10:18. [18]

'Memory is a root in the dark': Octavio Paz. See *Alternating Currents*, trans. H. R. Lane, New York 1973, and *The Labyrinth of Solitude: Life and Thought in Mexico*, trans. L. Kemp, New York 1961. [18]

'In the spring and the beginning of summer...': Charles Smith, op. cit., p. 112. [19]

The ocean 'not only put out the light...': T. G. Wilson, *The Irish Lighthouse Service*, Dublin 1968, p. 57. [205, note 2, Introduction]

'Fresh Spring...': Matsuo Bashó, *The Narrow Road to the Deep North and Other Travel Sketches*, trans. Nobuyuki Yuasa, Harmondsworth 1972, p. 78 [20]

'Raw and cold is icy spring...': 'The Four Seasons,' trans. Kenneth Jackson, in *A Celtic Miscellany*, Harmondsworth 1971, p. 67.

CHAPTER 1-NEWGRANGE

'we have no bridge...': Sean O'Faolain, *The Irish*, Harmondsworth 1969, p. 18. [21]

'we know almost nothing about them...': ibid., p. 15. [23]

The Stonehenge architect 'must almost certainly have been a man familiar with the buildings of the contemporary civilizations of the Mediterranean world': R. J. C. Atkinson, *Stonehenge and Avebury and Neighbouring Monuments*, London 1959, p. 22. [24]

Colin Renfrew, *Before Civilization: The Radiocarbon Revolution and Prehistoric Europe*, New York 1973, pp. 109, 249, 247. [24]

'The study of prehistory is in crisis': Colin Renfrew, 'Ancient Europe is Older Than We Thought,' in *National Geographic Magazine*, Vol. 152, No. 5, Nov. 1977, p. 615.[24]

'currant cake': M. J. O'Kelly, 'The Restoration of Newgrange,' in *Antiquity*, LIII, 1979, p. 209. [25]

'Bewildered bullocks': John Waddell, 'The Invasion Hypothesis in Irish Pre-history,' in *Antiquity*, LII, 1978, p. 123. [27]

'This most exquisitely carved stone...': W. R. Wilde, *The Beauties of the Boyne and its tributary the Blackwater*, Dublin 1850, p. 193. [29]

'2 men with crowbars': Richard Burchett, as quoted in Clair O'Kelly, *Newgrange and the other Boyne Monuments*, Cork, 1978, p. 5. [29]

'one of the most remarkable slabs...': Clair O'Kelly, ibid., p. 14. [30]

'We must no longer assert...': Alexander Thom, *Megalithic Lunar Observatories*, Oxford 1971, p. 5. [31]

'a field of quacks': John Eddy, 'Medicine Wheels and Plains Indian Astronomy', in *Astronomy of the Ancients*, eds. Kenneth Brecher and Michael Feirtag, Cambridge, 1979, p. 1. [31]

'We are now in the midst of a campaign...': Philip Morrison, 'Introduction', ibid., p. viii. [32]

'We seldom look at the sky...': Jerome Y. Lettvin, 'The Gorgon's Eye', ibid., p. 133. [32]

'consider the slow eastward slippage...': Harald A. T. Reiche, 'The Language of Archaic Astronomy: A Clue to the Atlantis Myth?' ibid., p. 155. [32]

'a refined academic version of astronaut archaeology': Glyn Danial, 'Megalithic Monuments', in *Scientific American*, Vol. 243, July 1980, pp. 85, 90. [32]

'Each time required the aid of the farmer's cart...': W. J. Knowles, 'Stone Axe Factories near Cushendall', in *P.R.I.A.*, No. 16, 1906, p. 384. [46]

'Spurious articles...': W. J. Knowles, ibid. [47]

'characteristic Antrim porcellanite': E. M. Jope, 'Porcellanite Axes from Factories in North-East Ireland: Tievebulliagh and Rathlin', in *U.J.A.*, Vol. 15, 1952, p. 31. [47]

CHAPTER 2-THE NATIONAL MUSEUM

'against the spells of women...': 'Breastplate,' trans. Rev. Charles H. H. Wright, in *The Writings of Patrick*, London 1889, p. 33. [52]

'Bronze is the best of all metals...': 'Advice to a Prince', trans. Tadhg O'Donoghue, in *Ériu*, Vol. IX, 1921-23, p. 54. [54]

CHAPTER 3-TARA

'Pinnacle of a hundred kings...': ascribed to Cuan O'Lothchain, 'Echtra Mac Echdach Mugmedóin', trans. Maud Joynt, in *Ériu*, Vol. IV, 1910, p. 93. [55]

'Today I buckle on a mighty strength': 'Breastplate', trans. D. A. Binchy, 'Varia III', in *Ériu*, Vol. XX, 1966, p. 234; 'The power of the birth of Christ...': trans. Wright, op. cit., p. 31. [56]

'it is not bravery...': Aristotle, *Ethics Eudemian*, III, 1, 25, trans. J. J. Tierney, in 'Celtic Ethnography', *P.R.I.A.*, Vol. 60, 1959-1960, p. 194. [56]

'whole race is madly fond of war...': Strabo, in 'Celtic Ethnography', ibid., p. 267. [57]

'They are exceedingly fond of wine...': Diodorus Siculus, ibid., pp. 249, 251. [57]

'Posidonius says he saw this sight in many places...': Strabo, ibid., p. 269. [57]

'exceedingly given to religious superstition...': Julius Caesar, *Bellum Gallicum*, trans. Tierney, in 'Celtic Ethnography', ibid., p. 272. [57]

'A king's chariot...': 'De Síl Chonairi Moir', trans. Lucius Gwynn, in *Ériu*, Vol. VI, 1912, p. 130, as quoted in Francis J. Byrne, *Irish Kings and High-Kings*, London, 1973, p. 63. [59]

'Posion is his satire...': *Cormac's Glossary*, trans. John O'Donovan, ed. Whitley Stokes, Calcutta 1868, p. 74. [62]

'A promise made...': 'Advice to a Prince', op. cit., p. 53; see also *Three Irish Glossaries*, trans. Whitley Stokes, London 1862, p. 162: 'Not stronger is the opinion of the multitude than the oath of one man.' [63]

'There are three periods at which the world dies...': *Senchus Mor*, trans. O'Donovan, O'Mahony, Hancock, edited by The Commissioners for Publishing the Ancient Laws and Institutes of Ireland, Dublin 1865, p. 51. [63]

'As the house...': ibid., p. 33. [63]

'It was the custom...': Henry of Saltrey, 'Tractatus de Purgatorio,' trans. George Philip Krapp, in *The Legend of Saint Patrick's Purgatory: its later literary history*, Baltimore 1900 p. 6. [63]

'it is normal experience...': Julius Caesar, op. cit. p. 272. [64]

'They consider it improper...': ibid. [64]

'the tradition of one ear to another': *Senchus Mor*, op. cit., p. 31. [64]

'Roman troops would be everywhere...': Cornelius Tacitus, *Agricola*, trans. Maurice Hutton, London, 1925, p. 211. [64]

'to think in terms of peripheral survival': Myles Dillon, 'The Hindu Act of Truth in Celtic Tradition', in *Modern Philology*, Vol. XLIV, Feb. 1947, No. 3, p. 140. [66]

'lowest common denominator of custom': D. A. Binchy, 'The Linguistic and Historical Value of the Irish Law Tracts', in *Proceedings of the British Academy*, Vol. XXIX, 1943, p. 199. [66]

'the penis of Fergus': George Petrie, 'On the History and Antiquities of Tara Hill', in *T.R.I.A.*, Vol. XVIII, 1837, p. 159. [66]

'a most filthy race...': Giraldus Cambrensis, *Topography of Ireland*, trans. Thomas Wright, London 1913, p. 134. [66]

'There is in the northern and most remote part of Ulster...': ibid., p. 138. [66]

'The wizard Lochru went angrily...': *The Tripartite Life of Patrick with Other Documents Relating to that Saint*, trans. Whitley Stokes, Vol. I, London 1887, p. 45. [68]

'Etymologically it is the verbal noun...': Byrne, *Irish Kings*, op. cit., p. 17. See also James Carney, *Studies in Irish Literature and History*, Dublin 1955, pp. 333-6; Tomás Ó Máille, "Medb Chruachna', in *Zeitschrift Für Celtische Philologie*, Vol. XVII, 1927, pp. 129-46; T. K. O'Rahilly, 'On the origin of the Names Érainn and Ériu', in *Ériu*, Vol. XIV, 1946, pp. 14-28; H. Wagner, 'Studies in Early Celtic Traditions', in *Ériu*, Vol. XXVI, 1975, p. 12. [68]

'The King who has not hostages in keeping...': 'Advice to a Prince', op. cit., p. 51. [68]

'Then the wondrous Wheel rolled onwards...': 'The Great King of Glory,' trans. T. W. Rhys Davis, in *The Sacred Books of the East*, ed. F. Max Muller, Vol. XI, Oxford 1881, pp. 252-4. [69, 71]

'O Muircheartach, son of valiant Niall...': Cormacan Eigeas, *The Circuit of Ireland by Muircheartach MacNeill, Prince of Aileach; A Poem Written in the Year DCCCCXLII*, trans. John O'Donovan, Dublin 1841, pp. 24-59. [71]

'curious remnant of paganism...': W. G. Wood-Martin, *Traces of the Elder Faiths of Ireland*, Vol. II, London 1970, p. 51. [71]

'Three shouts of victory...': 'Advice to a Prince,' op. cit., p. 51. [73]

CHAPTER 4-CRUACHAIN

'window on the Iron Age': Kenneth Jackson, *The Oldest Irish Tradition: A window on the Iron Age*, Cambridge 1964. [74]

The Ancient Irish Epic Tale Táin Bó Cūalnge, trans. Joseph Dunn, London 1914, pp. 212, 217, 218, 261, 300. [74, 76]

'a certain distaste...': J. R. R. Tolkien, 16 December 1937, in *The Letters of J. R. R. Tolkien*, ed. H. Carpenter, Boston 1981, p. 26. [205, note 1, ch. 4]

'Trusting in their horses and chariots': Byrne, *Irish Kings*, op. cit., p. 74. [77]

'The Intoxicating One': trans. Tomás Ó Máille, in 'Medb Chruachna', op. cit., p. 144. [78, 80]

'She who is the nature of mead': trans. H. Wagner, in 'Studies in Early Celtic Traditions,' op. cit., p. 12. [80]

'It is the custom amongst all the Irish...': Edmund Spenser, *A View of the Present State of Ireland*, ed. W. L. Renwick, Oxford 1970, p. 7. [81]

'Fedhlimidh son of Aedh son of Eoghan...': *Annals of Connaught*, as quoted in Myles Dillon, 'The Inauguration of O'Conor', in *Medieval Studies Presented to Aubrey Gwynn, S.J.*, Dublin 1961, p. 186. [81]

'To Cruachain of the purple-berried trees...': Giolla Iosa Mor Mac Firbis, 'Hereditary Proprietors of the Clan Fianchrach', trans. John O'Donovan, in *The Genealogies, Tribes, and Customs of Hy-Fiachrach, commonly called O'Dowda's Country*, Dublin 1844, p. 289. [81]

CHAPTER 5-DOWNPATRICK

'a ruin's devious career': Rose Macaulay, *Pleasure of Ruins*, London 1953, p. xvii. [85]

'We entreat thee, holy youth...': *The Writings of Patrick*, trans, Rev. Charles H. H. Wright, London 1889. All excerpts from 'The Confession' and the 'Epistle to Coroticus' are from this edition. As both are exceedingly short, no page references are given. [86]

'these wild and harsh men': Muirchú, 'Vita Patricii', trans. Ludwig Bieler, in *The Patrician Texts in the Book of Armagh*, Dublin 1979, p. 73. [86]

'To Patrick and his bishop...': G. A. Chamberlain, *Saint Patrick: His Life and Work*, Dublin 1959, p. 51. [86]

'unaided and alone': ibid., p. 53. [86]

'Capital of the realm of the Irish...': Muirchú, op. cit., p. 75. [86]

'It seemed good to St. Patrick...': Muirchú, trans. N. J. D. White, in *St. Patrick, His Writings and Life*, London 1921, p. 82; 'There, in the words of the Psalmist...': Muirchú, trans. Bieler, op. cit., p. 83. [86]

'could not fail to have heard...': Chamberlain, op. cit., pp. 73-4. [86]

'Which he loved beyond all other places...': Muirchú, trans. White, op. cit., p. 104. [87]

'Forasmuch as, my lord Áed...': Muirchú, trans. Kenney, in *Sources*, op. cit., p. 332.

'Their public and private accounts': Julius Caesar, op. cit., p. 272. [89]

'gesture alphabet': R. A. S. Macalister, *Corpus Inscriptionem Insularem Celticarum*, Dublin 1945, p.v. [89]

'The Romans declare to our country...': Gildas, *The Ruin of Britain*, trans. Hugh Williams, London 1899, pp. 37, 45. [90]

Their views 'never invited on any question': Caesar, op. cit., p. 271. [90]

'A female satirist': trans. Vernam Hull, as quoted in Byrne, *Irish Kings*, op. cit., p. 184. [91]

'Their Babylon': Muirchú, trans. Bieler, op. cit., p. 85. [91]

'at the instigation of the deacon Palladius': Prosper of Aquitaine, *Chronicon*, trans. Kenney, *Sources*, op. cit., p. 165. [93]

'overthrows the heretics...': ibid. [93]

'To the Irish believing in Christ...': ibid. [93]

'No one was found in those parts...': Giraldus Cambrensis, op. cit., p. 142. [93]

'those who dwell in desert places...': 'Catalogus Sanctorum', trans. Myles Dillon and Nora Chadwick, in *Celtic Realms*, London 1967, p. 180. [95]

'Palladius the first bishop sent here...': See D. A. Binchy, 'Patrick and his Biographers: Ancient and Modern', in *Studia Hibernica*, No. 2, 1962, p. 132. [95]

'When Patrick went aloft...': trans. Binchy, ibid., p. 124. [95]

These words 'simply reflect a contemporary belief...': Binchy, ibid., p. 125. [95]

'quaint': Chamberlain, op. cit., p. 13. [97]

'bad, ungrammatical, rude': Charles H. H. Wright, op. cit. pp. 22, 23. [97]

'a decidedly insufficient command of Latin': Christine Mohrmann, *The Latin of St. Patrick*, Dublin 1961, p. 46. [97]

'a real linguistic handicap...': ibid. [97]

'no traces of quotation or borrowings...': ibid., p. 8. [99]

'The scriptures are sufficient for our instruction': Athanasius, op. cit., p. 33. [99]

'truly a desert land': Giraldus Cambrensis, op. cit., p. 20. [100]

'The highest "grade" of king...': D. A. Binchy, 'Patrick and his Biographers', op. cit., p. 63. [100]

'Lord, I do not...': 2 Corinthians 12:15. [103]

'meant to copy': Chamberlain, op. cit., p. 12. [103]

Coroticus 'was ignominiously changed into a fox...': Muirchú, trans. Bieler, op. cit., p. 101. [103]

CHAPTER 6-THE ROCK OF DOON

'On the seventh day of December...': Manus O'Donnell, *Betha Colaim chille, Life of Columcille*, trans. A. O'Kelleher and G. Schoepperle, Urbana 1918, p. 451. [109]

The 'children that were wont to play with him...': ibid., p. 41. [109]

'Crimthan': L. Russell Muirhead, *Ireland*, London: Chicago 1962, p. 164. [109]

'To have it was his right by blood': Manus O'Donnell, op. cit., p. 3. [109]

'lewd customs hateful to God...': as quoted in D. A. Binchy, 'Irish Law Tracts', op. cit., p. 195. [109]

'rigdamnai, or "king-material"': Byrne, *Irish Kings*, op. cit., p. 35. [110]

'They say he setteth but one foot upon the stone...': Spenser, op. cit., pp. 7, 8. [110]

'The effusion of blood...': as quoted in D. A. Binchy, 'Irish Law Tracts', op. cit., p. 195. [110]

'tanistry is the undoubted parent...': Henry Maine, *Early Law and Custom*, London 1883, p. 128. As referred to by D. A. Binchy, ibid., p 196. [110]

'Christ is my druid': trans. John O'Donovan, in *The Miscellany of the Irish Archaeological Society*, Vol I, Dublin 1846, p. 13. [111]

'swept away the noblest third part...': The Four Masters, *Annals of The Kingdom of Ireland*, trans. John O'Donovan, Vol. I, Dublin 1851, p. 183. [111]

'One can scarcely avoid the conclusion...': Proinsias MacCana, *Celtic Mythology*, London 1970, p. 35. [206, note 1, ch. 6]

'Brigit was born...': trans. Whitley Stokes, 'Three Irish Homilies', in Kenney, *Sources*, op. cit., p. 357. [206, note 1, ch. 6]

'This is why I love Derry...': Manus O'Donnell, op. cit., p. 189. [111]

'naked in imitation of Christ...': The *Rule* of Columcille, op. cit., p. 119. [114]

'Testaments of God': ibid. [114]

'Three labours in thy day...': ibid., pp. 120, 121. [114]

'If any of the presbyters builds a church...': 'Canons Attributed to St. Patrick,' trans. John T. McNeill and Helena M. Garner, in *Medieval Handbooks of Penance*, New York 1938, p. 77. [116]

'For fifteen hundred paces...': Manus O'Donnell, op. cit., p. 47. [116]

'A most wise magician...': *The Life of St. Samson of Dol*, trans. Thomas Taylor, London 1925, pp. 14, 20. [118]

'Let the abbot's son enter the Church...': 'Advice to a Prince,' op. cit., pp. 53, 54.]118]

'No one bequeaths anything...': trans D. A. Binchy, in 'Irish Law Tracts,' op. cit., p. 218. [118]

'he was not a gentle hero...': 'The Bodleian Amra Choluimb chille', trans. Whitley Stokes, in *Revue Celtique*, Vol. XX, 1899, p. 137. [119]

'on a charge of offences that were trivial...': Ádomnan, *Life of Columba*, trans. A. O. and M. O. Anderson, London, 1961, p. 469. [119]

CHAPTER 7 - BENMORE HEAD

'the most beautiful landscapes...': William Thackeray, *The Irish Sketch Book*, London 1869, p. 298. [120]

'Sweet, wild and sad...': ibid., p. 250. [120]

CHAPTER 8 - GLENCOLUMBKILLE

'Three hundred churches...': Manus O'Donnell, op. cit., p. 435. [124]

'It extends into the ocean...': John O'Donovan, 'Letters containing information relative to the history and antiquities of the County of Donegal, collected during the progress of the Ordnance Survey', typescript, National Library, Dublin, entry for year 1835. [128]

'Right often': Manus O'Donnell, op. cit., p. 437. [128]

'There is a gray eye...': 'Bodleian Amra Choluimb chille,' trans. Whitley Stokes, op. cit., p. 39. [128]

'I have heard he gives no horses...': trans. Dillon and Chadwick, in *Celtic Realms*, op. cit., p. 230; see also Kuno Meyer, 'Miscellanea Hibernica', in *University of Illinois Studies in Language and Literature*, Vol. II, No. 4, Nov. 1916, p. 44. [129]

Áed 'had many questions here': 'Bodleian Amra Choluimb chille', trans. Whitley Stokes, op. cit., p. 47. [131]

'A tale I have for you...': *The Amra of Choluim Chilli of Dallan Forgaill*, trans. J. O'Beirne Crowe, Dublin 1871, p. 45. [135]

CHAPTER 9 - LOUGH ERNE

'Devenish of the Assemblies': *Leabhar Breac*, as quoted in J. E. Canon McKenna, *Devenish (Lough Erne): Its History, Antiquities, and Traditions*, Dublin: Enniskillen 1931, p. 23. [136]

'The Isle of Oxen': All excerpts from the cursing of Tara may be found in one of the following stories, unless otherwise noted — 'Life of St. Molasius of Devenish', 'A Story of Aedh Baclamh', 'This is the death of Dermot son of Fergus Cerrbeoil as the Book of Sligo tells it', trans. Standish H. O'Grady, in *Silva Gadelica: A Collection of Tales in Irish*, London 1892, pp. 18-34, 70-88. [136-9]

'A prison of hard narrow stone': *The Martyrology of Donegal: A Calendar of the Saints of Ireland*, trans. John O'Donovan, eds. J. H. Todd and William Reeves, Dublin 1864, p. 83. [136]

'his body, frozen with hailstone...': Tírechán, 'Collectanea', trans. Ludwig Bieler, in *The Patrician Texts in the Book of Armagh*, op. cit., p. 131. [136]

'Loved cursing': 'Cuimmín's Poem on the Saints of Ireland,' trans. Whitley Stokes, in *Zeitschrift Für Celtische Philologie*, Vol. 1, 1896, p. 67. Revised translation in Kenney, *Sources*, op. cit., p. 303. [138]

'detention...': Whitley Stokes, 'Sitting Dharna', in *The Academy*, No. 697, 12 Sept. 1885, p. 169. [138]

'Better be doomed to perish...': 'Advice to a Prince', op. cit., p. 51. [139]

'The people of this nation...': Giraldus Cambrensis, op. cit., p. 111. [139]

'Three chosen men...': *The Chronicle of Aethelweard*, trans. A. Campbell, London 1961, p. 48. [139]

These 'wanderers and strangers...': Celestine, Bishop of Rome, trans. Dillon and Chadwick, in *Celtic Realms*, op. cit., p. 167. [140]

'We, all the Irish...': trans. Kenney, *Sources*, op. cit., p. 193. [140]

'Bishops and monks have different vocations...': for translations of the letters of Columbanus, see *Sancti Columbani Opera*, ed. G. S. M. Walker, Dublin 1957, p. 3-59. [140]

'The Easter Question is not the most enthralling of subjects': J. F. Webb, *Lives of the Saints*, Harmondsworth 1970, p. 13. [140]

'in ritual were addicted to Jewish fables': Epiphanius, trans. P. Scaff, in *History of the Christian Church*, Vol. II, New York, 1873, p. 406. [141]

'We would have nothing in common...': Emperor Constantine, ibid., p. 405. [141]

'We ought not to keep Passover with the Jews...': Columbanus to Gregory the Great, 'Epistle CXXVII', trans. James Barmby, in *A Select Library of Nicene and Post-Nicene Fathers of the Christian Church*, eds. Philip Scaff and Henry Wace, Second Series, Vol. XIII, New York 1898, pp. 38-40. [142]

'Liberty was the tradition of my fathers...': *Sancti Columbani Opera*, op. cit., pp. 3-59. [142]

'I have not dared to come myself...': ibid. [142]

'The apostolic see...': the Venerable Bede, *The Ecclesiastical History of the English People*, ed. Bertram Colgrave and R. A. B. Mynors (Oxford 1969), p. 147. [143]

'To live with me (or) eat at the same table...': *The Confessions of St. Augustine*, trans. F. J. Sheed, New York 1942, p. 46. [207, note 4, ch. 9]

'No religion that succeeds...': Herbert Muller, *The Uses of the Past*, New York 1957, p. 191. [207, note 5, ch. 9]

'A 'rude structure...': *In State Care*, p. 131. [151]

'Lovely season of May...': 'Cétamon', trans. James Carney, 'Three Old Irish Accentual Poems', in *Ériu*, Vol. XXII, 1971, p. 45. [151]

CHAPTER 10-ARMAGH

'atmosphere of ancient dignity...': Muirhead, *Ireland*, op. cit., p. 122. [152]

'so hated the Saxons...': Anne Fremantle, *The Age of Belief*, New York 1954, p. 76. [207, note 1, ch. 10]

'Seized by a panic of foreboding...': See Bede, *Ecclesiastical History*, eds. Colgrave and Mynors, op. cit., Book 1, Chapter 23. [154]

'The Easter we keep...': Bede, *Ecclesiastical History*, eds. Colgrave and Mynors, op. cit., pp. 301, 307. Insert of 'Otherwise, when I come to the gates of heaven...': trans. Leo Sherley-Price, as quoted in Brendan Lehane, *The Quest of Three Abbots*, London 1968, p. 208. [155]

'because the Irish in summer time...': Bede, *Ecclesiastical History*, eds. Colgrave and Mynors, op. cit., p. 347. [207, note 2, ch. 10]

'Mayo of the Saxons': See Kenney, *Sources*, op. cit., pp. 463-4. [207, note 2, ch. 10]

'as I might say, a pimple...': Cummian, Abbot of Durrow (?), as quoted in Kathleen Hughes, *The Church in Early Irish Society*, London 1966, p. 107. [158]

'A 'good and wise man': Bede, *Ecclesiastical History*, eds. Colgrave and Mynors, op. cit., p. 507. [158]

'My heart is troubled...': Tírechán, trans. Kenney, in *Sources*, op. cit., p. 330. [159]

'His kin and his church to Patrick toll Doom': Tírechán, 'Additamenta', trans. Ludwig Bieler, *Patrician Texts*, op. cit., p. 179. [159]

'Once, therefore, S. Patrick went forth from the city Armagh...': 'The Book of the Angel', trans. Kathleen Hughes, in *The Church in Early Irish Society*, op. cit., pp. 275-81; see also Ludwig Bieler, *Patrician Texts*, op. cit., pp. 185-91. [161]

'Transfer of the relics...': *Annals of Ulster*, trans. Kenney, in *Sources*, op. cit., p. 335. [162]

'Any wretched, pitiful thing...': 'A Poem of Prophecies', trans. Eleanor Knott, in *Ériu*, Vol. XVIII, 1958, p. 69. [162]

'In the words of the Easter liturgy...': John Paul II, *The Pope in Ireland: Addresses and Homilies*, Dublin 1979, p. 17. [163]

CHAPTER 11-TALLAGHT

'Come to me, loving Mary...': *The Poems of Blathmac Son of Cú Brettan, Together With The Irish Gospel of Thomas and A Poem on The Virgin Mary*, ed. and trans. James Carney, Dublin 1964, p. 3. [167]

'Christ was born...': popularly ascribed to Oengus the Culdee, trans. Whitley Stokes, in *The Saltair Na Rann: A Collection of Early Middle Irish Poems*, Oxford 1883, p. v. [167]

215

'The laity and the people of the great old churches yonder...': 'The Monastery of Tallaght', trans. E. J. Gwynn and W. J. Purton, in *P.R.I.A.*, Vol. XXIX, July 1911, p. 137. [168]

'Take not the world, O cleric': *The Martyrology of Tallaght*, trans. Richard Best and Hugh Lawlor, London 1913, p. 113. [168]

'To abide always...': 'The Rule of Tallaght', trans. Edward Gwynn, in *Hermathena*, Vol. XLIV, 1927, p. 11. [168]

'We lift up a ready heart...': 'Metrical Rule of the Céli Dé', trans. William Reeves, in 'On the Céli-dé, commonly called Culdees', *T.R.I.A.*, Vol. XXIV, 1864, p. 200. [168]

'The lax folk'... et seq.: 'The Monastery of Tallaght', op. cit., pp. 148, 133, 141, 149. [168]

'The monthly disease...': 'Prose Rule of the Céli Dé', trans. John O'Donovan, in 'On the Céli-dé, commonly called Culdees', op. cit., p. 211. [207-8, note 2, ch. 11]

'Now the privy houses and the urine houses...': ibid., p. 209. [169]

'To fast with him on God': popularly ascribed to Oengus the Culdee, op. cit., p. iii. [208, note 4, ch. 11]

Freezing water 'up to his loins...': Bede, *Ecclesiastical History*, eds. Colgrave and Mynors, op. cit., pp. 497-9. [208, note 4, ch. 11]

'Until weary...': 'The Old-Irish Table of Penitential Commutations', trans. D. A. Binchy, in *Eriu*, Vol. XIX, 1962, pp. 61, 63. [169]

'Properly administered lashes': ibid. [169]

'The wise man's work is in his mouth...': 'Metrical Rule of the Céli Dé', op. cit., p. 201.

'it is not usual for a layman...': 'Penitential Commutations', op. cit., p. 61. [208, note 5, ch. 11]

CHAPTER 12-CLONMACNOISE

'O Shannon...': Tadhg Og O Huiginn, trans. Osborn Bergin, 'Two Poems on the Shannon', in *The Irish Review*, 1913, p. 16. [170]

'There was not left...': The Four Masters, op. cit., p. 1525. [170]

'When he knew that the day of his death was at hand...': trans. Kenney, in *Sources*, op. cit., p. 379; see also *The Latin and Irish Lives of Ciaran*, trans R. A. S. Macalister, London 1921, and *Lives of the Saints from The Book of Lismore*, trans. Whitley Stokes, Oxford 1890, pp. 262-80. [170]

'May Christ of the arts...': 'The Graves of the Kings at Clonmacnoise', trans. R. I. Best, in *Ériu*, Vol. II, 1905, p. 171. [170]

'Men will quake with terror...': Snorri Sturluson, *King Harald's Saga*, trans. Magnus Magnusson and Herman V. Pálsson, Harmondsworth 1966, p. 109. [171]

'Lo, it is nearly 350 years...': Alcuin to Ethelred, King of Northumbria. For more letters by Alcuin on the Norse raids see *Alcuin of York*, ed. Stephen Allott, York 1974, pp. 8, 36-41. [174]

'It is not known when or how they evolved the keel...': Tre Tryckare, *The Viking*, Gothenburg, Sweden 1966, p. 8. [174]

'The grey eagle's talons...': Snorri Sturluson, op. cit., p. 59. [175]

'gave heathen oracles': see Duald MacFirbis, *On the Fomorians and the Norsemen*, trans. Alexander Bugge, Christiania 1905, pp. 8, 16. [175]

'Burst, revealing a welter of meat...': Haakon Shetelig, *Viking Antiquities in Great Britain and Ireland*, Oslo 1940, p. 53. [177]

'There were Christian men here then...': Ari Thorgilsson, *The Book of the Icelanders*, trans. Halldór Hermannsson, Ithaca 1930, p. 60. [208, note 2, ch. 12]

'In this year many forsook their Christian baptism...': trans. John O'Donovan, in *Three Fragments*, Dublin 1860, p. 127. [178]

'combustio': A. T. Lucas, 'The Plundering and Burning of Churches in Ireland, 7th to 16th Century,' in *North Munster Studies: Essays in Commemoration of Monsignor Michael Molony*, ed. Etienne Rynne, Limerick 1967, p. 174; see also by the same author, 'Irish-Norse Relations: Time for a Reappraisal?' in *Journal of the Cork Historical and Archaeological Society*, Vol. LXXI, Nos. 213 and 214, 1966, pp. 62-75. [208, note 3, ch 12]

'the most beautiful book in the world': Muirhead, *Ireland*, op. cit., p. 9. [181]

'A ready method of testing the sanity of insanity...': William Stokes, *'The Life and Labours in Art and Archoeology of George Petrie*, London 1868, p. 142. [181]

'everything that is made from without...': Oscar Wilde, *De Profundis*, New York 1964, pp. 109, 110, 119. [184]

CHAPTER 13-MONASTERBOICE

'One of the rare isolated geniuses...': Muller, *Uses of the Past*, op. cit., p. 253. [185]

'Swarming with worms...': Pope Honorius III, as quoted in Robert Adamson and John M. Mitchell, "Johannes Scotus Erigena', in *The Encyclopedia Birttanica*, 13th edition, Vol. 9, London 1926, p. 743. [208, note 1, ch. 13]

'Strange human reaction to decay': Rose Macaulay, *Pleasure of Ruins*, op. cit., p. xv. [186]

'imperatoris scotorum': for full entry see Kenney, *Sources*, op. cit., p. 353. [188]

'most beautiful woman': *Njál's Saga*, trans. C. F. Bayerschmidt and L. M. Hollander, New York 1968, p. 350. [188]

'The best qualities in all matters...': ibid. [188]

'Were desperately entangled': Haakon Shetelig, op. cit., p. 75. [189]

'king of Ireland...': *Njál's Saga*, op. cit., p. 350. [189]

'And it will be one of the wonders...': *The War of the Gaedhil with the Gaill, or The Invasion of Ireland by the Danes and Other Norsemen*, trans. James H. Todd, London 1867, p. 175. [191]

'Where is Domhnall...': ibid. [191]

'Put the foreigner down under him...': ibid., p. 197. [191]

'Let it pass from mouth to mouth...': *Njál's Saga*, op. cit., p. 357. [191]

'slit open his belly...': ibid. [191]

'I never saw a battle like it...': *War of the Gaedhil and the Gael*, op. cit., p. 183. [193]

'No church or holy city...': 'A Poem of Prophesies', op. cit., p. 67. [193]

CHAPTER 14-MELLIFONT

'Wickedness in the crook of the pastoral staff': ibid, p. 73. [194]

'a 'damned race'...' and later excerpts: Bernard of Clairvaux, *Life of St. Malachy of Armagh*, trans. H. J. Lawlor, New York 1920, p. 51. [194]

'Love seeks no cause nor end but itself...': Bernard, as quoted Anne Fremantle, op. cit., p. 105. [194]

'It is said that husbands exchange their wives...': St Anselm of Canterbury, trans. Aubrey Gwynn, in *The Twelfth-Century Reform*, Dublin 1968, p. 17. [199]

'There is a dispute in Irish law...': 'Bretha Crólige', trans. D. A. Binchy, in *Ériu*, Vol. XII, 1938, p. 45; see also Binchy, 'Irish Law tracts', op. cit., p. 220. [199]

'Long rain of May...': Sóin, *The Narrow Road to the Deep North and Other Travel Sketches*, op. cit., p. 17. [204]

NOTES: source references relating to the notes will be found listed with the other references from the same chapter.

Further Reading on the Sites

TEXT REFERENCES

Moone Abbey. Frontispiece
1. Porter, Arthur K., *The Crosses and Culture of Ireland*, New Haven 1931, pp. 44, 110, 114, 117.
2. Stokes, Margaret, 'Notes on the High Crosses of Moone, Drumcliff, Termonfechin, and Killamery', in *T.R.I.A.*, Vol. XXXI, 1896-1901, pp. 542-50.

Skellig Michael. Introduction
1. de Paor, Liam, 'A Survey of Scelig Mhichíl', in *J.R.S.A.I.*, Vol. LXXXV, Part II, 1955, pp. 174-87.
2. *Dunraven I*, pp. 26-36.
3. Henry, Françoise, 'Early Monasteries, Beehive Huts, and Dry-stone Houses: Skellig Michael (Fifth Section)', in *P.R.I.A.*, Vol. 58, Section C, 1956-57, pp. 113-29.
4. *Leask I*, pp. 18-21.
5. Westropp, J. J., 'Skellig-St. Michael's Rock,' in *J.R.S.A.I.*, Vol. VII, 1897, pp. 308-15.
6. Wilson, T.D., *The Irish Lighthouse Service*, Dublin 1968.
7. For Skellig sea birds:
   Fitter, Richard, consulting ed., *Book of British Birds*, London 1973, pp. 248, 259, 454.

Abbey of Mona Incha. Introduction
1. Giraldus Cambrensis, *The First Version of 'The Topography of Ireland'*, trans. John J. O'Meara, Dundalk 1951, pp. 42-3, 114.
2. Leask, Harold G. and C. McNeill, 'Monaincha, Co. Tipperary', in *J.R.S.A.I.*, Vol. L, 1921, pp. 19-35.
3. *Petrie II*, pp. 35-37.

Clochán, Slea Head. Introduction
1. Aalen, F. H. A., 'Clocháns As Transhumance Dwellings in the Dingle Peninsula, Co. Kerry', in *J.R.S.A.I.*, Vol. 94, 1964, pp. 39-45.
2. Macalister, R. A. S., 'On An Ancient Settlement in the South-West of the Barony of Cockaguiney, County of Kerry', in *T.R.I.A.*, Vol. XXXI, Part VII, 1899, pp. 269-81.

Newgrange and the Boyne. Chapter 1
1. Eogan, George, 'Excavations at Knowth, Co. Meath, 1962-1965,' in *P.R.I.A.*, Vol. 66, Section C, No. 4, pp. 299-400.
2. Eogan, George, *Excavations at Knowth (I)*, Dublin 1984.
3. Herity, Michael, 'From Lhuyd to Coffey: New Information from Unpublished Descriptions of the Boyne Valley Tombs', in *Studia Hibernica*, No. 7, 1967, pp. 127-45.
4. Macalister, R. A. S., *Newgrange*, The Stationery Office, Dublin.
5. O'Kelly, Clair, *Illustrated Guide to Newgrange and the Other Boyne Monuments*, Cork 1978.
6. O'Kelly, Michael J., 'The Restoration of Newgrange', in *Antiquity*, Vol. LIII, 1979, pp. 205-10.
7. O'Kelly, Michael J., *Newgrange: Archaeology, art and legend*, London 1982.
8. Ó Ríordáin, Seán and Daniel, Glyn, *New Grange and the Bend of the Boyne*, New York 1964.
9. Patrick, J., 'Midwinter Sunrise at Newgrange', in *Nature*, Vol. 249, 1974, pp. 517-19.
10. Wilde, W. R., *The Beauties of the Boyne, and its Tributary, the Blackwater*, Dublin 1849.

For a discussion of Fourknocks:

11. Harnett, P. J., 'Excavation of a passage grave at Fourknocks, County Meath', in *P.R.I.A.*, Vol. 58, Section C, 1956-57, pp. 197-277.
12. Harnett, P. J. 'The Excavation of Two Tumuli at Fourknocks (Sites II and III), Co. Meath', in *P.R.I.A.*, Vol. 71, 1971, pp. 35-89.

Slieve na Calliagh. Chapter 1

1. Coffey, George, 'Notes on The Prehistoric Cemetery of Loughcrew, With A Fasciculus of Photographic Illustrations of the Sepulchral Cairns', in *T.R.I.A.*, Vol. XXXI, 1896-1901, pp. 23-38.
2. Frazer, W., 'Loughcrew Hills', in *J.R.S.A.I.*, Vol. V, 1895, pp. 303-16.

Carrowmore Area. Chapter 1

1. Borlase, William C., *The Dolmens of Ireland*, Vol. I, London 1897, pp. 142-74.
2. Burenhult, Göran, *The Archaeological Excavations at Carrowmore, Co. Sligo, Ireland, Excavation Seasons 1977-79*, Stockholm 1980.
3. Wood-Martin, W. G., 'The Rude Stone Monuments of Ireland', in *J.R.S.A.I.*, Vol. VII, 1885-86, pp. 470-87, 539-95; Vol. VIII, 1887-88, pp. 50-69.

Tievebulliagh. Chapter 1

1. Knowles, W. J., 'On Counterfeit Antiquities', in *J.R.S.A.I.*, Vol. VII, 1885-86, pp. 430-31.
2. Knowles, W. J., 'Stone Axe Factories Near Cushendall', in *J.R.S.A.I.*, No. 16, 1906, pp. 383-94.
3. Knowles, W. J., 'Prehistoric Stone Implements from the River Bann and Lough Neagh', in *P.R.I.A.*, Vol. XXX, Section C, 1912-13, pp. 195-222.
4. Jope, E. M., 'Porcellanite Axes From Factories in North-East Ireland: Tievebulliagh and Rathlin', in *U.J.A.*, Vol. 15, 1952, pp. 31-60.
5. Movius, Hallam L., *The Irish Stone Age: Its Chronology, Development & Relationships*, Cambridge 1942, pp. 222-227.

Carrowkeel. Chapter 2

1. Macalister, R. A. S., E. C. R. Armstrong, and R. Praeger, 'Reports on the Exploitation of Bronze-Age Carns on Carrowkeel Mountain, Co. Sligo', in *P.R.I.A.*, Vol. XXIX, Section C, No. 9, 1912, pp. 311-47.

Heapstown. Chapter 2

1. Wood-Martin, W. G., 'The Battle-ground and Ancient Monuments of Northern Moytirra', in *J.R.S.A.I.*, Vol. VI, 1883-84, p. 467.

Knocknarea. Chapters 3 and 4

1. Milligan, Seaton F., 'County Sligo', in *J.R.S.A.I.*, Vol. XXVI, 1896, pp. 307-9.
2. Wood-Martin, W. G., 'Rude Stone Monuments', op. cit., Vol. VIII, pp. 83-5.

Tara. Chapter 3

1. Macalister, R. A. S., *Tara*, The Stationery Office, Dublin.
2. O'Reilly, P. J., 'Notes on the Coronation Stone at Westminster, and the *Lia Fail* at Tara', in *J.R.S.A.I.*, Vol. XII, 1902, pp. 77-92.
3. Ó Ríordáin, Seán, *Tara: The Monument on the Hill*, Dundalk 1960.
4. Petrie, George, 'On the History and Antiquities of Tara Hill', in *T.R.I.A.*, Vol. XVIII, 1837, pp. 25-232.
5. Swan, D. L., 'The Hill of Tara, county Meath: The evidence of Aerial Photography', in *J.R.S.A.I.*, Vol. 108, 1978, pp. 51-66.

Aileach. Chapter 3

1. Bernard, Walter, 'Exploration and Restoration of the Ruin of the Grianan of Aileach', in *P.R.I.A.*, Vol. I, Series 2, 1879, pp. 415-23.
2. Crawford, H. S., 'Aileach', in *P.R.I.A.*, Vol. XLV, Part III, 1915, pp. 204-7.

Cruachain. Chapter 4

1. Ferguson, Samuel, 'On Ancient Cemeteries at Rathcrogan and Elsewhere in Ireland (as Affecting the Question of the Site of the Cemetery at Taltin)', in *P.R.I.A.*, Vol. 1, Series 2, 1879, pp. 114-28.
2. Knox, H. T., 'The Croghans and Some Connacht Raths and Motes', in *J.R.S.A.I.*, Vol. XLI, 1911, pp. 94-116.
3. Knox, H. T., 'Ruins of Cruchan Ai', in *J.R.S.A.I.*, Vol. XLIV, Part 1, 1914, pp. 1-50.
4. O'Donovan, John, *Letters containing information relative to the history and antiquities of the County of Roscommon, collected during the progress of the Ordnance Survey*, Bray 1927, pp. 86-9.
5. For Carnfree:
   Jones, Walter A., 'The Proclamation Stone of the Connaught Kings', in *Journal of the Galway Archaeological and Historical Society*, Vol. XII, Nos i & ii, p. 46.

6. Macalister, R. A. S., *The Archaeology of Ireland*, London 1928, p. 178.

St Columb's Rock. Chapter 4
1. *A Preliminary Survey*, p. 193.

Downpatrick. Chapter 5
1. *County Down*, pp. 98-100, 266-72.
2. *Leask II*, pp. 147-8.
3. Parkinson, R. E., *The Cathedral Church of Down* (Downpatrick).
4. Proudfoot, Bruce, 'Excavations at the Cathedral Hill, Downpatrick, Co. Down', in *U.J.A.*, Vol. 17, 1954, pp. 97-101.
5. Reeves, William, *Ecclesiastical Antiquities of Down, Connor, and Dromore, Consisting of A Taxation of Those Dioceses, Compiled in the Year MCCCVI*, Dublin 1847, pp. 223-32.

Dunmore Head. Chapter 5
1. Macalister, R. A. S., 'On An Ancient Settlement', op. cit., pp. 279-80.

The Book of Armagh. Chapter 5
1. Bieler, Ludwig, ed. and trans., *The Patrician Texts in the Book of Armagh*, Dublin 1979.

Clonmacnoise. Chapters 5 and 12
1. *Barrow*, pp. 173-5.
2. *Dunraven II*, pp. 95-105.
3. *Leask I*, pp. 61, 72, 146-50.
4. Lionard, Pádraig, 'Early Irish Grave Slabs', in *P.R.I.A.*, Vol. 61, Section C, No. 5, 1961, pp. 95-169.
5. Macalister, R. A. S., *The Memorial Slabs of Clonmacnoise, King's County; With an appendix on the Materials For A History of the Monastery*, Dublin 1909.
6. *Petrie I*, pp. 1-8, 15-84; Plates I-LXXIV.
7. Ryan, John, *Clonmacnoise: A Historical Summary*, Dublin 1973.
8. Westropp, T. J., 'A Description of the Ancient Buildings and Crosses at Clonmacnoise, King's County', in *J.R.S.A.I.*, Vol. XXXVII, 1907, pp. 277-306, 329-40.

The Dane's Cast. Chapter 5
1. *County Down*, pp. 144-46.
2. Davies, O., 'The Black Pig's Dyke', in *U.J.A.*, Vol. 18, 1955, pp. 29-36.

3. Evans, E. Estyn, *Prehistoric and Early Christian Ireland: A Guide*, New York 1966, pp. 58, 95, 140.
4. Kane, W. F. De Vismes, 'The Black Pig's Dyke: The Ancient Boundary Fortification of Uladh', in *P.R.I.A.*, Vol. XXVII, 1907-1909, pp. 301-28.
5. Norman, E. R. and J. K. S. St Joseph, *The Early Development of Irish Society: The Evidence of Aerial Photography*, Cambridge 1969, p. 88.
6. O'Donovan, John, *Letters Containing Information Relative to the History and Antiquities of the County of Down, Collected During the Progress of the Ordnance Survey in 1834*, Dublin 1909, pp. 27-38.

Rock of Doon. Chapter 6
1. Crawford, H. S., 'Doon', in *P.R.I.A.*, Vol. XLV, Part III, 1915, p. 225.
2. Kinahan, G. H., 'Additional List of Megalithic and other Ancient Structures, Barony of Kilmacrenan, County Donegal', in *J.R.S.A.I.*, Vol. IX, 1889, pp. 283-4.

Gartan. Chapter 6
1. Baille, R. C., 'Oratory of St. Columkille at Gartan', in *J.R.S.A.I.*, Vol. VIII, 1898, p. 275.

Movilla. Chapter 6
1. *County Down*, pp. 283-4.
2. *In State Care*, pp. 24-5.
3. *Petrie II*, pp. 71-2.

Gallarus Oratory. Chapter 6
1. *Dunraven I*, pp. 59-61.
2. *Leask I*, pp. 59-61.
3. *Petrie II*, p. 8.
4. Westropp, T. J., 'Gallerus', in *J.R.S.A.I.*, Vol. VII, 1897, pp. 297-8.

Canons' Island. Chapter 6
1. Norman, E. R., and J. K. S. St Joseph, *Early Development of Irish Society*, op. cit., pp. 104-5.
2. Westropp, T. J., 'Canons' Island', in *J.R.S.A.I.*, Vol. VII, 1897, pp. 286-90.

Ardfert Cathedral. Chapter 6
1. Anderson, William and Clive Hicks, *Cathedrals in Britain and Ireland, From early times to the reign of Henry VIII*, New York 1978, pp. 142-3.
2. *Barrow*, p. 113.
3. *Leask I*, pp. 124-6.

Crannóg, Benmore Head. Chapter 7
1. M'Henry, Alexander, 'Crannog of Lough na Cranagh, Fair Head, Co. Antrim', in *P.R.I.A.*, Vol. II, Second Series, 1879-1888, p. 462.

Glencolumbkille. Chapter 8
1. Anonymous Report, 'Proceedings and Papers', in *J.R.S.A.I.*, Vol. XXI, 1890, pp. 259-66.
2. Price, Liam, 'Glencolumbkille, County Donegal, And Its Early Christian Cross-Slabs', in *J.R.S.A.I.*, Vol. LXXI, Part III, 1941, pp. 71-88.

Iona. Chapters 8, 10 and 12
1. Cook, J., 'Scottish Archaeological Tour of the Royal Society of Antiquarians of Ireland in conjunction with the Cambrian Archaeological Association', in *J.R.S.A.I.*, Vol. IX, 1899, pp. 173-88.
2. Dunbar, John and Ian Fisher, *Iona*, Edinburgh, 1983.
3. O'Reilly, P. J., 'The Site of Columb's Monastery in Iona', in *J.R.S.A.I.*, Vol. X, 1900, pp. 334-42.
4. The Royal Commission on the Ancient and Historical Monuments of Scotland, *Argyll, An Inventory of the Monuments, Vol. 4, Iona*, Edinburgh, 1982.

The Mullagh. Chapter 8
1. Ryan, John, 'The Convention of Druim Ceat (AU. 575)', in *J.R.S.A.I.*, Vol. LXXVI, 1946, pp. 35-55.
2. Westropp, T. J., 'Druimceat', in *J.R.S.A.I.*, Vol. XLV, Part III, 1915, p. 171.

Devenish. Chapter 9
1. *A Preliminary Survey*, p. 161.
2. *Barrow*, pp. 92-6.
3. Hamlin, Ann, *Devenish*, Newry 1979.
4. *In State Care*, pp. 124-6.
5. Leask I, pp. 37-8.
6. Lowry-Corry, Lady Dorothy, 'St. Molaise's House at Devenish, Lough Erne, And Its Sculptural Stones', in *J.R.S.A.I.*, Vol. LXVI, Part II, 1936, pp. 270-84.
7. McKenna, J. E. Canon, *Devenish (Lough Erne): Its History, Antiquities, and Traditions*, Dublin: Enniskillen 1931.

Bobbio. Chapters 9 and 14
1. Stokes, Margaret, *Six Months in the Apennines, or A Pilgrimage in Search of Vestiges of the Irish Saints in Italy*, London 1892.

For reports on Annegrai, Luxeuil and Fontaines:
2. Stokes, Margaret, *Three Months in the Forests of France*, London 1895.

Killadeas. Chapter 9
1. Lowry-Corry, Lady Dorothy, 'The Sculptured Stones At Killadeas', in *J.R.S.A.I.*, Vol. LXV, Part I, 1935, pp. 23-33.

White Island. Chapter 9
1. Du Noyer, George V., 'Remarks on Ancient Irish Effigies Sculptured on the Walls of the Ancient Church on White Island, Lough Erne, Parish of Magheraculmoney, County of Fermanagh', in *J.R.S.A.I.*, Vol. III, 1860-61, pp. 62-9.
2. *Leask I*, pp. 157-8.
3. Lowry-Corry, Lady Dorothy, 'A Newly Discovered Statue at the Church on White Island, County Fermanagh', in *U.J.A.*, Vol. 22, 1959, pp. 59-66.
4. McKenna, James E. Canon, and Lady Dorothy Lowry-Corry, 'White Island, Lough Erne: Its Ancient Church and Unique Sculptures', in *J.R.S.A.I.*, Vol. LX, 1930, pp. 23-37.

Boa Island. Chapter 9
1. Lowry-Corry, Lady Dorothy, 'The Stones Carved With Human Effigies on Boa Island and on Lustymore Island, in Lower Lough Erne', in *P.R.I.A.*, Vol. XLI, 1932-33, pp. 200-4.

Inishmacsaint. Chapter 9
1. *In State Care*, pp. 131-2.
2. Wakeman, W. F., 'Lough Erne and Ballyshannon Excursion', in *J.R.S.A.I.*, Vol. XXVI, 1896, p. 288.

Armagh. Chapter 10
1. *A Preliminary Survey*, p. 66.

Jerpoint Abbey. Chapter 10
1. *Leask II*, pp. 29-32.
2. Hunt, John, 'Rory O'Tunney and the Ossory Tomb Sculptures,' in *J.R.S.A.I.*, Vol. LXXX, 1950, pp. 22-8.
3. Rae, Edwin C., 'Irish Sepulchral Monuments of the Later Middle Ages', in *J.R.S.A.I.*, Vol. 100, 1970, pp. 1-38; and Vol. 101, 1971, pp. 1-29 ('The O'Tunney Atelier'). Many illustrations.
4. The Stationery Office, *Jerpoint Abbey, Co. Kilkenny*, Dublin, p. 15.

Sleaty. Chapter 10
1. Kenney, James F., *The Sources for the Early History of Ireland: Ecclesiastical*, New York 1966, p. 340.

Emain Macha. Chapter 10
1. *A Preliminary Survey*, p. 65.
2. Elliot, John, 'Emania', in *J.R.S.A.I.*, Vol. VI, 1883-84, pp. 409-12.
3. Hughes, Felix J., 'Eamhain Macha', in *Seanchas Ardmhacha: Journal of the Armagh Diocesan Historical Society*, Vol. 1, No. 2, 1955, pp. 1-10.
4. *In State Care*, pp. 76-7.

St Gall. Chapter 12
1. Duft, Johannes and Meyer, Peter, *The Irish Miniatures in the Abbey Library of St. Gall*, Berne: Lausanne, 1954.

Ratto. Chapter 12
1. *Barrow*, pp. 109-13.
2. Petrie, George, *The Ecclesiastical Architecture of Ireland, An essay on the origin and uses of The Round Towers of Ireland*, Shannon 1970, pp. 398-400.

Monasterboice. Chapter 13
1. *Barrow*, pp. 150-53.
2. Macalister, R. A. S., *Muiredach, Abbot of Monasterboice 890-923 A.D., His Life and Surroundings*, Dublin 1914.
3. Macalister, R. A.S., *Monasterboice, Co. Louth*, Dundalk 1946.

Clontarf. Chapter 13
1. Ryan, John, 'The Battle of Clontarf', in *J.R.S.A.I.*, Vol. LXVIII, 1938, pp. 1-50. The maps are especially useful.

Christ Church Cathedral. Chapter 13
1. Anderson, William and Clive Hicks, *Cathedrals in Britain and Ireland*, op cit., pp. 156-8.
2. *Leask II*, pp. 43-5.

Clonkeen. Chapter 14
1. *Dunraven II*, pp. 113-15.
2. *Leask I*, pp. 127-9.

Clonfert Cathedral. Chapter 14
1. Crawford, Henry S., 'The Romanesque Doorway at Clonfert', in *J.R.S.A.I.*, Vol. XLII, 1912, pp. 1-7.
2. *Dunraven II*, pp. 106-10.
3. Hodge, Cecil J., *St. Brendan's Cathedral: A Short History and Guide*, Westport.
4. *Leask I*, pp. 137-42.

Cashel. Chapter 14
1. *Barrow*, pp. 182-85.
2. Dunraven II, pp. 71-80.
3. Leask, Harold G., *St. Patrick's Rock: Cashel*, The Stationery Office, Dublin.
4. *Leask I*, pp. 39-40, 113-21.

Mellifont Abbey. Chapter 14
1. Colmcille, Father, O.C.S.O., *The Story of Mellifont*, 1958.
2. de Paor, Liam, 'Excavations at Mellifont Abbey, Co. Louth', in *P.R.I.A.* Vol. 68, 1969, pp. 109-64.
3. *Leask II*, pp. 41-3.

Select Bibliography

The books and articles listed below are not meant to stand as a complete or definitive bibliography. Scholars and experts may well notice omissions. However, these were the sources primarily used in the preparation of this book. Asterisk (*) indicates a work heavily relied upon by the author. Most translations of Gaelic materials by O'Donovan, Stokes, Todd et al. are credited in References and not listed here.

Allott, Stephen, *Alcuin of York*, York 1974.

Anderson, A. O. and M. O., *Adomnán's Life of Columba*, London 1961.

Anderson, M. O., 'Columba and other Irish Saints in Scotland,' in *Historical Studies V*, Philadelphia 1965, pp. 26-36.

Anderson, M. O., 'The Annals,' in *Kings and Kingship in Early Scotland*, Edinburgh: London 1973, pp. 1-42.

Atkinson, R. J. C., *Stonehenge and Avebury and Neighbouring Monuments*, London 1959.

* Bannerman, John, *Studies in the History of Dalriada*, Edinburgh: London 1974.

Barraclough, Geoffrey, *The Crucible of Europe: The Ninth and Tenth Centuries in European History*, Berkeley: Los Angeles 1976.

Baudis, Josef, 'On the Antiquity of the Kingship of Tara', in *Ériu*, Vol. VIII, 1916, pp. 101-7.

Bayerschmidt, Carl F., and Lee M. Hollander, *Njál's Saga*, New York 1955.

Bernard of Clairvaux, *Life of St. Malachy of Armagh*, trans. H. J. Lawlor, New York 1920.

Best, Richard I., and H. J. Lawlor, *The Martyrology of Tallaght*, London 1931.

Bieler, Ludwig, *The Life and Legend of St. Patrick: Problems of Modern Scholarship*, Dublin 1949.

Bieler, Ludwig, *The Works of St. Patrick*, London 1953.

Bieler, Ludwig, *Ireland, Harbinger of the Middle Ages*, London 1963.

Bieler, Ludwig, *St. Patrick and the Coming of Christianity*, Dublin 1967.

* Bieler, Ludwig, *The Patrician Texts in the Book of Armagh*, Dublin 1979.

* Binchy, D. A., 'The Linguistic and Historical Value of the Irish Law Tracts', in *Proceedings of the British Academy*, Vol. XXIX, 1943, pp. 195-227.

* Binchy, D. A., 'The Fair of Tailtiu and the Feast of Tara', in *Ériu*, Vol. XVIII, 1958, pp. 113-38.

* Binchy, D. A., 'The Passing of the Old Order', in *Proceedings of the International Congress of Celtic Studies 1959*, ed. Ó Cuív, Dublin 1962, pp. 119-32.

* Binchy, D. A., 'The Background of Early Irish Literature', in *Studia Hibernica*, No. 1, 1961, pp. 7-18.

Binchy, D. A., 'The Old Irish Table of Penitential Commutations,' in *Ériu*, Vol. XIX, 1962, pp. 47-72.

* Binchy, D. A., 'Patrick and His Biographers: Ancient and Modern', in *Studia Hibernica*, No. 2, 1962, pp. 7-173.

Binchy, D. A., 'Bretha Déin Chécht', in *Ériu*, Vol. XX, 1966, pp. 1-66.

Binchy, D. A., 'Varia III,' in *Ériu*, Vol. XX, 1966, pp. 229-37.

Binchy, D. A., Book review of *The Church in Early Irish Society* by Kathleen Hughes, in *Studia Hibernica*, No. 7, 1967, pp. 217-19.

* Binchy, D. A., 'St. Patrick's First Synod', in *Studia Hibernica*, No. 8, 1968, pp. 49-59.

* Binchy, D. A., *Celtic and Anglo-Saxon Kingship*, Oxford 1970.

* Binchy, D. A., 'Irish History and Irish Law', in *Studia Hibernica*,

No. 15, 1975, pp. 7-36; No. 16, 1976, pp. 7-45.

Brecher, K., and M. Feirtag, eds., *Astronomy of the Ancients*, Cambridge, 1979.

Burl, Aubrey, *The Stone Cirlces of the British Isles*, New Haven: London, 1976.

Byrne, Francis, J., 'The Ireland of St. Columba', in *Historical Studies V*, Philadelphia, 1965, pp. 37-59.

Byrne, Francis J., *The Rise of the Uí Néill and the high-kingship of Ireland*, Dublin 1969.

Byrne, Francis J., 'Tribes and Tribalism in Early Ireland', in *Ériu*, Vol. XXII, 1971, pp. 128-66.

* Byrne, Francis J., *Irish Kings and High-Kings*, London, 1973.

Byrne, Francis J., 'Senchus: The Nature of Gaelic Historical Tradition', in *Historical Studies IX*, Belfast 1974, pp. 137-60.

Carney, James, *Studies in Irish Literature and History*, Dublin 1955.

Carney, James, *The Problem of St. Patrick*, Dublin 1961.

Chadwick, Nora, 'The Vikings and the Western World', in *Proceedings of the International Congress of Celtic Studies 1959*, op. cit., pp. 13-42.

Chamberlain, G. A., *St. Patrick: His Life and Work*, Dublin 1959.

Champneys, Arthur C., *Irish Ecclesiastical Architecture*, Dublin 1910.

Colgrave, Bertram and R. A. B. Mynors, *Bede's Ecclesiastical History of the English People*, Oxford 1969.

Collins, A. E. P., 'Settlement in Ulster, 0-1100 A.D.', in *U.J.A.*, Vol. 31, 1968, pp. 53-8.

Daniel, Glyn, 'Megalithic Monuments', in *Scientific American*, July 1980, pp. 78-90.

de Paor, Liam, 'The Aggrandisement of Armagh', in *Historical Studies*, ed. T. D. Williams, Dublin 1971, pp. 95-110.

Dillon, Myles, 'The Archaism of Irish Tradition', in *Proceedings of the British Academy*, Vol. XXXIII, 1947.

Dillon Myles, 'The Hindu Act of Truth in Celtic Tradition', in *Modern Philology*, Vol. XLIV, Feb. 1947, No. 3. pp. 137-40.

Dillon, Myles, 'The Story of the Finding of Cashel', in *Ériu*, Vol. XVI, 1952, pp. 61-73.

Dillon, Myles, *Early Irish Literature*, Chicago, 1958.

Dillon, Myles, 'The Inauguration of O'Connor', in *Medieval Studies Presented to Aubrey Gwynn, S. M.*, Dublin 1961, pp. 186-202.

* Dillon, Myles and Nora Chadwick, *The Celtic Realms*, London 1967.

Dillon Myles, ed., *Early Irish Society*, Dublin 1954.

Douglas, David C., 'Rollo of Normandy', in *English Historical Review*, Vol. LVII, 1942, pp. 417-36.

Duckett, Eleanor S., *The Gateway to the Middle Ages: Monasticism*, Ann Arbor 1938.

Duffy, Joseph, *St. Patrick in his own words*, Dublin 1975.

Easton, Stewart and Helen Wieruszowski, *The Era of Charlemagne*, New York 1961.

Evans, E. Estyn, *Irish Folk Ways*, New York 1957.

Evans, E. Estyn, *Prehistoric and Early Christian Ireland: A Guide*, New York 1966.

Evans, E. Estyn, *The Personality of Ireland: Habitat, Heritage And History*, Cambridge 1973.

Fremantle, Anne, *The Age of Belief*, New York 1962.

Graham-Campbell, James and Dafydd Kidd, *The Vikings*, London 1980.

Gwynn, Aubrey, *The Twelfth-Century Reform*, Dublin 1968.

Gwynn, Aubrey and R. Neville, *Medieval Religious Houses in Ireland*, London 1970.

Gwynn, E., 'The Rule of Tallaght', in *Hermathena*, Vol. XLIV, 1927, pp. v-109.

Gwynn, E. and W. J. Purton, 'The Monastery of Tallaght', in *P.R.I.A.*, Vol. XXIV, July 1911, pp. 17-179.

Gwynn, John, *The Book of Armagh*, Dublin 1913.

Hadingham, Evans, *Circle and Standing Stones*, New York 1975.

Hamilton, James, *Bangor Abbey Through Fourteen Centuries*, Bangor 1980.

* Hanson, R. P. C., *St. Patrick: His Origins and Career*, Oxford 1968.

Hawkins, Gerald S., 'Callanish, a Scottish Stonehenge', in *Science*, Vol. 147, No. 3653, 1 January, pp. 127-30.

Hawkins, Gerald S., *Stonehenge Decoded*, London 1966.

Hawkins, Gerald S., 'Photogrammetric Survey of Stonehenge and Callanish', in *National Geographic Society Research Reports - Abstracts and Reviews of research and exploration authorized under grants from the National Geographic Society during the year 1965*, ed. Paul Oehser, Washington, D.C. 1971, pp. 101-8. Technical data and maps.

Hayes-McCoy, G. A., *Irish Battles*, London 1969.

Henry, Françoise, 'The effects of the Viking invasion on Irish art', in *Proceedings of the International Congress of Celtic Studies 1959*, op. cit., pp. 61-72.

Henry, Françoise, *Irish Art in the Early Christian Period*, Ithaca 1965.

Henry, Françoise, *Irish Art During the Viking Invasion*, Itacha 1967.

Henry, Françoise and G. L. Marsh-Micheli, 'A Century of Irish

Illumination 1070-1170', in *P.R.I.A.*, Vol. 62, Section C, No. 5, 1962, pp. 5-164.

Her Majesty's Stationery Office, *Ancient Monuments of Northern Ireland: Not in State Care*, Belfast 1969.

Hern, Gerhard, *The Celts*, New York 1975.

Herren, Michael, 'Classical and Secular Learning Among the Irish Before the Carolingian Renaissance', in *Florilegium*, Vol. 3, 1981, pp. 118-57.

Hillgarth, J. N., 'Visigothic Spain and Early Christian Ireland', in *P.R.I.A.*, Vol. 62, Section C, No. 6, 1962, pp. 167-94.

* Hughes, Kathleen, *The Church in Early Irish Society*, London 1966.

Hughes, Kathleen, *Early Christian Ireland: Introduction to the Sources*, Ithaca 1972.

Hughes, Kathleen, *The Early Celtic Idea of History and the Modern Historian*, Cambridge 1977.

Hully, Vernam, 'Cáin Domnaig', in *Ériu*, Vol. XX, 1966, pp. 151-77.

Jackson, Kenneth, 'The Celtic languages during the Viking period', in *Proceedings of the International Congress of Celtic Studies 1959*, op. cit., pp. 3-11.

Jackson, Kenneth, *A Celtic Miscellany*, Harmondsworth 1973.

Joynt, Maud, 'Echtra MacEchdach Mugmedóin,' in *Ériu*, Vol. IV, 1910, pp. 91-111.

Keating, Goeffrey, *The History of Ireland*, trans. David Comyn, London 1902.

Kelleher, John V., 'Early Irish History and Pseudo-History', in *Studia Hibernica*, No. 1, 1961, pp. 113-27.

Kelleher, John V., 'The Rise of the Dal Cáis,' in *North Munster Studies: Essays in Commemoration of Monsignor Michael Moloney*, ed. Etienne Rynne, Limerick 1967, pp. 230-41.

Kelleher, John V., 'The Táin and the Annals', in *Ériu*, Vol. XXII, 1971, pp. 107-27.

Kelly, Fergus, 'A Poem in Praise of Columb Cille', in *Ériu*, Vol. XXIV, 1973, pp. 1-34.

Kendrick, T. D., *A History of the Vikings*, New York 1930.

Kenney, James F., 'Early Irish Church History as a Field for Research by American Students', in *Catholic Historical Review*, Vol. XVII, No. 1, April 1931.

Kenney, James F., 'St. Patrick and the Patrick Legend', in *Thought*, Vol. VIII, No. 1, June 1933.

* Kenney, James F., *The Sources for the Early History of Ireland: Ecclesiastical*, New York 1966.

Lawlor, H. J., 'Notes on St. Bernard's Life of St. Malachy, and His Two Sermons on the Passing of St. Malachy', in *P.R.I.A.*, Vol. XXXV, 1919-1920, pp. 230-64.

Leask, Harold G., *Glendalough*, The Stationery Office, Dublin.

Leff, Gordon, *Medieval Thought: St. Augustine to Ockham*, Harmondsworth, 1962.

Lucas, A. T., 'Irish-Norse Relations: Time for a Reappraisal?' in *Journal of the Cork Historical and Archaeological Society*, Vol. LXXI, Nos. 213 & 214, 1966, pp. 62-75.

Lucas, A. T., 'The Plundering and Burning of Churches in Ireland, 7th to 16th Century', in *North Munster Studies*, op. cit., pp. 172-229.

Macalister, R. A. S., *Studies in Irish Epigraphy*, London 1897, 1902, 1907.

Macalister, R. A. S., *The Latin and Irish Lives of Ciaran*, London 1921.

Macalister, R. A. S., *The Archaeology of Ireland*, London 1928.

MacCana, Proinsias, *Celtic Mythology*, London 1970.

* MacNeill, Eóin, *Phases of Irish History*, Dublin 1919.

MacNeill, Eóin, *Celtic Ireland*, Dublin 1921.

MacNeill, Eóin, *Early Irish Law and Institutions*, Dublin 1935.

MacNeill, Eóin, *St. Patrick*, Dublin 1964.

MacNeill, Marie, *The Festival of Lughnasa*, Oxford 1962.

MacNiocaill, Gearóid, *Ireland Before the Vikings*, Dublin 1972.

Magnusson, Magnus and Hermann Pálsson, *King Harald's Saga: From Snorri Sturluson's 'Heimskringla'*, Harmondsworth 1966.

Martin, F. X. and F. J. Byrne, eds., *The Scholar Revolutionary: Eoin MacNeill, 1867-1945., and the Making of the New Ireland*, Shannon 1973.

McNeill, John T. and Helena M. Garner, *Medieval Handbooks of Penance*, New York 1938.

The Metropolitan Museum of Art, *Treasures of Early Irish Art: 1500 BC to 1500 AD*, New York 1977.

Mohrmann, Christine, *The Latin of Saint Patrick*, Dublin 1961.

Moore, Donald, ed., *The Irish Sea Province In Archaeology and History*, Cardiff 1970.

Morris, Henry, 'The Circuit of Ireland by Muirchertach na gCoch All gCroiceann, AD 941', in *P.R.I.A.* Vol. LXVI, pp. 9-31.

Morris, John, *The Age of Arthur: A History of the British Isles from 350-650*, London 1973.

Muller, Herbert J., *The Uses of the Past: Profiles of Former Societies*, New York, 1957.

* Norman, E. R. and J. K. S. St Joseph, *The Early Development of Irish Society, The Evidence of Aerial Photography*, Cambridge 1969.

O'Connell, D. J., 'Easter Cycles in the Early Irish Church', in *P.R.I.A.* Vol. LXVI, pp. 67-106.

O'Connor, Frank, *The Backward Look: A Survey of Irish Literature*, London 1967.

Ó'Corráin, Donnchadh, 'Irish Regnal Succession: A Reappraisal', in *Studia Hibernica*, No. 11, 1971, pp. 7-39.

Ó Corráin, Donnchadh, *Ireland Before the Normans*, Dublin 1972.

Ó Cuív, Brian, ed., *Seven Centuries of Irish Learning*, Cork 1971.

Ó Cuív, Brian, ed., *The Impact of the Scandinavian Invasions on the Celtic-speaking Peoples c. 800-1100 AD*, Dublin 1975.

O'Donnell, Manus, *Life of Columcille*, trans. A. O'Kelleher and G. Schoepperle, Urbana 1918.

O'Dwyer, Peter, *Céli Dé: Spiritual Reform in Ireland 750-900*, Dublin 1981.

O'Faolain, Sean, *The Irish*, Harmondsworth 1969.

Ó Fiaich, Tomás, ed., 'The Patrician Year 1961-'62', in *Seanchas Ardmhacha: Journal of the Armagh Diocesan Historical Society*, Special Issue, March 1962. See also 'St. Patrick and Armagh — A Symposium', Vol. 2, No. 1, 1956, pp. 1-78.

O'Grady, Standish, *Silva Gadelica: A Collection of Tales in Irish*, London 1892.

Ó Máille, Tómas, 'Medb Chruachana', in *Zeitschrift Für Celtische Philologie*, Vol. XVII, 1927, pp. 129-46.

O'Rahilly, Thomas F., *Early Irish History and Mythology*, Dublin 1946.

O'Rahilly, Thomas F., 'On the Origin of the Names Érainn and Ériu', in *Ériu*, Vol. XIV, 1946, pp. 14-28.

*O'Rahilly, Thomas F., *The Two Patricks: A Lecture on the History of Christianity in Fifth-Century Ireland*, Dublin 1971.

Pagels, Elaine, *The Gnostic Gospels*, New York 1979.

Proudfoot, V. B., 'The Economy of the Irish Rath', in *Medieval Archaeology VI*, 1961, pp. 94-122.

Rees, Alwyn and Brinley, *Celtic Heritage*, London 1961.

Reeves, William, 'On the Céli-dé, commonly called Culdees', in *T.R.I.A.*, Vol. XXIV, 1864, pp. 119-263.

*Renfrew, Colin, *Before Civilization: The Radiocarbon Revolution and Prehistoric Europe*, New York 1973.

Renfrew, Colin, 'British Prehistory: Changing Configurations', in *British Prehistory: A New Outline*, ed. Renfrew, London 1974, pp. 1-40.

Renfrew, Colin, 'Ancient Europe is Older than We Thought', in *National Geographic Magazine*, Vol. 152, No. 5, Nov. 1977, pp. 614-23.

Richards, Melville, 'The Irish Settlements in South-West Wales', in *J.R.S.A.I.*, Vol. XC, 1960, pp. 133-62.

Roe, Helen M., 'The Irish High Cross: Morphology and Iconography', in *J.R.S.A.I.*, Vol. 95, 1965, pp. 213-26.

Ryan, John, 'Brian Boruma, King of Ireland', in *North Munster Studies*, op. cit., pp. 355-74.

*Scaff, Philip, *History of the Christian Church: Nicene and Post-Nicene Christianity*, Vol. III, New York 1884.

Shetelig, Haakon, *Viking Antiquities in Great Britain and Ireland*, Oslo 1941.

Smith, Charles, *The Ancient and Present State of the County of Kerry*, Dublin 1774.

Smyth, A. P., 'The Earliest Irish Annals: Their First Contemporary Entries and the Earliest Centres of Recording', in *P.R.I.A.*, Vol. 72, 1972, pp. 1-48.

Stokes, Whitley, 'Sitting Dharna', in *The Academy*, No. 28, 1885, p. 169.

Stokes, Whitley, 'The Bodleian Amra Choluimb chille', in *Revue Celtique*, Vol. XX, No. 1, 1899, pp. 30, 132, 248, 400.

Stokes, Whitley, 'On Two Irish Expressions for 'Right Hand' and 'Left Hand' ', in *Ériu*, Vol. III, Part I, pp. 11, 12.

Stokes, William, *The Life and Labours in Art and Archaeology of George Petrie*, London 1868.

Taylor, Thomas, *The Life of St. Samson of Dol*, London 1925.

Thom, Alexander, *Megalithic Sites in Britain*, London 1967.

Thom, Alexander, *Megalithic Lunar Observatories*, Oxford, 1971.

Thorgilsson, Ari, *The Book of the Icelanders ('Islendingabók')*, ed. and trans. Halldór Hermannsson, in *Islandica*, Vol. XX, 1930.

*Tierney, J. J., 'The Celtic Ethnography of Posidonius', in *P.R.I.A.*, Vol. 60, 1959-1960, pp. 189-275.

Todd, James, *St. Patrick Apostle of Ireland: A Memoir of his Life and Mission*, Dublin 1864.

Tryckare, Tre, *The Viking*, Gothenburg Sweden, 1966.

Turville-Petre, G., 'On the Poetry of the Scalds and of the Filid', in *Ériu*, Vol. XXII, 1971, pp. 1-22.

Waddell, John, 'The Invasion Hypothesis in Irish Prehistory', in *Antiquity*, Vol. LII, pp. 121-8.

Wagner, H., 'Studies in the Origins of Early Celtic Traditions', in *Ériu*, Vol. XXVI, 1975, pp. 1-26.

Walker, G. S. M., *Sancti Columbani Opera*, Dublin 1957.

Webb, J. F., *Lives of the Saints*, Harmondsworth 1970.

White, Newport J. D., *St. Patrick, His Writings and Life*, London 1920.

Wood, John Edwin, *Sun, Moon and Standing Stones*, Oxford 1968.

Wood-Martin, W. G., *Traces of the Elder Faiths of Ireland*, London, 1902.

Wright, Charles H. H., *The Writings of Patrick*, London 1889.

Index

228

tuatha, 63, 109, 116
Tulsk (Co. Roscommon), 74, 81
Turgesius, 175, 178

Uí Liatháin, 89
Uí Néill:
Columcille from, 109, 114, 131, 135; expansion of, 77, 102, 120, 131, 135; and the high-kingship, 69, 78, 159, 161, 165, 188; and St Patrick, 100, 102; other references, 73, 91, 107

Ulaid, 74, 77-8, 85, 100, 120, 131, 158
Ulster Defence Force (UDF), 148

Valentia Island, 1, 3, 20
Vikings:
artistic influence, 185; effects on the church, 178, 181; in England, 178; longships, 174; monastic attacks, 5, 8, 171, 174-5; settlements, 177-8; conflict with Brian Bóruma, 186, 188-9, 191, 193
Vulfilaic, 12-13

Waterford, 175, 193
Wexford, 175
Whitby, synod of, 155
White Island, 145, 148, 151
Wilde, Oscar, 184
Wilde, Sir William, 29, 33
Wilfrid of Canterbury, 155
William the Conqueror, 177, 197
William of Orange, 23

Acknowledgments

THIS book was begun in 1973, and an initial draft completed by autumn of the next year. To Robert Sweeney my thanks for the cheerless task of pointing out to me its grave deficiencies — as he said at the time, 'Honest friends are few'. My respect for his judgment has increased over the many years that have passed since then. Paul Lazarus, another old colleague, also worked with me that first year at Fortunes Rocks, in Maine. My appreciation to him.

To Penelope Preston, my oldest Irish friend, go thanks for countless occasions of hospitality during the seven visits to Ireland made in connection with this book. In the west, Margaret and Thomas Uniacke of Riverville, with their daughters Francis and Grace, never failed in assistance. My appreciation to the following for seeing me in Ireland, and sharing with a stranger the results of their many years of research into various arcane matters of the Irish past: D. A. Binchy, Dublin Institute for Advanced Studies; the late M. J. O'Kelly of University College, Cork; Joseph Duffy, Bishop of Clogher.

All the photographs in this book are the author's with the following exceptions: the Book of Armagh, courtesy The Board of Trinity College, Dublin (photo by Green Studio Ltd), and two aerial photographs of Armagh City and Canons' Island, by permission of the University of Cambridge Committee for Aerial Photography and Dr. S. K. J. St Joseph. To J. Fischer, my gratitude for his special detour and subsequent photograph at Ballysadare Bay of the extensive kitchen midden there.

The Ordnance Survey map on page 67 is reproduced by kind permission of the Director of the Ordnance Survey, Dublin. The illustration on page 28 is reproduced by kind permission of Mrs Claire O'Kelly author of the *Concise Guide to Newgrange*.

Special thanks are due to Dr P. Ochsenbein, Director of the Stiftsbibliothek in St Gallen, Switzerland, for his extremely generous cooperation in facilitating the photograph of Codex 51 during my visit of 28 September 1984; the custodians of the Abbey of Bobbio in Emilia-Romagna, Italy, for their patience on All Souls' Day, 1982; the staff of the National Museum of Ireland for allowing me to photograph axe heads from their collection.

I am especially grateful to the staffs of the Boston Public Library and the National Library of Ireland.

For assistance in manuscript preparation, a case of Barbera d'Alba is insufficient thanks to Susan Bailey and Ralph Brown. Without Carla Fergusson and William Lane this book might never have been completed. William H. Rudy, distinguished author of *Racing in America 1960-1979*, read over the final draft and saved me considerable embarrassment in his detection of several errors. And Fergal Tobin's careful stewardship in the editorial process proved indispensable.

For illustrations and cover, to say nothing of the many, many hours of personal frustration which this project generated, my deepest appreciation to Jan V. Roy.

Finally, I would like to emphasise to readers of this book that my own travels in Ireland did not follow the order in which they appear in the text. That arrangement is artificial to some degree, tailored to fit my own subjective decisions regarding the organisation of what is a substantial body of material. Seasoned visitors to Ireland may also notice several antiquated observations: the *Lia Fáil*, for instance, no longer is surrounded by an iron fence; the Caldragh graveyard on Boa Island, when last I passed it in 1984, was clearly marked from the roadway;

Valentia Island is now connected to the mainland by a bridge road, and so on. These minor discrepancies date my visits to be sure but do not affect, I believe, any of the judgments I formed.

JCR
7 January 1986
Newburyport, Massachusetts.